A History of

JESUS COLLEGE CAMBRIDGE

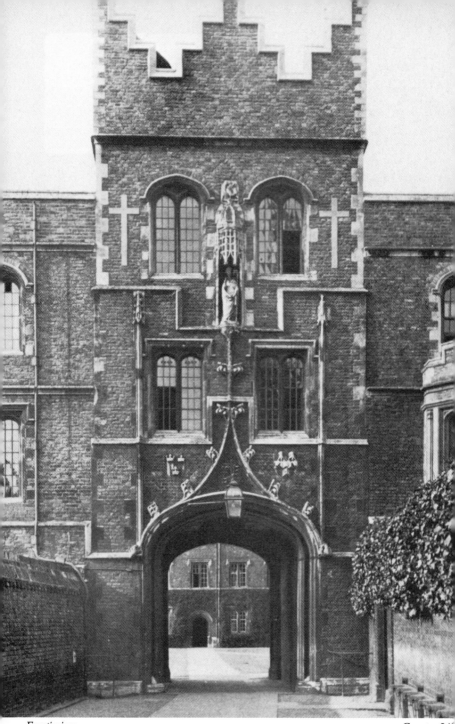

THE GATE-HOUSE

A HISTORY OF
JESUS COLLEGE
CAMBRIDGE

BY
ARTHUR GRAY, MA
Master of the College 1912–1940

AND

FREDERICK BRITTAIN LITT.D
Fellow of the College 1937–1969

SILENT BOOKS
CAMBRIDGE

Preface

ARTHUR GRAY's history of Jesus College, Cambridge, was published in 1902 as one of a series of histories of the various Oxford and Cambridge colleges. He died in 1940. The publishers F. E. Robinson and Company no longer exist and the copyright descended to the author's son, Mr W. A. Gray. The Council of Jesus College asked my husband, the late Dr Frederick Brittain, to revise the book making as few alterations as possible, to bring it up to date; and Mr W. A. Gray kindly gave his consent to publication which was made possible by the generous co-operation of Messrs Heinemann.

In his revision my husband made alterations where he believed the original work to be in error. There are not many of these and such as there are occur in the earlier part of the book. In the latter part of it he had to do little more than bring time-references and place-references up to date. However, he stopped short at the change of Masters in 1849, abandoned Arthur Gray's brief narrative of events from that date to 1902 and wrote an account of the history of the College from 1849 to 1960 himself.

This edition brings the history up to 1978 and contains some corrections left by my husband.

Jesus College, Cambridge 1978   M. BRITTAIN

The letters and numbers are those of the various staircases; shading represents passages under buildings.
*Chapter-house arches.
Compare with David Loggan's engraving of the College, about 1688

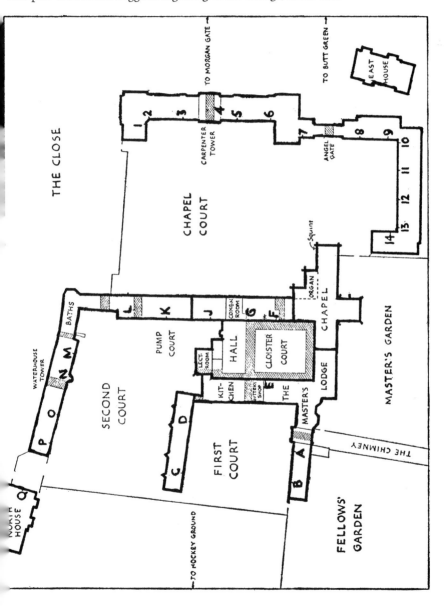

List of Illustrations

Contents

COLLE

.Collegium IESU, vulgo ità dictum, receßu ab oppido situq, amœnißimo, studijs et Musis (quæ seceßum et otia quærunt) accomodum hūt olim Cenobium velatarum Virginum à MAL
F: Ælwylio) et sponsa Clothary Regis Francorum, a qua tamen se subduxit clam, votum nuncupari sit Abbatiæ Cenobium hoc Recalende memorie Iohannes Alcock, Episcopus Elī
altera infamis) ac Monastery dignitate juribus, quibuscunq ex mandato, et expressā licentiā Serenißimi Regis HENRICI septimi primitus supprestis et deletis, in Collegium Student
duobus Discipulis, et à felicißimo illo CAROLI Secundi reditu augetur undeviginti Discipulis, et Exhibitionarys, qui laudißimis ornantur stipendijs, per munificentiam Tobiæ Rustat Arm
Speq, Henrici Brunsell LL:D et Canonici Ecclesiæ Eliensis, et Magistri Iohannis Sommervile. Tulit multos Viros egregios, dedit, tum Ecclesiæ, tum Reipul Præ ceteris autem, Tres 1
Custos, stil tum ante infames illos in Anglia motus Regnante, Gloriosißimo nunc Martyre, CAROLO Primo, tum post Reditum CAROLI Secundi 18° ΜΟΚΟΙ 18°. Multos habuit Aū
Westfeild Episcopus Bristollensis, Humfredus Henchman, Episcopus Londinensis, Gulielmus Boswell olim CAROLI Primi apud fœderatos Belgas, et Edmundus Foley Se
Collegy Trinitatis Magister, et ut cæteros omittam, Thomas Sutton Crœsus ille Anglorum, Fundator Domus apud Londinum Carthusianæ. Quod superest, votum absolvit

Cantab.

Reverendo,
Admodum Doctissimoq, viro
GUILIELMO SAYWELL
S.T.P. Archidiacono Elien: necnon
eiusdem Ecclesiæ Canonico, Collegy
Iesu apud Cantabrigienses Cus-
todi Meritissimo, et Ecclesiæ Angli-
canæ Defensori et Ornamento
D.D.C.Q.
Dav: Loggan.

A Capella.
B Bibliotheca.
C Refectorium.
D Magistri Hospitium.
E Culina.
F Hortus Magistri.
G Hortus Sociorum.

H.H. fecit 325.

edificatum Anno Domini 1150 et Sanctæ Virgini Rhadegundæ ab eodem dicatum. Fuit hec Rhadegunda Berthory Thuringiæ apud Germanos Reguli filia, unica belli merces, (Teste
ncellarius, regnantibus scil EDVARDO quarto et HENRICO Septimo, Abbatisse et existentium inibi monialium (quæ omnes emanserant ad duas, quarum una erat infans
g. Beatæ Mariæ Virgini, Sanctiq Iohanni Evangelistæ et Rhadegundæ. Benefactores habuit complures, eosq munificentissimos, ita ut jam alat Custodem, sedecim Socios cum viginti
stibus Reverendissimi in Christo Patris Ricardi nuper Archi-Episcopi Eboracensis Domine Margarethæ Boswell, Viduæ et Relictæ Domini Gulielmi Boswell, olim huius Collegy
bornienses suos urum Eboracensem, nimirum Thomam Crannmerum, Ricardum Bancroft et predictum Ricardum Sterne Quorum Primus bu hic Socius, Tertius Ec-
etteris eluxit Iosephus Bale et Grifith Williams, utrq Episcopi Ossorienses Thomas Goodrick, Episcopus Eliensis, Legatus, et Summus Angliæ Thesaurarius Thomas
d Seueros nunc temporis Orator. Dominus Ricardus Fanshaw, Poeta celebris, Doctissimus pariter ac Nobilissimus Iohannes North, Græcæ Linguæ Professor, et postea

To 1849

To 1849

CHAPTER I

THE NUNS OF ST RADEGUND

THROUGHOUT almost the whole of its existence Jesus College has been known by an alias. In the letters patent for its incorporation, which Bishop Alcock obtained from King Henry VII, it is licensed as 'the College of the Blessed Mary the Virgin, St John the Evangelist, and the glorious Virgin St Radegund, near Cambridge'. The now accepted name, 'Jesus College', has no place in the letters patent; yet it appears, beside the ampler form, in some of the earliest muniments of the new foundation, and even in the fifteenth century had supplanted it in common speech. For then, just as now, the road which leads from Cambridge to Barnwell was known as Jesus Lane; then, also, there was a now forgotten Jesus parish, wherein the College farmers dwelt, and, as contemporary evidence shows, 'heard their divine service' in Jesus church, and buried their dead in Jesus churchyard. Bishop Stanley, in the preamble of the statutes which he gave to the College about the year 1514, says that the College church was dedicated to the Name of Jesus; but he did not forget that it had an older ascription, and elsewhere he speaks of it as the church of St Radegund. Since the days of Henry II that had been its name; but Radegund herself usurped the honour due to a saint of older claim, and at best was but the junior partner of St Mary, whose patronage of the site dates from Stephen's reign.

With these two saints, Mary and Radegund, Bishop Alcock, in his dedication of the College, associated a third, his name-saint,

John the Evangelist. But the two former are the real θεοί ἐντόπιοι of Jesus College. An unbroken tradition of eight centuries connects their names with its site, and confers on it a better title to the epithets 'ancient' and 'religious' than can be claimed by any other college in the University—'ancient', for the antiquity of its origin far transcends that of the University itself, and 'religious', since the aspect of its buildings and the seclusion of its position recall unmistakably that religious household from which it sprang, the Benedictine nunnery of St Mary and St Radegund.

The story of this nunnery, which is to be the subject of the present chapter, may seem remote from the purpose of a college history. If it be so, the apology for its intrusion here must be partly its intrinsic interest, partly the light which it throws on some peculiarities which from the outset distinguished Jesus from other Cambridge colleges and are not altogether obliterated today. The nuns bequeathed a large mass of miscellaneous documents—charters, wills, account-rolls, etc.—to the College, and the scrupulous care with which they were originally housed and, not less, the wholesome neglect which long respected their repose in the College treasury, have fortunately preserved them intact to the present time. Their interest lies in the picture which they give us of pre-academic Cambridge; of an isolated women's community in an alien world of men; and of the depravation and decay which came of that isolation, and which ended in the first suppression in England of an indigenous house of religion. What is to be said in this chapter will also help to explain some of the curious monastic features which gave a picturesque distinction to Jesus College—the uncollegiate plan of its buildings, the church shared between College and parish, the free school in the entrance court, the Radegund tithes and Radegund Manor House, and the fair which invaded the College grounds.

The description of the College in Henry VII's letters patent as being 'near Cambridge' has a curiously retrospective look about it. In 1496 no burgher would have hesitated to say that Jesus College was *in* Cambridge, for the town boundary then marched with that of the suburb of Barnwell along the eastern margin of the Close. But this was not so in the earlier days of the nunnery.

Then the town limit was at the point in Jesus Lane where Park Street branches from it. Here the road was crossed by a water-course, which was probably at least as old as the Conquest. Its name was the Lang Rith—i.e. long channel—but in legal documents it was called the King's Ditch. This ditch, at its upper end, began at the mill near Queens' College, then called the King's Mill. It passed along Mill Lane and Pembroke Street, once known as Langrithes Lane; from thence it bent in a north-easterly direction to the site of the old post office, took the line of Hobson Street, and, passing through the grounds of Sidney Sussex College, crossed Jesus Lane, and so was carried along Park Street to the river, which it rejoined nearly opposite Magdalene College. As the nunnery was outside the ditch, it was often described as 'without' or 'near' Cambridge.

Outside the ditch, towards Trumpington and Barnwell, in a long band stretched a houseless tract which from primitive ages had been part of the Field of Cambridge. At its north-eastern end was the townsmen's common pasture-land, which we now call Midsummer Common, and which centuries ago was known as the Green Croft. The river-water was held up at a higher level then than now, and in winter time the Green Croft was a watery void extending, as a charter of Barnwell Priory describes it, 'in dry and in marsh from the street to the river'. On a dry gravelly spur projecting into the Green Croft the nuns planted their cell. The situation was waste enough, yet such as had strong attraction to the religious of monastic ages—*soli amoenitate satis delectabilis*, as the Barnwell chronicler describes the surroundings of the Augustinian priory, which occupied a corresponding declivity on the eastern margin of the Green Croft. Material advantages, too, were not wanting to the site. In a portion of the river skirting Jesus Green, and called Nunneslake, the nuns had exclusive fishing rights. A channel which was navigable by the small 'catches' of the fen waters gave them useful communication with the river, and no doubt served to bring to their doors the Barnack stone which they used in building their church. Enclosed within the walls of their kitchen was an excellent spring, which supplied the needs of the College down to the year 1895, when it pleased the town authorities, in the course of sewerage works, to divert its supply and to commit the College to the tender mercies and hard water of a company.

Who the nuns were that first settled by the Green Croft, when and whence they came thither, and by what title they became possessed of their original site, our documents do not record. They started house-keeping in a humble way, without a charter of foundation, with neither a church to serve nor a saint to give them name and countenance. What we do know is that they were already in occupation of a portion of the Green Croft site in the opening years of Stephen's reign, and that they found an early, perhaps their first, benefactor in a Bishop of Ely. Bishop Alcock, when he wished to obtain the King's sanction for the suppression of the nunnery, went so far as to claim that it was of the foundation and patronage of the Bishops of Ely. He may have been right, though it is not likely that he could have found chapter and verse to support his assertion. To Ely bishops the nunnery owed what material encouragement it received in the twelfth century, and if any man has the right to share with Alcock the founder's niche over Jesus gateway, that man was Nigellus, second bishop of the diocese. He succeeded the first bishop, Hervey, in 1133, and the first of several charters which he gave to the nuns must apparently be dated in one of the earliest years of his episcopate. It is addressed, with Norman magnificence, 'to all barons and men of Saint Etheldrytha, cleric or lay, French or English', and it grants 'to the nuns of the little cell lately instituted without the town of Cantebruge' certain land lying near to other land belonging to the same cell. From the Great Inquisition made in the reign of Edward I, generally referred to as the 'Hundred Rolls', we learn that the land given by the bishop consisted of four acres adjoining ten acres next the Green Croft, which King Malcolm granted to the nuns as a site for their church.

To the friendly interest of Nigellus it seems probable that the nunnery owed its first considerable benefaction, a grant by one William the Monk, otherwise le Moyne, of certain land, consisting of two virgates with six acres of meadow, and 'four cottars with their tenure', in the neighbouring village of Shelford. This le Moyne was in his day a man of might and a close friend of the bishop. The two were stout upholders of the cause of the Empress against Stephen, and thereby earned the bitter hostility of the Ely monks, who were on the King's side, and loudly complained that the militant bishop and his friend had despoiled the monastery and the shrine of St Etheldreda to provide themselves with funds for the war. Of le Moyne we are told by the writer of the *Historia Eliensis*, Thomas of Ely:

> With axes, hammers, and every implement of masonry, he profanely assailed the shrine, and with his own hand robbed it of its metal. But he lived to repent it bitterly. He, who had once been extraordinarily rich and had lacked for nothing, was reduced to such extreme poverty as not even to have the necessaries of life. At last, when he had lost all and knew not whither to turn himself, by urgent entreaty he prevailed on the Ely brethren to receive him into their order, and there, with unceasing lamentation, tears, vigils and prayers deploring his guilt, he ended his days in a sincere penitence.

After eight centuries the Shelford lands still remain the property of the nuns' heirs and successors—a remarkable instance of continuity of title. Domesday tells us that they had once belonged to 'Heraldus comes', more familiar to us as King Harold. After the fatal day of Senlac they passed to the Conqueror, and by Henry I were granted to le Moyne. His benefaction to the nuns was for the souls of King Henry and all the faithful in God, and its object was to be the maintenance of one nun for ever. He is described in the charter as a goldsmith (aurifaber), and it was apparently for services in that capacity that he obtained the land from King Henry, for it is recorded that in the reign of Edward I a descendant of his held land at Shelford by the singular serjeanty of repairing the King's crown whenever required.

The nuns obtained a confirmation of le Moyne's grant from King Stephen. The date of the confirmation is fixed by the curious circumstance that the charter was given at a Bedfordshire village, Meppershall, 'in the siege'. Stephen was engaged in besieging a refractory baron, Milo de Beauchamp, at Bedford in January 1138. In Stephen's charter the nuns are styled 'the nuns of St Mary'.

The next benefactor of the nunnery was the Countess Constance, sister of Louis VII of France and widow of King Stephen's only son, Eustace of Boulogne. She granted the nuns certain exemptions from the royal 'customs' for all their lands within and without the borough, as well as all the fishing rights which had been possessed by her husband and herself in the waters belonging to the borough. Her grant, which may be dated about the year 1154, was for the souls of her husband, Eustace, and of Stephen's Queen, Maud, and for the good estate of King Stephen. Her solicitude for her dead husband derives a touch of living interest from the characters given to the royal pair in the Peterborough version of the Anglo-Saxon Chronicle:

> He was an evil man, and did more harm than good wherever he went: he spoiled the lands and laid thereon heavy taxes. She was a good woman, but she had little bliss of him, and it was not the will of Christ that he should long reign.

Sherman, in his *Historia Collegii Jesu*, says that the nuns always regarded Malcolm IV, King of Scotland, as their founder. If they did so, it was, as Dyer observes, on the principle, κορυφοῦται ἐν βασιλεῦσι, for neither as the first nor as the chief of their benefactors did he deserve such consideration. His interest in the nunnery is to be ascribed to the fact that he was Earl of Huntingdon, the two counties of Cambridge and Huntingdon being then linked in one earldom, as to this day they have a common sheriff. The King's first charter, dated at Huntingdon and addressed 'to all his men, cleric and lay, of the Honour of Huntingdon', gave the nuns of Grantebrige ten acres next the Green Croft whereon to build their church. The King stipulated for a formal rent of two shillings per annum, and directed his 'minister' to offer the money, when received, at the altar of the nuns' church. In a second charter he released the nuns from all payment or service on account of the land. The two charters are to be dated within the years 1157 and 1164.

In the first of these charters the nuns are styled simply 'the nuns of Grantebrige'; in the later they are 'nuns of Saint Mary and Saint Radegund of Cantebrug'. This is the earliest occurrence in a charter of the name of St Radegund, and its appearance is to be explained by a then recent historical circumstance. In the year 1159, King Malcolm took a Scottish army overseas to help Henry II in his Toulouse campaign against Louis VII. The English and Scottish kings met, we are told, at Poitiers, and during his stay there we must suppose that Malcolm made acquaintance with the cult of St Radegund. Poitiers is still 'a great worshipper' of the glorious Virgin; thither she retired after deserting her consort, the Merovingian Lothar, and there she founded her celebrated Abbey of the Holy Cross. Her fame spread to many foreign lands, and not least to England. Five English parish churches are dedicated to her. She had a chapel in old St Paul's, London, and in Gloucester, Lichfield, and Exeter Cathedrals. St Radegund's Abbey at Bradsole, near Dover, was founded in her honour in 1191. In later times the Cambridge nunnery, the church, and the parish came to be known simply as St Radegund's. But in strictness the church was dedicated to St Mary, and the Priory took its name from a chapel of St Radegund contained in the church—no doubt, in the Norman portion erected immediately after Malcolm's gift.

The curious parish of St Radegund, whose shadowy existence as a civil parish ended with the Cambridge Award Act of 1857, did not come into being until nearly a century after King Malcolm's foundation of the church. The twelfth-century charters of the nunnery do not tell us in what parish the Green Croft site was included. The town boundary was drawn at the King's Ditch, and the nunnery, being outside it, may have been extra-parochial; certainly it was never held to be in Barnwell. The Cambridge parishes which bordered the nuns' demesne were All Saints' in Jewry—so-named as being in the Jews' quarter, and to distinguish it from All Saints' next the Castle—and St Clement's. Attachment to a parish, with consequent liability to tithes and altar dues and restriction of the right of sepulture, was strongly repugnant to monastic ideas of independence, and the nuns sought their emancipation at an early period in their history. At some time in the reign of Henry II they acquired the advowson of All Saints' Church from a certain Sturmi of Cambridge, who inherited the patronage from his ancestors. In 1180 they obtained the rectorial rights from Geoffrey Ridel, Bishop of Ely. The advowson of St Clement's was given to the Almoner of St Radegund about the year 1215, by Hugh, son of Absalon, who appears to have been Alderman of the Gild Merchant of Cambridge. The rectory of the same church was appropriated to the nuns by John de Fontibus, who was Bishop of Ely from 1220 to 1225. These two advowsons still belong to Jesus College, and the rectorial tithes survive in an attenuated form as 'Radegund tithe' to the present day.

As was invariably the case where a living was absorbed by a religious house, the parochial clergy starved on the meagre pittance which was left to them, and the nuns were at constant feud with their vicars on money matters. The vicars of St Clement's had not even a proper 'manse' to live in, and at times of episcopal visitation made repeated complaints of the leanness of their living. They had a special grievance in the fact that they were required to furnish an annual sum of five marks out of altar-offerings, to provide the sisterhood with the clothing of their order. Such is the persistence of English institutions, even when they have passed through the mill of revolution, that we find this 'clothing money' regularly paid by the vicars for more than half a century after the feminine beneficiaries had given place to scholars of the other sex. When it became the practice to present resident members of the College to the livings, the complaints of the vicars, which in 1248 were loud enough to reach the ears of Pope Innocent IV at Rome, were quieted, if not satisfied. All Saints' parish acquired a fine new church and a commodious vicarage during the nineteenth century, but the curates of St Clement's have as good cause now as centuries ago to complain of the easy liberality of the Bishop of Ely who robbed Clement to enrich Radegund.

With the degree of independence obtained by the impropriation of the two parishes which might reasonably have claimed their allegiance the nuns were for a while content; but not for long. Their neighbours, the Augustinian canons of Barnwell, had got permission to detach their priory precincts from the parish in which they were situated, and to make of them a 'peculiar' parish, i.e. one whose revenues were the *peculium*, or possession, of a monastic body, and which was exempt from the jurisdiction of the archdeacon. The nuns copied the example thus given them about the year 1250. The church founded by Malcolm was long in building; its main fabric, Professor Willis says, was completed about 1245. In dimensions it was very different from the torso which we see today. Its great length—about 190 feet, far transcending that of any now-existing parish church in Cambridge—possibly indicates an original design, such as was common in monastic churches, to set apart a portion of the nave for parish purposes. At all events, when their church was completed, the nuns lost no time in getting sanction to make it parochial.

At the time when the detachment took place, the nunnery demesne had come to be regarded as parcel of All Saints' parish, and the nuns had to compensate the vicars of that parish for the loss of income which they thereby sustained. Of the ancient cleavage a surviving memorial existed in the yearly payment of 40s. which the College made to the vicar of All Saints' until the church was closed and the parish united with that of Holy Sepulchre in 1973. Save for the benefit which they may have derived from the offerings of the nuns, it is not to be supposed that the vicars suffered any considerable pecuniary loss when St Radegund's parish set up for itself, for the latter, from first to last, was a parish in little but in name. It had, indeed, a 'curate', appointed by the nuns without presentation to the bishop, and receiving from them a yearly stipend of £5; the church had a font, and the wills of the parishioners were proved by the nuns' sacrist and deposited in their treasury. But the parish was very small. At the time of the Great Inquisition of Edward I in 1278 it contained four messuages only, all of them the property of the nuns. The parishioners seem to have been for the most part clergy or servants attached to the nunnery.

This 'peculiar' parish existed far into the lifetime of the College, but its later history may best be told while we are dealing with the affairs of the nunnery. The reconstitution of Alcock, as we shall hereafter see, was brought about with the minimum of change that the circumstances allowed. Such features of monastic usage as it was possible for a practically-minded founder, not unconscious of the dawning of new lights in learning, to adapt to College purposes he showed himself anxious to preserve. The parish of St Radegund was retained, and the earliest surviving statutes of the College, given by Bishop Stanley, Alcock's successor at Ely, in 1514, provide that one of the Fellows shall be annually elected curate of the parish church of St Radegund annexed to the College and shall have the cure of souls of all dwelling there. But the need for a separate parish ceased when the servants of the College were housed within its walls. The farmers of the nunnery demesne lands, which after the dissolution were known as the Manor of St Radegund, still, indeed, claimed their right to attend the church within the College and, even so late as the reign of Queen Mary, it is covenanted for them in an extant deed that

> both the colledge and the vicare of Alhallows shall suffer hereafter the farmers to come and frequent the colledge church to hear their divine service, accordinglie as it is specified in a payre of indentures betweene the sayde master and fellows and the sayde vicare, except it be in the plaigue tyme.

But the farmers were few, and even the primitive College society, *pusillus grex*, as Bishop Stanley calls it, required far more house-room than the thirteen sisters of St Radegund had done. Alcock, therefore, converted into college rooms the portion of the nave which had belonged to the parishioners. Instead of the old western door, portions of which still exist, buried in the walls of the Master's lodge, he made a new door at the south-west angle of the shortened nave. It opened on the parish churchyard, which, as 'Jesus churchyard', was the burial-ground of the parishioners far into the sixteenth century and now forms part of the Master's garden.

When and how the parish became absorbed again into that of All Saints' is not clear. Both parish church and curate disappear in the revised statutes which Bishop West (1515–33) gave to the College. But one long-abiding trace of the former remained in the fair celebrated in the churchyard yearly at the Feast of the

Assumption. This fair, known in post-nunnery times as Garlick Fair, was a very ancient institution, for the charter which granted the nuns the privilege of holding it was given to them by King Stephen. Originally it was held on two days, viz. on the vigil and on the feast of the Assumption—i.e. 14–15 August—but a charter of Henry VI extended it to a third day. The nuns' accounts show that at fair time they hired an extra cook to help in the kitchen, and besides the profits derived from catering they took tolls of the booth-keepers. Profits from tolls, indeed, continued to be accounted for by the College bursars down to the year 1709. But on the whole the fair did not bring in any substantial returns either to the nuns or to the College, and the competition of the two neighbouring fairs, 'Pot' Fair, on Midsummer Common, and the more celebrated Sturbridge Fair, near Barnwell, carried off all but local custom from Garlick Fair. So King Stephen's fair sank to the level of a village feast, and a self-respecting College felt that its dignity was compromised by the annual exposure of the wares of Autolycus under the chapel walls. Puritanic masters of the College, whose dividends were no longer augmented by the sale of 'cakes and ale', from over the mud wall which parted their private garden from the 'Fair Close' looked sourly on the vulgar merry-making of their humbler neighbours, and the decree went forth that the fair should be exiled to the furthest western margin of the Close, where it gave its name to Garlick Fair Lane, now called Park Street. Removed from the vicinage of its patron saint, it protracted an obscure existence there until the beginning of the nineteenth century.

The three centuries which followed King Malcolm's donation brought with them very little to record in the nuns' affairs. Had the Priory possessed a chronicler the events on which she would have dwelt would have been the sudden downfall of the bell-tower in 1277; the dreadful fires which devastated their house and goods in 1313 and in 1376; and the equally disastrous gale which 'prostrated' their buildings in 1390. One hundred and fifty years after the first settlement on the Green Croft the sisters no doubt became aware that the neighbouring town had drawn to itself a miscellaneous lot of scholars, and that something called a

University was beginning to make a local figure there. Certain of the scholars dwelt in houses rented from the nunnery, which were henceforth known as hostels; but except in a business aspect their arrival did not greatly interest the sisters. As their names show, the Cambridge nuns were drawn exclusively from the families of local squires and burgesses, and they did not affect a learning beyond their times or their class. The account-rolls which the departing sisters left behind them in 1496 reveal pretty fully the routine of their lives. Books—save for the casual mention of the binding of the Lives of the Saints—were none of their business; and works of charity, excepting the customary dole to the poor on Maundy Thursday and occasional relief to 'poor soldiers disabled in the wars of our lord the King', scarcely concerned them more. The duties of hospitality in the Guest House make the Cellaress a busy woman. They cost a good deal, but are not unprofitable; the nuns take in 'paying guests'—daughters of tradesmen and others. Being ladies, the sisters neither toil nor spin; but the Prioress and the Grangeress have an army of servants, whose daily duties have to be assigned to them; carters and ploughmen must be sent out to the scattered plots owned by the nunnery in the open fields about Cambridge; the neatherd has to drive the cattle to distant Willingham fen; the brewer has instructions for malting and brewing the 'peny-ale' which serves the nuns for 'bevers'; and the women-servants are dispatched to work in the dairy, to weed the garden, or to weave and to make candles in the hospice. Once in a while a party of the nuns, accompanied by their maid-servants, takes boat as far as to Lynn, there to buy stock-fish and Norway timber, and to fetch a letter for the Prioress.

Occasional glimpses are given us in episcopal registers at Lambeth and Ely of larger occurrences that ruffled at times the quiet of the cloister. Great was the stir when a Visitor deputed by the archbishop or the bishop came on his rounds to inspect the nunnery. One such Visitor, Thomas de Wormenhale, commissioned by the Archbishop of Canterbury in the year 1373, when the see of Ely was vacant, gives us a curious 'snapshot' picture of the little life in St Radegund's cloister. The sisters are privately and separately examined. Tongues are loosed, and old grievances on that day have privilege to air themselves. The Prioress, Margaret Clanyle, is' unpopular; she spends, and the nunnery is poor. The refectory roof will not keep out the weather, and when it is wet the sisters must take their meals where they can. The clerical staff is unpaid, and celebration for benefactors is scandalously pretermitted. Moreover, discipline is lax, and the nuns, or some of them, get easy permission to gad outside the cloister. Worst is the case of Dame Elizabeth de Cambridge. Being a lady of rank, the daughter, indeed, of that eminent burgess Sir Thomas de Cambridge, she escapes that correction which her reprehensible conduct calls for. For the Prioress herself does not deny that Elizabeth is in the habit of withdrawing herself from divine service and allowing friars of different orders, as well as scholars, to visit and converse with her at inopportune times, to the scandal of religion. Furthermore, it is alleged that she murmurs at correction (though the complaint is that she does not get it), and provokes discord among the sisters; and, lastly, that she does not trouble to get up (*non curat surgere*) to attend matins, as she is bound to do. For the remedying of these abuses the Visitor, easy man, has only two suggestions to make: first, that the Prioress must pay her way, when and how she may; and, secondly, that Dame Elizabeth had better give up quarrelling with her sisters, and get up for matins when she can (*cum poterit*); if she does not mend her ways she must look to be excommunicated.

Scandal is generally the key which unlocks the cloister gate and permits a glance into the interior shadows. *Bene vixit quae bene latuit*. Not such was Margaret Cailly, whose sad story was the gossip of the nuns' parlour in 1389. She came of an old and reputable family which had furnished mayors and bailiffs to Cambridge and had endowed the nuns with lands at Trumpington. For reasons sufficiently moving her, which we may only surmise, she escaped from the cloister, discarded her religious garb, and sought hiding in the alien diocese of Lincoln. But it so happened that Archbishop Courtenay that year was making metropolitical visitation of that diocese, and it was the ill fortune of Margaret, 'a sheep wandering from the fold among thorns', to come under his notice. The archbishop, solicitous 'that her blood be not required at our hands', handed her over to the keeping of his brother of Ely. The bishop, in turn, passed her on to the custody of her own Prioress, with injunctions that she should be kept in close confinement, under exercise of salutary penance, until she showed signs of contrition for her 'excesses'; and, further, that when the said Margaret first entered the chapter-house she should humbly implore pardon of the Prioress and her sisters for her offences. The story ends for us at Margaret's prison door; but it may be hoped that a second elopement relieved the sisterhood of a situation which may well have been as embarrassing to them as it was distressful to the apostate who had tasted the sweet poison of secular liberty.

Another scene within the nunnery walls, of which the Ely registers permit us to be spectators, is the election of a Prioress in September 1457. The proceedings in chapter-house and church are set down in much detail, and the vote cast by each of the eleven sisters is duly recorded. The choice of the majority fell on the Sacrist, Joan Lancastre, but we are told that she only accepted the burden laid on her under much pressure and with many protestations. The grounds of her reluctance are not far to seek. Though the nuns, so lately as in the year 1451, were fairly paying their way, their financial outlook had clouded in the dark years of civil war which followed. The bell-tower was again in trouble and, a few months before the election, the Bishop of Ely invited the faithful to lend a helping hand to its repair and to supply the nuns with church books and vestments.

Twenty years pass, and Prioress Elizabeth Walton, in 1478, has to confess that the nuns are 'destitute of money for our pore lyffing', and that they owe their butcher £21 of lawful money of England. To remedy this unsatisfactory state of affairs they adopt the unthrifty course of assigning to him, for a term of nineteen years, the profit of two nunnery tenements in Cambridge. Next the nunnery seal disappears, sold, no doubt, or pawned. The nunnery lands are untilled, or at least yield them no profit. Joan Key in 1482, finding bankruptcy past concealment, vacates her office of Treasuress three months before her term expires, and leaves a heavy tale of debt for her successor to liquidate. Poverty and the growing temptations which come of the proximity of the University bring sad moral depravation. The better sisters withdraw to other religious houses. Elizabeth Butlier, aged only sixteen, finds that she cannot serve God at St Radegund's with as much devotion as she wishes, and seeks a new home at St Helen's nunnery, London; another nun goes to Davington, Kent.

Matters had reached this desperate pass when, in 1486, John Alcock succeeded Bishop Morton in the see of Ely. Next year the Prioress of St Radegund's died, and the bishop availed himself of the opportunity to attempt a reformation of the nunnery. His proceedings are narrated in his register:

On the twelfth day of October, A.D. 1487, the Bishop visited the house or monastery of the nuns of St Mary and St Radegund, then destitute of a Prioress and vacant by the death of the late Prioress, Mistress Joan Cambrigge . . . and sitting in the chapter-house of the foresaid monastery, on the tribunal, delivered his decree as follows:

In the name of God Amen. We, John, by divine permission Bishop of Ely, on the 12th day of October, visiting in our right as ordinary the nunnery of St Mary and St Radegund, Cambridge, destitute of the solace of a Prioress, for certain true, just, notorious, and manifest causes, find all and singular the nuns unfit and disqualified to elect their future Prioress, and therefore decree that in such manner of election they are justly deprived of voice. Wherefore we take upon ourselves the task of providing from some other like religious place a fit person for the vacancy in the said nunnery, the right of electing and providing for the same nunnery having devolved canonically upon us, and having the fear of God before our eyes we thus proceed.

And you, Mistress Joan Fulborne, duly and lawfully professed of the order of St Benedict and long time laudably conversant in the same, for your good religion and integrity, sincere virginity and other merits of prudence and holy conversation credibly reported to us, we appoint and provide to be Prioress of the same house. . . .

And consequently, by mandate of the Bishop, the reverend Master William Robynson, bachelor in either law, conducted the same Joan

Fulborne to the High Altar, while the nuns, with others, chanted *Te Deum*, and assigned to her the stall in the choir and the place in the chapter anciently and of custom appointed to the Prioress, and canonically inducted her into the same with all its rights and appurtenances.

Whether Alcock, when he attempted the moral reformation of the Priory, did anything towards the repair of its finances or fabric we do not know. His plans, whatever they were, resulted in blank failure. John Mair, who was resident at Cambridge when the facts were fresh in memory, describes the morals of the sisterhood as all that they should not be. Sherman says that they cast off the veil and voluntarily withdrew, and that the buildings lay for some time deserted and desolate. The little parish of St. Radegund, once tenanted by the clergy and servants attached to the nunnery, shared in its depopulation. Nine tenements in Jesus Lane lay vacant in 1497-8, when the collectors of the newly-founded College took stock of the property which fell to them from the nuns' portion.

While the house was in this derelict condition it was visited by the bishop, in 1495-6. The evidence of what he saw there is given in the letters patent for the foundation of the College, dated 12 June 1496. The buildings and properties of the house are dilapidated and wasted owing to the improvidence, extravagance, and incontinence of the nuns resulting from their proximity to the University of Cambridge. Two nuns only remain: one of them is professed elsewhere, the other is of ill fame (*infamis*). They are in abject want, utterly unable to maintain divine services or the works of mercy and piety required of them, and are ready to depart, leaving the house desolate.

The two last unhappy sisters departing took with them whatever of portable property they could find; or perhaps there was nothing to take. Certain it is that they left nothing behind—nothing except some bundles of deeds, inconsiderable to them, valuable to the incoming scholars and the historian in times to come. One legacy, more important, they left us—their church and domestic buildings. At the end of the fifteenth century Cambridge was chiefly remarkable for its monastic establishments.

Their great churches and spacious courts were immeasurably grander than anything which the colleges had to show. Of the men's religious houses, save an insignificant fragment of the Priory at Barnwell, not a vestige is left. The nunnery of St Radegund remains, disguised and curtailed, but in its main features fairly complete. With the help of documentary evidence from the nuns' muniments and the early College records, it is not difficult to reconstruct its plan and to identify its principal parts with the existing buildings.

Between the nunnery and Radegund Lane we may picture a considerable stretch of vacant ground. Beneath the church walls was the parish churchyard; beyond it, eastward, the Fair Yard, with gates opening to the lane. A footway—the present 'Chimney' —which was parted from the churchyard by a mud wall, conducted to the western door of the nave and the outer gates of the monastery. Above the gates was a low building containing a single chamber, and next it, westwards, a small attached block, later the school-house, which was probably the nuns' almonry. Within the gates was the *curia*, or outer court of the monastery, which, perhaps, had farm-buildings and offices of various uses irregularly grouped about it. On its eastward side it was flanked by a long range of buildings, substantially the same as we see today. But its walls of weathered clunch are now encased in brick, its height has been increased by a second upper floor, and its thatched roof has disappeared. At one end stood, as it still stands, the kitchen, lighted then by narrow lancet-headed windows, but otherwise much as we see it still. In a walled space, still existing, the nuns probably piled their stock-fish in a stack, as it may be seen piled in Norwegian warehouses today. The room to the south of the kitchen was then most likely, as it was in early College days, the *pincerna*, or pantry. Next it, southwards, was the present entry to the cloister; but the entry was formerly further to the south, in what is now a part of the Master's lodge. In the wall of this modern entry, then a chamber, we may note an ancient aperture, somewhat widely splayed, which had once been closed by a shutter, of which the hinge remains. It communicates with the pantry, but did not serve the purpose of a window. It is a feature seen in various forms in many monasteries, and called the *rota*, or turn. Here a nun might, by permission, obtain a stoup of beer from the servant in the pantry. It appears to have been passed to the opening down a box-like case horizontally attached to the pantry wall in such a manner that the two parties could not see or converse with one another.

The ground-floor rooms below the Old Library were probably occupied by the Cellaress. Above them was the *aula*, or hall, for the lodging of the nuns' guests. It did not communicate with the cloister, but was reached by a 'porch', or covered staircase, ascending from the *curia*. The ancient apartment which became the hall of the Master's Lodge was the *camera*, or dwelling-room of the Prioress. For long known as the Old Hall, it was renamed 'The Prioress's Room' when separated from the Lodge in 1946. The handsome wainscoted room over it, called the Conference Room, was her solar, or upper chamber. Next it was her oratory, a small room which is now distinguished by a large window of three lights looking into the cloister. On the ground-floor, next the north aisle of the nave, was a room called the vestibule, from which the Prioress had a private access to the church. It is now occupied by the staircase of the lodge.

The south walk of the cloister was flanked throughout its length by the nave of the church. The west front contained a central doorway of a thirteenth-century type. Aisles, north and south, lined the nave, that on the north side occupying the position of the present south walk of the cloister. The pier arches of the nave, seven in number on each side, were in character like those in the north transept, but loftier. There was a screen, which probably extended to the full height of the nave and stood in the position of the present west wall of the chapel; it served to separate the parochial church from the more eastern portion reserved to the nuns. The upper story of the central tower is an addition of Alcock's time; the bell-tower of the nuns was probably covered with a low conical roof. The roofs over the four arms of the church were all of high pitch, as is shown by the weather markings on the tower. The transepts each had a chapel on the eastern side. The northern one occupied the position of the present organ-chamber; that on the south side, if we may judge from the mouldings of the arch opening into the transept, was put up about the time when the steeple fell, in 1277.

In the chancel there was an often-mentioned altar of St Katherine and other virgins, standing on the north side of the high altar. External to the north wall of the presbytery there was a building of two stories, the upper of which must have obscured the lower part of the lancet windows. It was evidently the Sacrist's abode, and the aperture is still to be seen on the outer wall, near the north-east angle of the chancel, through which she watched the light before the high altar.

In the north transept may be seen the square-headed doorway, now built up, through which the nuns entered the church from their dormitory. The room immediately outside the door was probably a vestry, through which the nuns passed from the foot of the dormitory stairs. The dormitory must have occupied the whole length of the upper floor of the eastern cloister range. Below it was the chapter-house, the square ending of which projected into what is now the Chapel Court. As was often the case, the floor of the chapter-house and the adjoining walk of the cloister were lowered in order to give a dignified height to this important building without breaking the level of the dormitory floor above. Outside the entrance of the chapter-house we may remark the stone bench, where on Maundy Thursday sat the twelve poor men (or women, perhaps) whose feet were washed by the sisters.[1] A passage under the daïs of the refectory—in College days called the Dark Entry—conducted to a prolongation of the cloister northwards from the Hall. On the eastern side of the Dark Entry was a room containing a fireplace, which seems to have been the warming house, to which the nuns were permitted to retire from the cloister in cold weather; westward of the passage were store-rooms beneath the refectory. The walls of the latter are preserved in the present Hall. The building which continued the eastern cloister range northwards from the refectory contained on the upper floor a large room which may have

---

[1] An estate at Madingley, called Maundy Sylver, provided the thirty pence which the nuns doled on this occasion.

been the novices' dormitory, and next it, at the extremity of the
building, was the *latrina*—the last a hardly altered example of
thirteenth-century masonry. East from the cloister stretched the
nuns' graveyard. The infirmary, a detached building which has
wholly vanished, most likely was placed near it.

CHAPTER II

THE FOUNDER AND HIS WORK

THE early Tudor period in university history was the day of great episcopal foundations. Within a space of forty years from the date of Bosworth Field six important colleges were planted—three at either university—and all of them were either founded by bishops, or to bishops owed the suggestion for their foundation. The earliest of the group was Jesus, Cambridge (1496), the creation of a Bishop of Ely, John Alcock. Next came the twin colleges of Christ's (1505) and St John's (1511) at Cambridge, which owed their origin to Fisher of Rochester, just as Christ Church, Oxford (1525), was in all but name the foundation of Wolsey of York. Prior in date to Christ Church were the Oxford colleges of Brasenose and Corpus Christi (both in 1512), the former founded in part by Smyth of Lincoln, the latter by Fox of Winchester. And to these illustrious men we may add one who, in the wide field of his munificence, surpassed them all, as in its scale he rivalled even Wolsey—Wolsey's predecessor at York, John Rotheram, re-founder of Lincoln, Oxford, benefactor of King's and Pembroke and the University Library at Cambridge, and founder of Jesus College at Rotherham. In the fact that of these six episcopal founders five—Wolsey being the exception—were natives of the northern counties, we perhaps see an indication of the remarkable revival of religious feeling witnessed at this period in Northern England, and of an awakening among the rulers of the Church to a sense of its responsibilities and of its shortcomings in those parts. The three Cambridge founders, Rotheram, Alcock, and Fisher, were all Yorkshiremen; all of them, moreover, connected with the ancient town of Beverley and its collegiate church. Rotheram, who took his name from his birthplace, and there went to school, was Provost of Beverley

Church, 1468–72. Alcock and Fisher were both of them born and educated at Beverley. Each of the three received his later education at Cambridge; but the Cambridge of Fisher's youth had already taken colouring from the New Learning, and inspired him with educational ideals other than those of his two predecessors. In the lives, the aims, and, it would seem, in the characters also of Rotheram and Alcock, there is a resemblance so close that each reflects the other, and it is not unreasonable to conjecture that in Rotheram's completed foundation at his native town we see the suggestion of what Jesus College, Cambridge, should have been had Alcock lived to carry out his designs.

Of the two men Rotheram was somewhat the older. He was admitted in theology in 1462, and Alcock in canon law in 1469–70. Rotheram was one of the original Fellows of King's, and subsequently became Master of Pembroke; Alcock's college is uncertain, but there is some likelihood that it was Pembroke. About the same time they were instituted to London rectories: Rotheram to St Vedast's, Alcock to St Margaret's, Fish Street, and to St Stephen's, Westminster. Rotheram was consecrated Bishop of Rochester in 1468; Alcock succeeded him there in 1472. In 1471 Rotheram went on an embassy to Burgundy, and in the same year Alcock was appointed a commissioner to treat with the King of Scots. From April to September 1474 the two bishops, by an arrangement of which no similar instance is known, jointly held the office of Lord Chancellor. Rotheram was translated successively to Lincoln in 1471 and to York in 1480; Alcock to Worcester in 1476 and to Ely in 1486. Each was conspicuous for his devotion to the cause of Henry VII. Rotheram, dying in May 1500, nominated Alcock supervisor of his will; Alcock died on 1 October of the same year.

Not the least noteworthy point in these singularly parallel lives is the fact that each of the friends founded in his diocese a college dedicated to the Name of Jesus. The licence to found Jesus College, Rotherham, was obtained in 1481; but the Archbishop only made final provision for its establishment in his will, dated 1498. Alcock, who obtained letters patent for the erection of his college in 1496, was less fortunate in completing his designs for its constitution. The letters patent provide that the College shall consist of a Master, six Fellows, and 'a certain number' of scholars to be trained in grammar. Bishop Nicholas West, in the preamble to the statutes which he gave to the College, says that Alcock designed that it should consist of a Master, six Fellows, and six boys, but he adds that the premature death of the founder prevented him from carrying his pious intentions into effect, that the endowment had subsequently proved insufficient for the maintenance of the number which he had designed, and that he had not lived to frame, *perfecte et sufficienter*, statutes for its governance. That statutes of some temporary kind were drafted by him seems certain. The earliest extant statutes of the College are those given to it in 1514-15 by James Stanley, Bishop of Ely, and they expressly abrogate all previous statutes. In the interval between Alcock's death and 1514, endowments, large in relation to the primitive foundation, had come to the College, and a somewhat extensive remodelling of the founder's plans was inevitable. Bishop Stanley, however, in his preamble, declares that he 'adheres to the footprints of his most devout predecessor', and in his palimpsest we may probably read the outlines of Alcock's scheme.

Rotheram's college, in the parish church of his native town, consisted of a provost, six choristers, and three masters, who were to teach respectively grammar, music, and writing. Its objects, stated in the licence for its foundation, were twofold: 'To preach the Word of God in the parish of Rotherham and in other places in the diocese of York, and to instruct gratuitously, in the rules of grammar and song, scholars from all parts of England, and especially from the diocese of York.' Alcock's foundation, as we have seen, was designed for a Master, six Fellows and six boys. Rotheram's college was to consist of ten persons for the fanciful reason that, whereas its founder had offended God in his ten commandments, he might benefit by the prayers of the society. Alcock's motive for fixing on a society of thirteen looks like a piece of conservatism, characteristic of the man. In many monasteries thirteen was the complement of professed members, the number having reference to the original Christian society of our Lord and his Apostles. Probably St Radegund's nunnery consisted of that number; eleven sisters are named as having *jus eligendi* at the election of a Prioress in 1457.

Rotheram's college, according to its measure, was intended to meet two pressing needs of his time, and especially of Northern England—a preaching clergy and boys trained for the service of the Church. At the end of the fifteenth century 'both theology and the art of preaching seemed in danger of general neglect. At the English universities, and consequently throughout the whole country, the sermon was falling into almost complete disuse.' [1] The disfavour with which it was regarded by the heads of the Church was largely due to fear of the activity of the Lollards, which had brought all popular harangues and discourses under suspicion. When the embers of heresy had been extinguished, here and there a reforming Churchman sought to restore among the parish clergy the old preaching activity. In the wide, unmanageable dioceses of the north the lack of an educated, preaching priesthood was most apparent. Bishop Stanley is probably only echoing the language of Alcock when he begins and closes his statutes with an exhortation to the society, whom he addresses as 'scholars of Jesus', so to conduct themselves 'that the Name of our Lord Jesus Christ may be honoured, the clergy multiplied, and the people called to the praise of God'. He enacts that of the five foundation Fellows (one of Alcock's six having been suppressed) four shall be devoted to the study of theology, and he requires that they shall be chosen from natives of five counties, which, owing to the imperfections of the existing copies of his statutes, are unspecified. If, as is likely, this county restriction was re-introduced by Stanley from the provisions made by Alcock, it is natural to surmise that the founder's native county was one of those preferred. Certain it is that his small society had a Yorkshireman, Chubbes, of Whitby, for its first Master. He had been a Fellow of Pembroke, and probably from the same society and county came one of the original Fellows of Jesus, William Atkynson.

[1] Mullinger, *The University of Cambridge*, vol. i, p. 438.

The same fear of Lollardism which had stifled preaching had caused the teaching profession to be regarded with jealousy by the authorities of the Church.[1] In a limited part of North-eastern England William Byngham, about the year 1439, found seventy schools void for 'grete scarstee of Maistres of Gramar', which fifty years previously had been in active use. His foundation of God's House at Cambridge was designed to supply trained masters to these derelict schools. The boys' schools attached to Rotheram's and Alcock's foundations were intended to meet the same deficiency. Presumably Alcock meant that one or other of his Fellows should supply the teaching, for his foundation did not include a schoolmaster. The linking of a grammar school with a house of university students was, of course, no novelty; the connexion of Winchester with New College had been copied by Henry VI in the association of Eton and King's. But Alcock's plan of including boys and 'dons' within the same walls, and making them mix in the common life and discipline of hall and chapel, if not absolutely a new thing, had no nearer prototype in an English university than Walter de Merton's provision in the statutes of his college for a *Grammaticus* and *pueri*.[2] Though the school was meant to supply a practical need, the pattern of it seems to have been suggested by Alcock's medieval sentiment. There is, indeed, no evidence or likelihood that St Radegund's nunnery maintained a school, but the same monastic precedent which Alcock apparently followed in fixing the number of his society prescribed the type of his school. It stood in the quarter where monastic schools were always placed, next the gate, in the old building which had served the nuns as their almonry.

In the endowment of the College Alcock had little part. Whatever his plans may have been, they were frustrated by his death, little more than four years after he had obtained the King's letters patent. As Bishop West says in his statutes, the College was by him, not *fundatum*, but *fundari coeptum*. From the wreckage of the

---

[1] Mullinger, *The University of Cambridge*, vol. i, p. 349.
[2] Merton's boys were placed in Nunhall, a building detached from the college; they were educated, in some cases, till they were capable of taking a degree.

nunnery a good deal was recovered. Indeed, under the competent management of the first Fellows the estates of the dispossessed priory brought in at least as large a sum as the nuns' Treasuress had gathered in times comparatively prosperous. The income of the nuns from all sources in the two years 1449–50 and 1450–1 had amounted, respectively, to £77 and £72 odd. Though many of the lands and houses were unlet in 1497–8, and many tenants remained in arrears or disputed payment, William Pykerell, the collector, managed to put by a net sum of over £70 in that year. His payments were few and formal; the rebuilding of the dilapidated house had either not begun, or its charges were borne by the bishop and his friends. We are accustomed to regard Alcock as not only the founder, but also the architect of Jesus; and for that belief we have the warrant of Bishop West's statement that the College was 'newly built and constructed, almost from its very foundations', by Alcock. Of the competence of the founder as an architect there can be no question. He was comptroller of the royal works and buildings under Henry VII, and his skill and taste are evidenced by his work at Ely, Westbury, Malvern, and at Great St Mary's Church, Cambridge. But the literal acceptation of West's assertion is subject to certain qualifications. First, the nunnery buildings were so far from being removed by Alcock that we now know that he retained them almost entire. Secondly, though the recasting of the old into the newest Perpendicular fashion was no doubt accomplished through his agency, the builder's hand was in some cases that of one of his friends, Sir Reginald Bray or Sir John Rysley.

What Alcock and his friends did to adapt the nunnery buildings to College uses may be briefly described. The great church was obviously beyond the requirements of his little community of thirteen, and he wisely decided not to lay on his College the costly burden of its maintenance in its full proportions. The western part of the nave was converted into a three-storied range of chambers. It had once been the parish church, and Alcock, careful as ever of the type, retained for parish uses the shortened nave and the transepts, and made a new door for the use of the parishioners at the south-west corner of the present nave. He destroyed the nave aisles and the transept chapels, and increased the area of the cloister court by adding to it the space occupied by the northern aisle of the nave. The thirteenth-century pier arches of the nave and chancel were filled up, and large Perpendicular windows of the plainest pattern were inserted in the upper part of the walls and in the gables of the south transept and choir. Most of this work was done by Sir John Rysley, who, on the testimony of Bishop Stanley, 'built the nave of the church, and covered the cloister with wood, lead, and fabric'. He died in 1512, and by his will left the College £160 for completing this work and glazing the windows. The bell-tower again needed the helping hands which Bishop Gray had invited for it forty years before. Its upper story had to come down, and was rebuilt in the same plain style as the nave. If in their recasting of the nuns' work Alcock and Rysley worked under disadvantages which, from an aesthetic point of view, are to be regretted, in wood, glass, and those interior adornments which were the glory of fifteenth-century builders, they enriched the church beyond all previous knowledge. Sufficient fragments remain of the beautiful stalls and screen of the founder to justify the judgment of Dr Shorton, a Jesus man transplanted to the Mastership of St John's, when he adopted 'the stalles in the southe parte of the Qwyer in Jhesus College in Cambridge' as the model of those to be put up in the chapel of his adopted college. They also demonstrate the marked superiority of the original to the copy.

In the hall the fine roof of Spanish chestnut with its beautiful corbels, the charming oriel, and the quaint window in the western wall were the additions of Alcock to the nuns' refectory; or it may be that they were the work of Sir Reginald Bray, whose arms are still displayed in the window opposite the oriel. The time-worn clunch walls of the nuns' refectory and domestic buildings were faced with brick, and the long galleries which furnished interior communication to the different quarters of the nunnery, and the porch, or pentis, ascending from the outer court to the Guest Hall, gave place to staircases. The lodging of the Prioress, with little structural alteration, became the Master's *mansum*, and her oratory, altered by the insertion of a Perpendicular east

window, was used as the Master's oratory from the days of Dr
Reston, Master from 1546 to 1551 until at least the Mastership of
Richard Sterne, appointed in 1634. Its use probably ended in
1644, when the Puritan, Thomas Young, was intruded into the
Mastership. The hands which unscrupulously walled up the
beautiful Early English work of the chapter-house (discovered in
1893) made atonement in the erection of the picturesque gate-
tower and the doorcase, bearing Alcock's rebus, in the eastern
wall of the outer court. One nunnery building, the sacristy,
described in the last chapter, was retained by Alcock to serve as a
lodging for distinguished guests of the College, but disappeared
early in the sixteenth century. Alcock's adaptation of the whole of
the conventual buildings to the requirements of a college was so
ingeniously effected that Bishop West, living in the next generation, seems to have thought the College buildings were entirely
of his creation, and Sherman, writing in the seventeenth century,
credited him with having deliberately adopted the monastic plan.

The formal title given to the College in the royal letters patent
was 'The College of the most Blessed Virgin Mary, Saint John
the Evangelist, and the Glorious Virgin Saint Radegund'. But
there can be no doubt of the truth of Sherman's statement that
it was the intention of the founder from the first that it should
be generally known as 'Jesus College'. The church was re-dedi-
cated by him to the Name of Jesus; the Fellows and scholars are
styled *Jesuani* in Bishop Stanley's statutes; the neighbouring street
took the name of Jesus Lane so early as 1497; and in legal phrase
the words 'commonly called Jesus College' were customarily
added at a very early date to the formal style. Indeed, it would
seem that the title first decided on was 'The College of Jesus, the
Blessed Virgin Mary, and Saint John the Evangelist'; for in
an address of the Master and Fellows to Henry VII, belonging, apparently, to the year 1497, that is the name which they
give to their society. Moreover, the original seal of the College
has for legend, SIGILLVM COLLEGII IHV: MARIE ET IOHIS: EVAG:
CANTEBR. It represents under canopies the Virgin and St John
standing on either side of the Saviour, and the base displays a
shield bearing the emblems of the Five Wounds. In Stanley's

statutes it is ordained that the Mass of the Name of Jesus shall be celebrated weekly throughout the year, and far into the nineteenth century the College allowed 'exceedings' on Festum Jesu.

From Alcock we now pass to the men who formed the small society of his newly constituted College, and to those of his friends who aided his work and continued it when he had been removed by death.

William Chubbes, the first Master, was, as we have seen, a native of Whitby, and had been a Fellow and President of Pembroke. He was about seventeen years junior to Alcock, for he was admitted to incept in theology in 1486-7, on which occasion he deposited as his caution a volume of Scotus, an author on whom he wrote a commentary; he was likewise author of an Introduction to Logic. It was at his suggestion that Alcock converted the nunnery into a college. Along with Chubbes the account toll of 1497-8 gives the names of Edward Griggson, William Pykerell, and Henry Lecheman, who either then or soon afterwards were Fellows; besides these, William Atkynson, Thomas Greyne, and William Plombe were apparently original Fellows. William Atkynson seems to be identical with a Pembroke man of that name, who was successively a prebendary of Southwell and a canon first of Lincoln and then of Windsor. Plombe was appointed by the founder to supervise the building of the College, and in 1497-8 a Grace of the Senate was passed excusing him from attendance at congregations, general processions, and funerals of the dead while he was engaged in the building of Jesus College.

Within a few years of its inception, and partly within the lifetime of the founder, the meagre endowment of the College was increased by the piety and liberality of a group of benefactors, most of whom were Alcock's friends, and who contributed to carry out his plans. Of the part taken in the building of the College by Sir John Rysley and Sir Reginald Bray something has already been said. Rysley furthermore founded a readership in theology, and designed other benefactions to the College had he lived. Sherman ascribes the foundation of the readership to John Batemanson, LL.D., and it would seem that its endowment was given jointly by the two. By the Visitors in the third year of Elizabeth this readership was converted into four College preacherships. It was once held by Cranmer.

In adjoining windows in the Priory Church of Great Malvern were once to be seen the figures of Alcock, the bishop of the diocese, and of Sir Reginald Bray, the architect who, under his direction, had re-edified the church. At the court and in politics we find the two men constantly associated in the reign of Henry VII, and Bray's fame and skill in architecture—he completed St George's Chapel at Windsor, and is credited with the design of Henry VII's Chapel at Westminster—must especially have brought him into close relation with Alcock, who was comptroller of the royal buildings. In Bray Jesus was again linked with the *domus antiqua et religiosa* of Pembroke, for he was a benefactor of both colleges, and his widow, the Lady Katherine Bray, in 1506 appointed the Master and Fellows of Pembroke parties to the covenant which she made with Jesus College for the maintenance of a master in grammar for the school in the latter College.

The school-house, we are expressly told in this deed, had already been built by Alcock. It stood between the gate and the Fellows' garden; on the upper floor was the boys' dormitory, and a chamber in the gate-tower was allotted to the schoolmaster. He was required to teach gratuitously the College boys and any others resorting thither from elsewhere. He was to receive from the College an annual stipend of ten marks, together with meat and drink, wine and wax for divine offices, and the services of the College barber and laundress, as any Fellow of the College. The usher was to teach the smaller and lower boys, and was paid forty shillings annually. He was lodged in the College proper, i.e. in the cloisters. The statutes of Bishop Stanley require that the four College *pueri* shall be under fourteen years of age at admission, having been previously sufficiently trained in singing, and shall serve as choristers. They are to be maintained by the College and attend grammar-school for four years, unless any should before then be sufficiently learned in grammar, in which case he may study arts or otherwise, as the Master of the College may direct. The boy promoted to the study of arts thereupon took rank as a *juvenis.* These College *juvenes*, four in number, were required to be *grammatici* and *dialectici*, skilful in singing and apt for divine services. One of the four was to serve as organist, the others respectively as sacrist, bible-clerk, and gatekeeper, and at refections all of them were to wait at the table of the Master and Fellows.

The school, as has been said, bore a very important relation to the College as first constituted. The stipend of the schoolmaster, £6 13s. 4d., was as large as that assigned to the Master of the College by Bishop Stanley's statutes, and the usher, with £2 per annum, was actually better off than a Fellow, who had no money stipend until 1549. Bishop West gave boys trained in the school a preferential claim to Fellowships after they had attained B.A. The school survived the Reformation, but the special purpose which Alcock meant it to fufil, viz. the training of boys as acolytes and choristers, ceased to exist after the medieval ritual disappeared. When the ancient Trivium was remodelled by the Visitors of Edward VI in 1549, grammar was discarded as a subject of university teaching, and Jesus was the only college permitted to give instruction in it. The Visitors of Elizabeth originally made the same exception. In the statutes which they drafted in 1569 it was ordained:

Nemo Grammaticam in ullo Collegio deceat nisi in Collegio Jesu tantum et in Collegiis Trinitatis et Regio quoad choristas.

But in the revised code of 1570 the exception in the case of Jesus was omitted. The College had anticipated this conclusion by ceasing to pay the stipends of the schoolmaster and usher at Christmas 1567.

In the fourteen years which intervened between Alcock's death and the date of Stanley's statutes four Fellowships were added to the six of the original foundation. Two of the new Fellowships were given in the fifteenth year of Henry VII: the first by Thomas Roberts of Over, in the county of Cambridge, endowed with lands in that parish; the second by will of Roger Thorney, maintained out of certain tenements in Southwark. The third Fellowship, on the authority of Sherman and a manuscript of 1557 called

Fundationes Collegii Jesu Cantabrigiae, is set down to the credit of Richard Pigott of London, serjeant-at-law. But the Fellow called Pigott's Scholar in the Stanley statutes was otherwise known as the Hastings Fellow, and his endowment was almost certainly provided by the Lady Jane Hastings, whose first husband was Richard Pigott. Her second husband was Sir Richard Hastings, summoned to Parliament in 1482 as Baron Welles and Willoughby. He died in 1503, and his wife in 1505. The fourth of the additional Fellowships was founded upon the rectorial tithes of Great Shelford, which were given to the College by Bishop Stanley in 1506. The same endowment furnished the stipends of the Master of the College and the schoolmaster. The costs of the appropriation having been borne by the Lady Katherine Bray, the College reserved to her during her lifetime the right of nominating the schoolmaster, and bound itself to celebrate yearly for her and her husband. This was the most valuable benefaction received by the College since its foundation; it brought in an annual sum of £26 13s. 4d. Bishop Stanley made it a condition of the grant that the nomination of the Fellow called Stanley's Scholar, and also of the Master of the College, should be reserved for ever to the Bishops of Ely. This limitation remained in force until the statutes of 1882 gave the right of election in both cases to the Master and Fellows. On the whole, the Bishops of Ely showed honesty and discernment in their appointments to the Mastership. Though they had no scruples about putting their own relations into the Fellowship, they kept the Mastership for men of some academic eminence. The election to the remaining Fellowships rested with the Master and Fellows, but Stanley's statutes prescribe that the Fellow elected by them must be presented to the bishop and instituted by him.

The ten Fellowships so far founded were reduced by Bishop Stanley to eight. Besides the Master and Fellows, the society, as enumerated by him, consisted of the four *juvenes*, the four boys, the schoolmaster and usher, the Master's servant, the cook and undercook. No stipends were provided for the Fellows of the Old Foundation; the accounts show that they received their commons and no more, and the same was, of course, the case

with the *juvenes* and *pueri*. After Bishop Stanley's grant of the
rectory of Great Shelford a long interval followed before the
stream of benefactions to the College was renewed. Its empty
channels were not filled until the cyclone of the Reformation had
broken on the University. The liberality of benefactors in the
generation which succeeded Alcock was not drawn to his old-
world ideals and schoolboy types in education; it flowed more
easily in the direction of the Lady Margaret's twin foundations.
Only one new endowment fell to the College in the long reign
of Henry VIII, that of a Fellowship, given in 1518 by Sir Robert
Rede, Chief Justice of the Common Pleas, and once a Fellow of
King's Hall. But 'Rede's scoler the Justis', as he desired that his
Fellow should be described, though he shared the liberties of
the other Fellows, was, in fact, no more than a chantry priest,
charged not with study or teaching, but only with the formal task
of celebrating for the founder's soul. More hopeful was his other
foundation, which is perpetuated in the well-known Rede Lecture. By his will (1518) he left in trust to the Master and Fellows
of Jesus an annuity of 20 marks, paid by the Abbey of the Holy
Cross at Waltham out of an estate at Babraham, for the maintenance of three 'ordinary' readers in the University schools—
viz. in Humanity, Logic, and Philosophy, moral and natural—and
for the keeping of his anniversary in St Mary's Church. The
Reader in Humanity was commonly called the Terence Reader,
a title which savours of the old learning, and Duns Scotus and the
old translations of Aristotle may have been the text-books of the
readers in Logic and Philosophy. But the date of Rede's foundation coincides with the first movement in favour of Greek studies,
and Mullinger regards it as giving an additional sanction to the
New Learning. At least, Rede shares with the Lady Margaret the
credit of being the first among university benefactors who recognized the need for an endowed Professoriate.

The statutes of Bishop Stanley did not serve the College for
long. He was succeeded at Ely by Bishop Nicholas West, who
at some time during his episcopate (1515-33) revised his predecessor's code. The statutes traditionally ascribed to him remained in force until 1841. They were first printed in 1852 in

Documents relating to the University and Colleges of Cambridge. The four manuscript copies of them which existed in the College in Sherman's day are described by him as 'all without date, all imperfect and interpolated, teeming with the careless *errata* of copyists, inconsistent with themselves, fortified with no episcopal authority'. Sherman's strictures are not undeserved. The *marginalia* and interpolations in these copies leave the original text in some places conjectural. In the Mastership of Dr Sterne (1633–44) the society, by collation of the existing copies, agreed upon a *textus receptus*, but it does not appear that this was ever approved by the Visitor. The fact is that the statutes, which have been hitherto regarded as West's, and which are prefaced by his preamble, are in reality a radical recension of his work by the commissioners of Edward VI in the year 1549. This is made abundantly clear by comparing the statutes with the return made by the same commissioners to Henry VIII in 1546, which latter shows that in their general outlines the provisions made by Stanley were then still in force. From the return we learn that in 1546 the College maintained nine Fellows, viz. the eight mentioned by Stanley and Rede's Fellow; that the foundation Fellows had no stipend, and the others received severally the sums prescribed by Stanley's statutes; that Stanley's allowance of 14*d.* for the weekly commons of each Fellow was unchanged; and that West had seen no cause to diminish the burden of exequies. The so-called West statutes present to us quite an altered state of affairs. They give the number of Fellows as eleven; they make no distinction as regards emolument between the Fellows of the original foundation and those subsequently added; they assign to each Fellow a yearly stipend of 26*s.* 8*d.*, and allow him 16*d.* weekly for commons. Of exequies they make no mention.

If it could be assumed that the statutes called West's were really his work, it might be concluded that the *pusillus grex* of 1514 had grown considerably in size and wealth before West's death in 1533. But in the truth-telling return of the Commissioners of 1546 we read not progress but paralysis. The College is indeed richer by one Fellowship than in 1514, but, instead of Stanley's four boys and four *juvenes*, it maintains six *discipuli* only. Even

so its statutable outgoings exceed its income from endowment by
£10 7s. 4d. The Bursars' accounts of the reigns of Henry VIII and
Edward VI tell an equally lamentable tale of stagnation and
penury. It was the practice of the Bursars of that time to give a
complete list of all the chambers in College, the names of their
occupants, and the rent paid by those who were not on the
foundation. Consequently, it would be possible to present a complete 'List of Residents' for most of the years 1535–51. The list
for the year last named may be taken as a specimen. Excluding
the schoolmaster and boys, who lived outside the College proper,
or cloisters, it enumerates the Master, eight Fellows (five M.A.,
three B.A.), five graduates other than Fellows (two M.A., three
B.A.), eleven *discipuli* (either five or six of whom are on the
foundation), the cook, undercook, and butler. Nine chambers,
including, it would seem, the usher's, are empty, several of them
per defectum reparacionis. The Fellows and graduates, and some
even of the *discipuli*, occupy each a separate chamber of his
own, and there is room to spare. The student-scholar, or undergraduate, is clearly as yet a rare visitant to the void spaces of the
College cloister.

The Reformation was as much a revolution in domestic
manners as in religion. Perhaps the change was less marked in
college society than elsewhere, but Bancroft's pupils would have
seen much to wonder at in the routine of life that Cranmer led
as undergraduate and Fellow. Of that life some glimpses are seen
in the statutes of Stanley and West. It is consciously monastic;
the individual has no place in it; the community is absolutely
self-contained. The barber, the two cooks, and the janitor, as
much as the Master himself, are statutable members of the foundation, with their allotted chambers, their places in chapel, their
allowances in hall. On rare occasions, and for the honour and
advantage of the College, the Master, taking with him some of
the Fellows, may have *prandium* or *coena* in the parlour, otherwise
all meals are taken in the hall. The *juvenes* wait upon the Master,
Fellows, and Fellow-Commoners (i.e. graduates and others not
on the foundation). During the meal a boy or a *juvenis* reads a
passage of Scripture or of some 'authentic' book. Only Latin is

to be spoken within the limits of the College. Besides the two common meals there are 'bevers' (*biberia*), when all Fellows and others (except the Master and all Doctors in College, who are each entitled to a pint of drink and a small portion of bread) assemble silently in the hall, and withdraw as soon as they have drunk. But anyone by payment may get bread and drink when he will. Each Fellow is allowed a chamber to himself, unless the number of Fellows should ever exceed that of chambers, in which case two Fellows may occupy one chamber, but in separate beds. Each class of residents is to be dressed decently, according to its rank, and those in Orders are to be *tonsi et coronati*. They are not to frequent huntings or taverns; not to keep hunting dogs, falcons, or sparrow-hawks; not to play at dice or other games not permitted to the clergy. If any Fellow or scholar strike another —*ita quod sanguis in aliqua quantitate notabili emanaverit*—he is to be fined 6s. 8d.; but if the bloodshed be not *notabilis, nec sit atrox laesio*, he is to be punished as the Master and Fellows direct; after three warnings he is to be expelled. No questionist at his B.A. degree, nor any scholar at the *prandium* at the beginning of Lent, is to be required to spend more than 6s. 8d. on food and drink, nor any M.A. or B.D. more than one mark on the occasion of his degree, unless he has a benefice or patrimony, or wishes to do so.

CHAPTER III

THE REFORMATION

ON the very threshold of the history of Jesus College we are confronted with the name of Cranmer. The College had scarcely been seven years in existence when he entered it.

Left an orphan by the death of his father, a Nottinghamshire gentleman, he was entered at Jesus in 1503, at the age of fourteen. We do not know what circumstances may have determined the choice of his College. His age shows that he could not have been one of the boys of the grammar school, and it is doubtful whether the College as yet had any exhibitions for *discipuli*, or undergraduates. Of the quality of the teaching which he received at Jesus we should be in no doubt, even if we had not the testimony of Foxe. Alcock, as his sermons prove, was a man learned for his times; but he had not, like his eminent predecessor at Ely, Bishop Gray, drunk from the springs of Greek learning. His training, like that of every Cambridge man of his generation, had been in the 'frivolous questions and obscure glosses' of Duns Scotus and the schoolmen, and when he looked about him for a Head for his new College, William Chubbes, then or later noted for a re-weaving of the old cobwebs in his commentary on Scotus, was a natural selection to make. Cranmer may or may not have come under the direct tuition of Chubbes, but we are told that at Cambridge 'he was nursled in the grossest kind of sophistry, logic, philosophy, moral and natural (not in the text of the old philosophers, but chiefly in the dark riddles of Duns and other subtle questionists), to his age of 22 years'. Neither was his tutor a person to inspire enthusiasm. 'The scholar of such an one I was,' he wrote, 'who when he came to any hard chapter, which he well understood not, would find some pretty toy to shift it off, and to skip over to another chapter, of which he could better skill.'

37

With such an instructor, and such a routine of study, he attained the degree of B.A. in 1511–12. After that, we are told, he gave himself to the study of Faber and Erasmus and good Latin authors. The new bent given to his studies was doubtless due to the influence of Erasmus, who began to lecture in Cambridge as the Lady Margaret's Reader in 1511. About that year Cranmer was elected to a Fellowship at Jesus, and then, as his secretary and biographer, Ralph Morice, quaintly remarks, 'it chanced him to marry a wife'. Foxe's account of the matter is that she was a gentleman's daughter, and that she was of affinity to the wife of the innkeeper of the Dolphin. It was objected to Cranmer at his last trial 'that he, being yet free, and before he entered into Holy Orders, married one Joan, surnamed Black or Brown, dwelling at the sign of the Dolphin in Cambridge. Whereunto he answered that whether she were called black or brown he knew not, but that he married there one Joan, that he granted.' The insinuation that the marriage was in some way discreditable to Cranmer may be set down to malevolent gossip. The Dolphin, which stood at the Bridge Street corner of All Saints' Passage, on ground now occupied by the Master's Courts of Trinity, was then the principal inn of Cambridge. The innkeeper was a tenant of Jesus College, and at sundry times we find that the College paid for the lodging and entertainment there of guests of consequence. But if the marriage of the young and unknown scholar to the distant connexion of an innkeeper, according to the views of the time, was not necessarily an ill-assorted one, it was, nevertheless, clearly improvident. Celibacy was a condition of the tenure of a Fellowship at Jesus under the statutes of 1514–15 and in all probability from the foundation of the College. In any event, residence in College was strictly insisted on, and in consequence Cranmer vacated his Fellowship by marriage. He appears to have lived with his wife at the Dolphin, and he maintained himself by lecturing in theology at the small Benedictine house of Buckingham College, which occupied the site of Magdalene College. But within a year from his marriage his wife died in childbed, and immediately 'the Master and Fellowes of Jesus Colledge, desirous again of their old companion, namely for his towardlinesse in learning, chose him againe fellow of the same Colledge'. He took the degree of M.A. in 1515, and then, as the College statutes required, devoted himself to the study of theology. By good fortune Erasmus's Greek Testament was published in the following year. Cranmer was still a layman, and did not face the responsibilities of ordination until his judgment had been confirmed by five years of study of the Scriptures in the light of the new scholarship. His fame as a theologian was then high in the University. He was appointed by his own College to the readership in theology founded by Sir John Rysley, and by the University was commonly chosen to examine for degrees in divinity, in which capacity he insisted on a competent knowledge of the Scriptures.

Historians of the University of Cambridge, from Fuller to Mullinger, have dwelt with legitimate and patriotic pride on the contrast at this period in the attitude of the two Universities towards the Reformation of Learning. At Oxford the new scholarship 'stormed an entrance'; 'barbarous fellows railed against the Greek tongue with great and heinous revilings'; in the streets 'Grecians' were mobbed by crews of young Priams and Hectors. At Cambridge hardly a spark of controversial heat was engendered by the collision of the old and new methods. The course of the transition is traceable at Jesus. The Scotist, Chubbes, was succeeded in the Mastership in 1505 by John Eccleston, evidently a man of the old ideas. He was rector of Great Shelford, and merited commemoration for having induced the dunce Bishop of Ely, Stanley, to appropriate his rectory to the College. William Capon, who followed in the Mastership in 1516, after the brief tenure of Eccleston's immediate successor, Thomas Alcock, was of more stirring quality. His brother John, who preceded him at Cambridge, passed from the abbacy of Hulme in Norfolk, to which he was elected in 1516, to the see of Bangor in 1533, and to that of Salisbury in 1539. John took the King's side when the divorce question was agitated at Cambridge, and for Cranmer's Bible he translated the Epistles to the Corinthians. William, though he owed the Mastership to Latimer's enemy, Bishop West, was, like his brother, strongly progressive in his views. Wolsey made him his chaplain and the first Dean of the college which he founded at Ipswich, and afterwards invited him to nominate rising Cambridge scholars for posts in Cardinal College at Oxford, and, as an indication of his leanings, it may be mentioned, on the authority of Strype, that no fewer than eleven of those selected by him were subsequently imprisoned for heresy. Strype's list does not include Cranmer, who declined an offered canonry there. Dr Shorton, then Master of Pembroke, but originally of Jesus, acted along with Capon in the selection of Cambridge scholars, and among those nominated to canonries at Cardinal College was Richard Harman of Jesus, who graduated M.A. in the same year as Cranmer and was afterwards his chaplain.

Of Cranmer's other Jesus friends and contemporaries several were noted theologians of the reforming party. Geoffrey Downs, who, as a Fellow of Jesus, was somewhat senior to Cranmer, was his lifelong friend and correspondent. John Bale, afterwards Bishop of Ossory, called 'bilious Bale' by Fuller for the rancour of his attacks on his papal opponents, was another contemporary of Cranmer's at Jesus. He seems to have come thither from John Capon's Benedictine house at Hulme, and in his *Illustres Britanniae Scriptores* he says that in his first years at Cambridge he 'wandered in ignorance and blindness of mind, without instructor or patron'. That, it would seem, was in the early, unawakened days of the College, for he gratefully commemorates the acquaintance which he formed at Jesus with many *viri doctissimi*, notably with Cranmer and Geoffrey Downs, 'once my most worthy father in theology'. Thomas Goodrich, originally of Corpus, was elected a Fellow of Jesus in 1510. He, too, threw in his lot with the Reformers, though not with the whole-heartedness of Cranmer or Bale. He was promoted to the see of Ely in 1534, was one of Edward VI's Commissioners to visit the University in 1549, and became Lord Chancellor in 1551. His best title to remembrance is that he revised the Gospel of St John for Cranmer's Bible, and took part in the compilation of the *Book of Common Prayer*. Goodrich and Downs assisted Cranmer in the production of the *Institution of a Christian Man*, and among the editors of the same work were two other Jesus divines: John Edmunds, Fellow in 1517 and at a later date Master of Peterhouse, and Robert Okyng, who was commissary to John Capon when the latter was Bishop of Salisbury.

What individual part was borne by other members of the society in the reform of letters and religion we cannot say; but that the College, as a whole, maintained friendly relations with Cranmer in the controversial period of his primacy is seen in the genial tone of the letters which he addressed to the Master and Fellows. From Croydon he writes to Dr Capon:

In my right hearty wise I commend me to you. And so certifying you that I send you here a buck to be bestowed amonges your company within your college. And, forasmuch as you have more store of money, and also less need than I at this season, therefore I bequeath you a noble of your purse towards the baking and seasoning of him. And whensoever I have so much money beforehand as I am now behindhand, I shall repay you your noble again. And thus fare you well.

At another time we find him kindly interceding with the College in behalf of a certain John Jackson, tenant of St Radegund's Manor farm, whose goods had been distrained by the College for arrears of rent; and, writing to Cromwell, whose displeasure for some reason had been drawn upon the Master and Fellows for this action, he begs him to suspend his judgment until he (Cranmer) has made inquiry into the matter.

Capon retired from the Mastership in 1546. His successor, John Reston, previously a Fellow of the College, and later a Canon of St Paul's, London, held it until his death in 1551. His period of office was memorable chiefly for the visitation of the University in 1549 and the recasting of the statutes of the College by the Royal Commissioners. The contemporary account of the proceedings of the Commissioners relates that in their tour of inspection of the colleges they came to Jesus on Sunday 26 May,

and commawnded six awlters to be pulled down in the body (i.e. the nave and transepts) of the churche, and wente from the churche into a chamber wher certayn images were, and cawsed them to be broken; and upon complayntes made unto the vysytors of sir Haryson, inceptor in artes and felowe ther, for incontinensye proved he was expulsed his fellowshyppe, and the president, Mr Hunt, discharged of hys office; and Mr Badcock had an excommunicacon sette uppe for hym, whereunto he appeard within ii days and was discharged. On the monday they went agayne to Jesus College and ther spente all that daye in examynynge the presydentes and Masters accounts.

Comparing this account with the proceedings of the Visitors at other colleges, it is evident that they found more to reform at Jesus than at any other College in the University. Of the revision of the College statutes something has already been said. Jesus, with the veteran foundations of Peterhouse and Clare, we are told, took up most of the Visitors' time; drastic changes were evidently required in its antiquated code. What has here to be noticed is the anticipation of the iconoclasm of the seventeenth century in the treatment of the chapel. Jesus was the only College so treated by the Visitors, and the reason must be either that, in spite of the reforming spirit shown by the society in Capon's time, the old ritual had maintained itself there with fewer changes than elsewhere, or that the Master and Fellows were tainted with reactionary views. The latter conclusion seems the more probable. Of Reston's opinions we know little. Sherman says he had an oratory consecrated for himself in the College—none other, in fact, than the former oratory of the Prioress—and perhaps it was this 'chamber' which provoked the iconoclastic zeal of the Visitors. The stipulation in his will that the College should maintain an obit for his soul perhaps implies that his sympathies were with the old order of things. His Fellows, with the single exception of Richard Goodrich, nephew of the Bishop of Ely, and a distinguished lawyer in the reigns of Mary and Elizabeth, were men of no eminence. Why Mr Hunt was discharged of his office does not appear; 'sir Haryson's' offence was one often laid to the charge of clerics of the Anti-Reform party. In Mr Badcock we recognize John Badcock, last of the Priors of Barnwell. He was not a Fellow, but occupied chambers in the College, and farmed the monastery lands and tithes in Cambridge; as late as 1562 he was incumbent of the parish of Barnwell.

The Reformation period, however rich in its promise of future vitality, was marked at Cambridge, as at Oxford, by all the out-ward signs of depression and decay. The unsettled condition of the Church, combined with the fear that the Universities would suffer the spoliation which had befallen the monasteries, brought a severe decline in the number of students—a decline from which there was no recovery until the reign of Elizabeth. 'No college', says Fuller, speaking of this time, 'had more scholars therein than hardly those of the foundation; no volunteers at all, and only persons pressed, in a manner, by their places to reside.' At Jesus, facts fully corroborate this statement. In the six years, 1535–40, seventeen students, all inferior commoners, or sizars, paid fees on admission. The accounts of only eight years between 1540 and 1559 are extant; in none of these years is any such fee recorded to have been paid. But even in this, its darkest hour, there were indications that a fairer future was opening for the College. From 1519 onwards, through the long reign of Henry VIII, the College had received not a penny of new endowment. Now begins a stream of new benefactions. About the year 1547 Dr John And-rews, a Canon of St Paul's, left by will to the College estates at Over and Steeple Morden for the maintenance of two Fellows and two scholars. This legacy was followed by two others—the first in 1551, when Dr Reston founded by will one Fellowship and eight scholarships; the other in 1558, when Dr Fuller be-queathed to the College the manor of Graveley to endow four new Fellowships. Including the Fellows and *discipuli* of the older foundations, the College was thus constituted on the basis of a Master, sixteen Fellows, and eighteen scholars. The number of the latter class still compared unfavourably with the forty-seven scholars maintained on the foundation of the Lady Margaret at Christ's; but the endowments of Andrews and Reston at last permitted Jesus to take its place among the other colleges as a place of education. When the door was opened to the scholar he was followed by the pensioner, and with the accession of Elizabeth the void places in the cloister began to fill rapidly. In the five years beginning with 1560 eighty-two admission fees were paid.

Eight years only separated the visitation of King Edward's

Commissioners from that of the Commissioners deputed by Cardinal Pole in the third year of Queen Mary (January 1557), and in the brief interim the whole society had been changed. The sweating sickness, whereof many died in Cambridge in 1551, 'patients ending or mending in twenty-four hours', seems to have been accountable for the disappearance of several of the old names from the list, for Dr Reston and two, at least, of the Fellows died in the summer of that year. Reston's successor in the Mastership, Edmond Perpoynte, B.D., lived only five years after his appointment; he died in January 1557, only two days before the Marian Commissioners came to Cambridge. Their advent was looked forward to with great apprehension by the Vice-Chancellor and authorities, who sought to find a claim for exemption among the bulls of the University, 'but fownde not pregnant matter'. That their alarm was not unreasonable was proved by the brutalities of the Pope's Datary, Ormanet, especially in the exhumation and burning of the bodies of the Reformers, Bucer and Fagius. The diary of John Mere, one of the esquire-bedells, graphically describes how the Visitors progressed through the colleges, making inquisition for heretical books, and rating Masters and Fellows for their bungling attempts to revive the half-forgotten rites of the Roman Church. The masterless society of Jesus seems to have passed its examination pretty well; at least, there is no record of angry comment on its shortcomings. College tradition connects one abiding feature with this visitation—the two stone crosses, set up, it is said, by the Commissioners' orders, in the highest story of Alcock's gate-tower.

Whatever deficiences the Visitors may have noted in the chapel appointments and ritual, clearly the Fellows, under their new Head, John Fuller, LL.D., made haste to repair them. Dr Fuller was of All Souls, Oxford, and he brought with him to Cambridge the uncompromising rigour of the Roman party then dominant at the sister University. He was indeed a generous benefactor of the College, *vir non sine honore nominandus*, as Sherman says. But in the pages of the *Acts and Monuments* he figures as the relentless suppressor of heresy in the diocese of Ely, of which he was Chancellor. When he first entered the Master's Lodge at Jesus the grass had scarcely yet grown on the spot where John Hullier, by his sentence, had been burnt on Jesus Green. From Oxford presumably came the suggestion for the splendours which in the two years of his sway distinguished the chapel ritual at Jesus. In these years, as in no other, the chapel expenses rank first in the Bursar's payments, preceding even the stipends of the Master and Fellows. The following are a few out of a long list of items of expenditure on the services of the *sacellum* and relate to the last fifteen months of his rule.

1557–58—For wine and singing bread[1] the hole yeare, 5ˢ.
    For Mʳ Smythe for 7 *lib.* and a qr. of waxe, whereof 5 *lib.* was in beting candle,[2] and 2 *lib.* and a qr. in yᵉ tapers, with yᵉ making, 7ˢ 3ᵈ.
    For 4 antiphonars mending, and a masse book and a psalter binding, 4ˢ.
    The trindle,[3] 12ᵈ.
    At Easter for 9 *lib.* waxe put into 6 tapers for the sepulchre, 9ˢ.
    A paschall[4] of 3 *lib.* with the making, 3ˢ 4ᵈ.
    4 *li.* of beting candles for Judas,[5] 4ˢ.
    For a cope of blewe damaske with flowers and an orfres of dunne velvet, 20ˢ.
    For a cope of greene bawdkin[6] with an orfres of grene, 10ˢ.
    To Willᵐ Alain, of Rysbroke, for 3 newe feasts, *videl.* yᵉ transfiguration, Jesus feast, and yᵉ visitation, and 4 leves of yᵉ newe antiphonar, and one to the olde, after 18ᵈ the leafe, 22ˢ.
    To yᵉ stationers for binding bookes for pricksong, 10ᵈ.

1558–59—To Willᵐ Alain, of Risbroke, for binding of an anthiphonar, with all stuff, carridge and recarridge, 16ˢ 8ᵈ.

[1] I.e., the host.
[2] *Beting candle*, tapers for kindling.
[3] A roll of consecrated wax.
[4] A large candle burnt before the altar from Easter-Eve to Ascension Day.
[5] The triangular candlestick, used at the service of *Tenebrae* in Holy Week. Candles were arranged on it, and successively put out as the service proceeded.
[6] Gold-embroidered silk from Baldach or Bagdad.

1558–59—Smithe, ye chandeler, for tenne pound of beting candell
   spent between Ester and Saint Nicholas daie, 10^s.
A dagge of yron waying 2 *li. et di.* for Saint Christopher,
   7^s 5^d.
To Bell, the carpenter, hanging up Saint Christopher, 20^d.
At tenebre Wenesdaie, 4 *li.* of beting candell, 3^s.
To three processioners in Englishe, 6^d.

From the meridian effulgence betokened by these entries we
descend at one plunge into the chillest of Puritanism. The extraordinary suddenness of the transition is evidenced by the accounts
of the very next year, 1559–60. There is no need to select among
the items of expenditure on the *templum*; the list stands briefly
thus:

For a communion table, 7^s.
   For 2 deskes, 3^s.
To the deane for candel for wynter, 6^s.
To the deane for wyne and breade, 10^d.

We rub our eyes and ask whether in twelve months the whole
Marian society has been carried off by 'the sweat', or outed by
another Commission. Nothing of the kind. The Fellows of the
last year of Mary are the Fellows of the first year of Elizabeth; no
new name is added to the list, no old name disappears. Fuller,
indeed, is Master no more; within a month of the deaths of Queen
Mary and Cardinal Pole, he followed them to the grave (December 1558). In his place Thirleby, the Marian Bishop of Ely, at
once (January 1559) appointed Thomas Redman, B.D., one of
the original Fellows of Trinity. But Redman, described in 1561 as
an unlearned Popish recusant, was deprived in the early months
of 1560, and nothing that he could effect prevented the new Commissioners who visited the University in September 1559 from
making short work of the 'superstitious rags' left by the late
Master. Fuller's body, laid in the choir of the chapel, was yet
'green in earth' when the undoing of his work there began. At
the foot of those very accounts of 1558–9 which witness to the
magnificence of the ritual at Jesus in the earlier year there are

appended three notes of expenditure, which are as a finger-post to mark the parting of the ways:

Item, a comunyon boke to baxter, 5ˢ 4ᵈ.
Item, to the same for eight psalters, after 2ˢ the pece, 16ˢ.
Item, for carrying dust out of the chappell, 2ᵈ.

Pulveris exigui jactu: with the removal of that twopenny dust-load ended, as far as Jesus was concerned, the Reformation broils. When the noise of battle was renewed the opposing camps were not Reformed and Roman, but Puritan and Anglican.

The statutes given to the College in 1549 were revised by the Visitors of 1559, and this recension remained in force until 1841. The changes were few, and were embodied in a single supplementary statute. The number of Fellowships was fixed at sixteen, five having been added by Reston and Fuller since 1549. Each Fellow had a fixed yearly stipend of £2 in addition to commons, a small increase of the 1549 allowance. The Visitors made no provision for an alteration in the value of money; the number of Fellows was to be increased or reduced as the revenues of the College might require. Pedantic conservatism stereotyped the Elizabethan arrangement and, until the principle of the 'dividend' was brought in by the statutes of 1841, the Bursars in their accounts kept up the fiction of the £2 stipend. The real income of the Fellows was derived from fines on beneficial leases and from certain adventitious sources, included in an informal supplement to the Audit accounts, known as the 'Dividend Paper'. The scholarships were to be fifteen in number. Though the amount allowed to the scholars for commons was progressively increased, they received no money stipend until 1861.

One change introduced by the Visitors of 1559 was of more than domestic interest. Four Fellows were assigned by them to the faculty of Civil Law, for the reason given that that study is *in republica pernecessarium*. The attention of the Commissioners of 1549 had been drawn to the neglect of the study at Cambridge and, with the object of supplying competent jurists for the diplomatic service of the State, a proposal was made by them to combine the two halls of Clare and Trinity into a single College of Civil Law. By the statutes of Bishop Stanley one of the original Fellowships at Jesus was reserved to law; a second was afterwards added on Andrews's foundation; by Queen Elizabeth's Visitors two of Fuller's four Fellowships were allotted to Civil Law.

The statutes of 1559 seem never to have been confirmed by the Bishop of Ely as Visitor. They were obviously hastily executed and left untouched many of the arrangements of 1549, which had been rendered obsolete by recent endowments. The discrepancies and deficiencies of the manuscript copies rendered a strict compliance with their provisions, in some matters, impracticable. But as they prescribed a constitution which, in form at least, the society maintained for 280 years, it is worth while giving an outline of their principal features.

The MASTER or KEEPER (*custos*) must be a Doctor either in Divinity or in Civil Law, or at least a Licentiate or Bachelor in Divinity. The appointment of the Master rests with the Bishop of Ely. He must reside three weeks in each quarter, but may have leave of absence from the Bishop *ad placitum*, provided that he resides forty days in all in each year. This was a relaxation of the statute of West, which required the Master to reside continuously except for two months in the year. The Mastership nearly always until 1885 was held along with some benefice in the diocese of Ely, and the intention of the statute of 1559 was to allow him to reside for the greater part of the year at his cure. Among his duties the Master is charged with the collection of the College revenues. He may employ a Receptor, but is personally responsible for disbursements, and is required to submit his accounts each year to an Auditor, appointed and paid by the society. The statutes recognize no such officer as a Bursar. In the absence of the Master, his duties were performed by the President, one of the Fellows nominated by him.

The FELLOWS are to be unmarried; this condition, which in all probability dated from the foundation of the College, had already been exacted in the statutes of Stanley, since these required all the Fellows to be priests. On the occurrence of each vacancy the Master and Fellows are to present to the Bishop of Ely two persons of whom he is to select one. Those presented must be B.A., at least, necessitous and, among other conditions, sufficiently trained in singing. The Fellows are required to reside continuously, except for fifty days in each year, when they are permitted to visit their parents and benefactors, and obtain 'exhibition' for their maintenance; otherwise they are not allowed to spend the night outside the College or to walk or ride more than one mile beyond the University. There must not be two Fellows of the same county, and the number from the northern counties (which are specified) must be the same as from the southern. The Fellow on the Shelford foundation is to be nominated and elected exclusively by the Bishop of Ely.

The SCHOLARS are to study grammar, rhetoric, logic, mathematics, or philosophy, and that they may give their time specially to these studies, they must be properly instructed in singing before their admission so that they may take part with the Fellows in divine services. They are elected by the Master and Fellows, and if they attain to the degree of B.A. within six years, and are fitted by character and learning, they are to be preferred to *extranei* in nominations to Fellowships.

The GRAMMAR MASTER is to be appointed by the Master of the College, with consent of the Bishop. The other conditions of his office, and that of the USHER, have been already stated. The school and its masters ceased to exist in 1570. The Master's servant is to have 'second commons'—i.e. the same as the scholars—and is to act as janitor. The wages of the barber and laundress are to be determined by the Master. The barber survived as a College functionary until the beginning of the nineteenth century.

The annual officiaries are to be a Seneschal and a Dean. The Seneschal is to provide fuel, kitchen necessaries, salt fish, salt, beer, etc. The Dean is to preside at all disputations, and to have charge of all books, church vestments, jewels, ornaments, etc.

One of the Fellows is to be Lector, and is to give daily lectures in metaphysics and philosophy, and once a week in mathematics, at which last all Fellows and Bachelor Fellow-Commoners are to attend. The auditors are to repeat the substance of the lecture on the following day. The lecturer is to receive a yearly stipend of

26s. 8d. from the College, as well as 8d. quarterly from each Fellow-Commoner, 6d. from scholars, and 4d. from sizars.

Of sizars the Master may have two, but no Fellow or Fellow-Commoner may have more than one.

So many Fellow-Commoners or Perendinants may be admitted as there are vacant chambers in the College. They are to pay room-rent, and a sum of 5s. on admission. The Fellow-Commoner who is admitted to second commons pays an admission fee of 1s. The class of Fellow-Commoners, it is to be noted, included at that time all grades of paying members of the College.

CHAPTER IV

ELIZABETH AND JAMES

THE promptness with which the Fellows of Jesus accepted the
new ritual and the articles of faith on Elizabeth's accession has
already been remarked. The same easy compliance with the
latest pattern of orthodoxy was to be witnessed in every one of
the colleges of Cambridge. Here and there a Head who refused
the oath of supremacy was removed, among them Thomas
Redman, the newly appointed Master of Jesus; but of the bulk
of the Fellows it would seem that no test was exacted, and none
were expelled.[1] The alacrity with which they passed over to
the victorious camp has been, not altogether unjustly, ascribed to
servility and self-interest, but something also may be set down to
mere indecision resulting from a decade of incessant variations in
the pole of authorized belief. The Fellows of those days were
mostly young men; indeed, at Jesus not one of the society had
been a member of it ten years previously. They had not grown
up in religious beliefs consecrated by tradition, and, unlike the
Heads, they did not stand committed by their record in the past
to any particular creed. At Jesus, moreover, there were special
reasons which made conformity to the views that found favour
in high places at all times a natural, and in the sixteenth century an
almost inevitable course. The nominee of the Bishop of Ely in
the Master's lodge at Jesus was not likely to be out of harmony
with the views of his patron, and, backed by the Visitor, the
Master was omnipotent in the Fellows' parlour. Some of the

[1] The Senior Fellow of Jesus, Dr Edyll, disappears from the list of Fellows in
1559. He died that year, and his will (dated in April) shows some dubiety as to
the rites appropriate for his commemoration. He directs his burial in Jesus
College Chapel, 'with masse or other prayers as the Church shall appoynt to be
songe or saide' for his soul.

Fellows, we may believe, coerced by Marian Masters, yet cherished a genuine, if timid sympathy with Protestant ideas. For when Fuller died they did not wait for the arrival of the Queen's Commissioners, but, as we have seen, made a particularly clean sweep of the Roman garnishings of the chapel before the Bursar had made up his books in September. Their zeal may have been sincere, for, at the time, it was questionably politic. The new Master and the Visitor were pronounced Romanists. But the power behind them was gone. Thirleby was deprived in 1559, and Redman in February 1560, and it is doubtful whether the latter ever occupied the Master's lodge. The date of his successor's appointment would imply that he was put into the Mastership by Bishop Cox, but Edward Gascoyn was scarcely the man to find favour with so Puritan a Bishop; it is more likely that he owed his place to the Crown, acting in the vacancy of the see. In the *Acts and Monuments* he is pilloried as a persecuting inquisitor, sadly routed in theological dispute by godly Alice Driver, the Ipswich martyr. Bishop Cox, though Gascoyn was his Chancellor and a prebendary of Ely, coldly certifies: 'Master Edward Gascoyn there [i.e. at Ely] is a Deacon; does not much reside there, but at Cambridge, where he lives; is LL.D.; not qualified for preaching, nor has he any special licence for it; nor does he keep hospitality there.' His tenure of the Mastership was brief; he retired in 1562. His successor, John Lakin, barely held office for a twelvemonth.

If Gascoyn retained any private leanings to the old faith, he was impotent to control the Protestant zeal of his Fellows. How it fared with the outward forms of religion under his rule is plainly shown by the following among many similar entries in the Bursar's books:

> 1559–60—*Templum.* For wyne and bread, 10^d (this is for the whole year).
>   For a comunyon table, 7^s.
> 1560–61—*Promptuarium.* Payed to Mr Rynsted in exchange of ye broken challys for a silver salte percell gylte, 50^s.
> 1561–62—For pasting ye table of ye comaundements, 2^d.

The item for sacramental bread and wine in 1559–60 is significant. In 1557–8, when the old ritual was triumphant, the year's expenditure under this head was five shillings. In the whole of Elizabeth's reign, in contempt of the rubric which prescribed that there shall be in all colleges a communion 'every Sunday at the least', it appears that the communion was only celebrated on the three great festivals. In 1560–1 the charge for bread and wine was actually only fourpence, and in 1565–6, and again in 1576–7, there were only two communions. In 1643–4, when the leanings of the Master and Fellows were strongly Anglican, the number of celebrations was six.

Since Capon's retirement in 1546 six Masters had successively come and gone in the space of seventeen years. Thomas Ithell, LL.D., who succeeded Lakin, held office for sixteen years and, as he was a man of character and intelligence, his comparatively long reign makes an epoch in the history of the College. He had been a Fellow of Magdalene, was an absentee prebendary of St Patrick's, Dublin, and, along with the Mastership, held the usual variety of preferments in Ely diocese. By the Puritan party at Cambridge he was reckoned 'a faint professor', identified with 'enemies unto God's gospel', such as Dr Caius. It was even alleged that he countenanced, or at least concealed, his brother, a 'Lovainist', and an emissary sent by the Church of Rome to corrupt the scholars. Of this brother Strype says:

> At length he was discovered; and the Vice-Chancellor sent Intelligence of it to the Chancellor, the Lord Treasurer Burleigh; and he was put into the Custody of his Brother, in order to reform him. But he was too well principled at Lovain, that any good should be done to him. So that his Brother was rather to proceed to some Restraint and Punishment. But he escaped soon, and was gone; which gave some just Cause of Suspicion of the Brother himself.

There were undoubtedly some of the Heads to whom the suspicion that they favoured the cause of Rome, and looked for a restoration of its rites, might justly apply; but it does not seem that Ithell was one of them. In Puritan times he might be described as a High Churchman, and when clerical discipline in the

University verged on dissolution, he gave a firm support to the authority of Archbishop Parker and the Chancellor Burleigh. When Cartwright, the leader of the ultra-Calvinistic party at Cambridge, was arraigned before the Heads for schismatic opinions, Ithell concurred in the sentence which deprived him of the Lady Margaret Professorship. The Chancellor regarded him as a trustworthy, capable man. He was appointed Commissary of the University, a Visitor of King's College in 1569, a Commissioner for the revision of the University statutes in 1570, and for those of St John's College in 1576.

In his own college Ithell's rule was accepted without question or cavil. He was content to leave the chapel ritual as he found it. The highly Protestant pattern which it took in 1558 was retained until long after Elizabeth's death. On the other hand, Jesus was spared the fanatical displays of Puritan zeal which brought on some colleges the stern rebuke of Burleigh. In 1565 many of the Fellows and students of Trinity and St John's rejected the use of the surplice in chapel; in many colleges the painted windows were destroyed. At Jesus small indications in the Bursar's books show that a more moderate spirit prevailed. 'Albs' and 'chapel gear' are washed; windows containing pictures of St Peter and St Ignatius are tolerated, and even repaired. And though we gather from the same source that the introduction, in the year 1567, of 'the Geneva psalmes in meter' in the chapel services was followed at no long interval by the sale of 'the orgaines', it would be rash to infer from this and like symptoms of slight regard for ceremonial beauty that Jesus in the last half of the sixteenth century was a particularly Puritan college. 'High' views of church discipline were then compatible with what would now be deemed a very 'low' type of ritual. During the latter part of Ithell's reign there was no question about the side on which the society of Jesus was ranged; it was uncompromisingly hostile to the Protestant extremists.

An indication of this, clearly traceable to Ithell's influence, is to be seen in the migration of Richard Bancroft, afterwards Archbishop of Canterbury, from Christ's to Jesus at the end of 1569. Bancroft and Ithell were apparently related through their

Country Life

THE OLD LIBRARY

Plate II

Above: THIRTEENTH-CENTURY PISCINA AND ARCADING IN THE CHAPEL

Below: THE PRIORESS'S ROOM DURING THE MASTERSHIP OF ARTHUR GR.

mothers, whose family name was Curwen or Corren. Through them they claimed kinship with Hugh Curwen, who was Archbishop of Dublin from 1555 to 1567 and afterwards Bishop of Oxford; and Bancroft, as well as Ithell, was a prebendary of St Patrick's, Dublin. Bancroft, after taking his B.A. degree, left Christ's because it lay under suspicion of 'Novelism'—i.e. Puritan doctrine—and he was apparently attracted to Jesus as much by the unquestioned orthodoxy of its society as by his relationship to the Master.[1] He was never elected to a Fellowship but, as Sherman says, had almost as much power as the Master, was eminent as a tutor, and advanced many of his pupils to Fellowships. He lived in College, on the staircase next the oriel of the Hall, until the year 1586. From his tutor's chamber at Jesus he took with him to the see of London something too much of the tone and temper of a 'don'. At the Hampton Court Conference he rated the Puritan divines for appearing before the King 'in Turkey gowns, not in their scholastic habits sorting to their degree'; and in their attitude he could see nothing but a wilful insubordination. But, in a nobler sense, he was in his high place a tutor to the last. 'It is undeniable', says S. R. Gardiner, 'that, within the limits prescribed by the Elizabethan system, the clergy were advancing under his superintendence in intelligence and vigour.'

Almost simultaneously with Bancroft's migration from Christ's, Jesus adopted as a Fellow one who, in his time, was not less celebrated as a tutor than Bancroft, and, like him, was the lifelong antagonist of the Puritans. This was the well-known Dr Legge, who came from Trinity in 1568, and was destined to be Dr Caius's successor in the Mastership of Caius College. The mere circumstance that Caius, whose 'perverse stomach to the professors of the gospel' was so notorious, should in his will have nominated Legge, 'his trusty and well-beloved friend', as his successor is a sufficient indication of the sympathies of the latter, and marked him out for the railing attacks of the Calvinist party

[1] Another migrant from Christ's to Jesus was Hugh Bellot, afterwards Bishop of Bangor and of Chester. He came to Jesus in 1566, having been elected a Fellow in that year.

in the University. 'An horrible papist' he seemed to the recalci-
trant Fellows over whom he presided. Among other items of
complaint which they brought against him it was alleged that
'the master hathe used continuall and expressive loud singinge
and noyse of organs to the great disturbance of our studies', a
practice which seemed to them inconsistent with the spirit of
their statutes, which did not permit small birds to be kept in
College, 'for troubling the students'. Legge is best remembered
now for his Latin play, *Richardus Tertius*, a subject in which he
anticipated the tragedy of Shakespeare. But Legge's play was
acted at St John's, not at Jesus, and only after he had ceased to be
a Fellow of the latter College. Plays, usually Latin, were regularly acted at Jesus twice or thrice a year in the last half of the
sixteenth century, but the name of Legge is not mentioned in
connexion with any of them.

Shortly after Legge became Master of Caius he was followed
to that College by another Fellow of Jesus, Richard Swale, who
was admitted a Fellow of Caius in 1577 and became its President
in 1581. The same charges of papistical tendencies were brought
against him as against Legge. Both of them long outlived the
attacks made upon them, and Swale, as a civilian, attained to
eminence in the service of the State. With Bancroft he served
in a diplomatic mission sent to Emden in 1600 to confer with
ambassadors from Denmark, and he was selected for his learning
to assist at the Hampton Court Conference. He was knighted by
James I in 1603.

Conspicuous among the Jesus worthies of Ithell's time was
Fulke Greville, the poet-philosopher, afterwards Lord Brooke,
'Servant to Queen Elizabeth, Conceller to King James, Frend to
Sir Philip Sidney', as, in words of his own choosing, he is described in his epitaph. Tradition connects his name with Trinity,
and his arms are in a window of the hall of that college; but there
is no record of his admission there. At Jesus he was entered as a
Fellow-Commoner in 1568, under the tutorship of Mr Legge,
and as it was in that year that Legge removed from Trinity to
Jesus, it is possible that Greville had been originally placed under
his care at Trinity, and accompanied his migration to Jesus. His

friend and schoolfellow, Philip Sidney, went to Christ Church, Oxford, at the same time that he came to Cambridge. To the memory of Sidney he dedicated his monumental volume of grave, sententious verse, which was not published until long after both the friends were dead. Greville survived Sidney for a whole generation, and died by an assassin's hand in 1628. At Cambridge he established a Professorship of History, and appointed to it the celebrated Dorislaus; but the endowment which should have maintained it was 'lost by the iniquity of the times' of the Rebellion. Among the records of Jesus there is a curious letter, addressed by him in 1617, when he was an old man, to the then Master, Dr Duport. In it he protests his love to the College, his 'old nurse', and expresses his wish to be allowed, at his own expense, to convert the west end of the chapel into College chambers. His well-meant scheme never took effect. Some fortunate obstacle, which we cannot guess at, preserved the ancient nave. A few years previously, in 1612, he visited his old College, and received from it a gift of 'a par gloves' costing sixteen shillings.

Dr Ithell's Mastership ended with his death in 1579. The firmness and capacity of his government had brought the College into high repute, and the number of its students more than doubled during his tenure of office. The number of admissions was largest in 1567-8, the year in which Legge became a Fellow, when it reached a total of forty-four. So large a number was never reached again during the next three centuries. The cloister court, with the small building which extended its eastern range northwards from the Hall, had previously provided ample room for the members of the College. About this year the deserted schoolhouse in the entrance court was converted into chambers to provide for the increased number of residents. The gross revenue of the College had risen from £245 in 1559-60 to £323 in 1569-70, the increase being due solely to improvement in the letting value of houses and land, for the College had received no fresh endowment. Nevertheless, it would have been altogether unable to meet the extraordinary expenditure involved in the building operations necessitated by its growth in numbers had it not hit upon an inexpensive method of providing for its needs. The church of St

Clement, the rectory and advowson of which belonged to the Master and Fellows, had lately fallen on evil days. Its steeple, about this time, 'was much decayed and vanished quite away'; its timbers of heart of oak helped to build the house of an alderman next the churchyard. It occurred to the Master and Fellows that the chancel, for the maintenance of which they were responsible, might be converted into a source of profit. They accordingly pulled it down, and carried '93 lode of stone' to the College, where it was employed in alterations in the school-house and offices. All Saints' Church had been pillaged in a similar fashion in 1563, when 'six lode of tyle-stone from Allhallowes' had been brought to the College and applied to its uses. Such devices in building were nothing accounted of in the days of Elizabeth.

Dr John Bell, who succeeded Ithell, was not a man of conspicuous abilities. Educated at St John's, and from thence elected to a Fellowship at Peterhouse, he passed through the ordinary curriculum of preferments in Ely diocese and attained to the Deanery in 1589, when he resigned the Mastership. His successor, John Duport, D.D., was not appointed until the following year. After the death of Bishop Cox, in 1581, the see of Ely remained vacant for eighteen years, during which time Elizabeth received its whole profits. Dr Duport was probably appointed by the Commissioners for the administration of the diocese, one of whom was his predecessor, Dr Bell. He was, it would seem, the first Master of Jesus who had been both an undergraduate and a Fellow of the College. He was admitted in 1563, the year when Ithell became Master, and he came from Ithell's county, Leicestershire. He was elected to a Fellowship in 1571, but resigned it and ceased to reside in 1582. Of Masters of Jesus he was the first who could lay claim to distinction as a scholar, and he helped in the production of the Authorized Version of the Bible. He died about Christmas 1617.

In the religious controversies which divided the University during the Masterships of Bell and Duport, Jesus, to use the phrase of Kingsley in describing the attitude of Cambridge towards *Essays and Reviews*, 'lay in magnificent repose'. Outside its walls the drift in the direction of Puritanism was with difficulty checked by authority. Among the older colleges it was especially strong at Christ's and St John's, and the foundation of Emmanuel in 1584 was destined to give it a fresh and powerful impetus. At Jesus the rule of Anglicanism was accepted without any hint of dissent, and from Ithell's day was maintained as an unbroken tradition until the ejection of its society by the Earl of Manchester at the outbreak of the Rebellion. The only notable member of the College who took the Puritan side was John Dod, who became a Fellow in 1578. Dod, it is said, was one of the Puritan leaders, including Cartwright, Chaderton, and Fulk, who attended secret meetings in St John's College, when Travers's *Ecclesiastical Discipline* was considered and adopted by the party as the authoritative exposition of its theory of a Christian Church. But Dod was no violent partisan: *Puritanus, verum modestus, pacificus* is Sherman's description of him. 'He was a *Passive Nonconformist*,' says Fuller, 'not loving anyone the *worse* for difference in judgment about *Ceremonies*, but all the better for their unity of affections in *grace* and *goodness*. He used to retrench some hot spirits when enveighing against *Bishops*, telling them how *God*, under that government, had given a marvelous increase to the Gospell, and that godly men might comfortably comport therewith, under which *learning* and *religion* had so manifest an Improvement.' He was a man of learning, and, in his day, 'an exquisite Hebrician'. He never broke away from the Established Church, though, on account of his views, he was suspended in all the benefices which he successively held. He died, at the age of eighty-six, in 1645, 'with whom', says Fuller, 'the *Old Puritan* may seem to expire, and in his grave to be interr'd'.

An interesting and somewhat enigmatical personage belonging to this period of Jesus history was William Petty, elected to a Fellowship in 1612. His original college was Christ's, where he had taken his M.A. degree; and before he was elected at Jesus he had been for some years Master of the grammar school at Beverley, the same school which had given Bishop Alcock his education. From thence we are told that he brought to Jesus many pupils, sons of *generosi* as well as sizars. He was perhaps the first

Englishman who visited Greece with the express purpose of exploration and the recollection of classical antiquities, and his career—unrecorded in the *Dictionary of National Biography*—was a foreshadowing in the early seventeenth century of that of another eminent Jesus Fellow, Professor E. D. Clarke, at the end of the eighteenth. He was chaplain to that Earl of Arundel who collected the Arundel marbles, and he accompanied the Earl's eldest son on his travels in France, Spain, and Italy. Afterwards he was sent abroad frequently by the Earl, with the object of searching for manuscripts, coins, and sculptures, and in 1624 we hear of him 'turning of old stones' at Constantinople, Troy, Pergamus, and elsewhere. The graphically interesting story of his diggings and researches is told in the letters of Sir Thomas Roe, Ambassador at Constantinople, to the Earl.[1] Sherman says that he afterwards settled at Athens, and there in some sort became a public professor of Greek—an illustration of the proverb γλαῦκ' Ἀθήναζε—and this remarkable association in letters of Cambridge and Athens reminds him of the old legend, whereof Lydgate sang, that Anaximander and Anaxagoras were amongst the first teachers in the university founded by the mythical prince, Cantaber of Spain. Petty returned to England, and when he died left £200 to Jesus College; but, owing to the dishonesty of his executor, the College never received his bequest.

The monotonous Mastership of Dr Duport was only relieved by formal events, chief among which were the two visits of King James I to Cambridge in March and May 1615. It was the first time that the College had received a sovereign, for Elizabeth, when she was at Cambridge in 1564, had omitted to go to Jesus 'because it stood far out of the way'. When English sovereigns began to attend race-meetings at Newmarket, Jesus proved to be not so far out of their way. King James's visits were preceded by one from Prince Charles and his brother-in-law, the ill-starred Elector Palatine Frederick, in March 1613. They came to Jesus as they were leaving the town for Newmarket, and were entertained with 'Rennish wine' and a Latin oration, still extant in

[1] *Ancient Marbles in Great Britain*, by A. Michaelis, pp. 185–205 (English translation).

manuscript. Nor were they spared elegiac effusions, the quality of which may be illustrated by the following specimen:

> Anglo-Britannus eram, sed venit Carolus hospes:
> Anglo-Britannus eram, Scoto-Britannus ero.
> Scoto-Britannus eram, Fredericus venit at hospes:
> Scoto-Britannus eram, Rheno-Britannus ero.
> Quisquis eram, vel ero, Fredericus Carolus adsunt:
> Anglo-Brito-Scoto-Rheno-Jesuanus ero.

The Elector Palatine, the Protestant hero who had married the Princess Elizabeth a month before the Cambridge visit, was vastly popular at the time, and in this year the College had helped the insolvent King James to provide a dowry for his daughter by a vote of the remarkable sum of seventeen shillings and sixpence 'for yᵉ princesse yᵉ Lady Elizabeth aide'. The King was so pleased with the reception of the two princes that he announced his intention of gracing the University with his royal presence in the winter of 1614–15. The Bursar's accounts show that elaborate preparations were made 'against yᵉ Kings comming' (March 1615). 'Musitions' were hired for the eventful day, the chapel windows were mended, the tapestry in the Hall was taken down, mended and brushed, snow and dirt were carried out of the College, and the Hall and cloisters were strewn with rushes. James repeated his visit later in the same year, and on both occasions was at Jesus. His Majesty was pleased to bestow special commendation on the aspect and surroundings of the College. *Musarum Cantabrigiensium Museum* was his name for it, and College memories fondly treasured the royal utterance that, 'were he to choose, he would pray at King's, dine at Trinity, and study and sleep at Jesus'.

The harmony which had previously marked the relations between the Master and the Fellows of Jesus was destined to be broken when Duport was succeeded in the Mastership by Dr Roger Andrewes. Andrewes had some titles to distinction. He had been a Fellow of Pembroke, of which college his brother, the amiable and pious Lancelot Andrewes, was Master from 1589 to 1605. Like his predecessor, Duport, he was one of the Cambridge divines selected to make the translation of the Bible known as the Authorized Version. He owed his advancement to the Mastership to the offices of his brother, who was Bishop of Ely and Visitor of the College from 1609 to 1619. But Roger had none of his brother's grace of character. He was overbearing and quarrelsome, and for the well-being of the College he showed the most contemptuous disregard. He held several canonries and other preferments, and seems to have resided little at Cambridge. The statutes assigned to the Master the management of the College estates and finances, and his neglect and incapacity led to an intolerable condition of affairs which is revealed in a series of papers in the University archives belonging to the year 1628. The first is a petition addressed by the Fellows to the King, the date of which is not given:

To the King's Most Excellent Majesty: The Humble Petition of the Fellows of Jesus Colledge in Cambridge

HUMBLY SHOWETH that whereas Dr Andrewes, Master of the said Colledge, by his detaining the monies due unto the Colledge Treasury and the Fellows' dividends, which are their whole means and Maintenance: As also by divers other breaches of their local statutes is like to bring the Society to Dissolution unless some present Course be taken for the redress of the present Evils and preventing the future imminent Dangers which his bad Government doth threaten: And whereas in the Vacancy of the See of Ely (the Bishop whereof being the Visiter of the said Colledge) your Majesty's petitioners have no way of Redress but to your Majesty.

Their humble Petition is your Majesty would be graciously pleased of your Princely Zeal and wonted Royal Care of the good of such Foundations and seminaries of Piety and Literature to refer the hearing of the Society's Grievances to the Vice-Chancellor and some other Masters of Colledges who may have power to examine and reform the present Enormities and prevent future Disorders. And (as in duty bound) they will not cease to pray for your Majesty's Long and Happy Reign, etc.

The King, in his reply, dated from Newmarket, 29 February 1627–8, referred the Fellows' petition to the Vice-Chancellor and Heads of Houses of the University, authorizing them to call the

Master and the Fellows before them to examine the truth of the complaints, and to certify His Majesty what they thought fit to be done for the righting of the society and the better government of the College in the future. In consequence of the King's reference, the Vice-Chancellor, Dr Bainbrigge, Master of Christ's, together with the Heads of Peterhouse, Corpus, and Queens', summoned Dr Andrewes and the Fellows before them. The Fellows submitted two long lists of grievances to them. The chief article which they laid to the Master's charge was that he detained various sums of College money, amounting in all to £500, of which part should have been carried into the Treasure-house, and part should have supplied the Fellows' dividends. The Master, they said, had given no account of the Treasury for the past two years, and when he last came to the College, three months after the proper time for the Audit, he refused to pay any of the Fellows their dividends—amounting to £11 11s. 10d. each—unless they would 'sett their hands' to the Audit Book, affirming that a certain sum due to the Treasury had been paid to it, which was not the fact. Seven of the Fellows, being reduced to destitution, were unable to discharge their debts to the College, and so were put out of commons. 'Extraordinary entreaty' was made to the Master to pay the dividends, but he absolutely refused to do so, 'except they would yeld to borrow them of him, wch some for extreem necessity yeelded unto, and so they gave him Bills of y^{r} hands for y^{r} owne; and yet he payd not above half, notwithstanding that ye Fellowes were contented to let him have in his hands 145^{lib}, taken then for Leases, set a purpose to supply his want'. Notwithstanding the direction of the statutes that the Master should supply the Steward with money for the purchase of household necessaries, for eighteen months past he had neglected to do so, and in consequence the Steward had been obliged irregularly to borrow sums amounting to £30 from the Treasury. The College officers and labourers could not get their wages at the due time, and the College was brought into such discredit that 'neither Butcher, Baker, Collier, Sedgeman nor Peutrer would trust it without the personall engagement of particular Fellowes'. The Master had never rendered any account of the Library; he did not view, or appoint any of the Fellows to view, the repairs on College estates, and by his neglect the fabric of the College was 'very much ruinated'. In general matters his conduct was not less injurious to the interests of the College. By the disrespect which he had shown to benefactors he had given 'just occasion of discouragement to all present well-willers'. He had used the Fellows 'most contemptuouslie, making them come 4 or 5 tymes before he will speake with them, and, when they have accesse, revileing, threatning and factiouslie irritating them one against the other'. He had pronounced one of the Fellows Dean, though only a minority of the Fellows had voted for him. He had not dined or supped in the Hall for more than seven years. He kept no discipline, and had 'done no act of justice upon just complaints, disclaiming the charge of (i.e. responsibility for) Fellow-Commoners and Pensioners'. Lastly, he was charged with making false entries in the register, and with having torn a whole statute (we are not told which) out of the Statute-Book, so that it was never read with the others in the chapel at the time appointed by the statutes.

Andrewes's answer to the objections of the Fellows amounts to a confession of the general truth of the facts alleged, and his attempted avoidance of them serves only to emphasize the unscrupulous character of the man. The dividends, he said, were not due until the accounts had been passed by the Fellows. In spite of their obstinacy in declining to sign the Audit Book, he had paid some part of them, and had offered to lend the rest. His omission to make up the accounts at the proper time and to provide the Steward with funds he excuses by the statement that he had been called to London by the news of the death of his brother the Bishop, and had been detained there by sickness. Some of his answers are redolent of the contemptuous usage which the Fellows found so hard to bear. Among other matters, they had objected to him that he had not delivered six yards of velvet 'wch was in exchange of an old cope, wch by importunity he optayned two years since, promising to bring them ye next tyme he came, notwithstanding he hath been often demanded it'. To which the Master replied 'that indeed he promised *five* yards of velvet, but since he findeth he hath no use of the coape, if the Fellowes persist in their unkindnesse, he will restore it againe'.

In March or April the delegated Heads reported to the King the result of their inquiries. They find that the Fellows have good cause for petitioning for their relief. For the righting of their grievances they recommend that Dr Andrewes be required immediately to make up all his accounts with the College, to deliver any sums which he owes into the Treasury, and to pay the Fellows and others their dividends and dues; that, notwithstanding the provision of the statutes, which assigned to the Master the collection and control of the College revenues, the Master and Fellows should at once and ever hereafter appoint one of the society to be Bursar, and to account for all receipts and disbursements; and, finally, that the Fellows should subscribe their names to the unaudited accounts, and that this subscription should be a sufficient discharge to Dr Andrewes. The other defects complained of, they suppose, may easily be redressed by the Visitor.

The King ordered the Vice-Chancellor to take immediate steps to right the society and remove its grievances. But the recommendations of the Heads seemingly bore no fruit. No Bursar was appointed; the Fellows did not sign the Audit Book, and in no single year from 1626 to the end of his Mastership were Andrewes's accounts approved by them. It does not appear what steps the Fellows took to call attention to the Master's contumacity. Four years passed before they were relieved of his tyranny. At last the King wrote a letter to him—the date is not given—to the effect that 'whereas he had, contrary to statute, absented himself from Jesus College two years at the least, he had given just cause why he should be made an example of Justice; but the King, remembering the favour he bore to his late worthy Servant, the Doctor's Brother, was pleased to forbear public disgrace, so as the Doctor made presentlie a voluntary Cession and Surrender of that Mastership'. Andrewes accordingly resigned in 1632, ἑκὼν ἀέκοντί γε θυμῷ, as Sherman puts it. He died three years later.

The falsification of the College register was one of the counts in the indictment against Andrewes; in one case an entry signed with his name only has been scored out, presumably by the Fellows. Nevertheless, against his many failings may be set the one redeeming merit, which may apparently be credited to him, of having introduced, probably from Pembroke, the practice of keeping an official College register. It dates from the first year of his Mastership (1618), and has been continued without interruption ever since. Its entries are, for the most part, formal—admissions, sealings, elections to scholarships, presentations to livings, nominations and inductions of Fellows, licences, testimonials, etc.; but it is none the less invaluable to the College historian.

John Eliot probably entered the College before the first date in the new register, for his admission does not appear in it, though he is recorded as taking his B.A. in 1622, and as obtaining College testimonials for ordination in 1625. Religious motives caused him to join the new settlement in Massachusetts in 1631. He was not the first member of the College who for conscience' sake sought a home in the New World. Francis Higginson, admitted at Jesus in 1608, but B.A. of St John's in 1609, and afterwards minister of the church of Salem, had died there in the year before Eliot's arrival. He was a scholar as well as an eloquent preacher, and his *New England's Plantation* is a valuable record of early settlement days. Eliot's famous Bible, in the language of the Massachusetts Indians, the earliest of missionary Bibles, was completed and printed at Cambridge, New England, in 1663. The first edition is very rare, and has been sold for large sums. A copy of it, presented by Eliot himself, and bearing his autograph and a dedicatory Latin distich, is one of the most treasured possessions of the College library. In memory of the 'Apostle to the Indians' an Eliot Prize for theology was founded in 1898 at Jesus by the liberality of his descendants and other donors in the United States.

The Bursars' accounts furnish us with a wealth of suggestion for reconstructing life at Jesus during the reigns of Elizabeth and James I. The age of the tradesman and his bills had not yet come in. The College bought its own materials, and hired its own labour. Consequently, every item of expenditure in the way of building, repairs, and housekeeping is faithfully recorded in the Audit Books. Very often the 'scholars' were glad to eke out their small allowances by doing odd jobs, for which the Bursar paid them. Trifling sums might be earned by keeping the wood-yard or coalhouse, or by winding the chapel clock, or by attending to the buttery in the butler's absence, or by carrying the clippings of the hedge, which served for fuel, from the Close into the College. Very often a Fellow employs his 'puple' to glaze his windows.[1] This was mostly about the years 1571–8, previous to which time it seems that windows in chambers were mostly unglazed. Chimneys and fireplaces in rooms came in much about the same time.

Frequent mention is made of the 'studies'. These were spaces partitioned off in two or three corners of the chamber, each, as a rule, lighted by its own window, and occupied in the daytime by a student, while the middle space served in common for sleeping purposes. Some of these, perhaps, survive in modern gyp-rooms. Some rooms in the Master's lodging were wainscoted or lined with 'buckrom', and Fellows sometimes bequeath their 'hangings' to their friends; but the walls were often left bare. Sometimes the tenants painted them with patterns or texts, still discoverable under modern wallpapers. A transient occupant of rooms that once were Bancroft's adorned his walls with the text in large Roman capitals: NON HABEMVS HIC MANENTEM CIVITATEM SED FVTVRAM INQVIRIMVS. HEB. 13. Heavy doors at the foot of the staircase shut it off from the court at night. The illumination of the cloister court was provided by a 'great and litle lanthorn', which required to be periodically horned.

The common life centred in the Hall. There the lectures were given. There (not, perhaps, only there) Fellow and pupil washed, using the 'bason and ewer customably sett upon ye borde over ye stocks'. There on winter evenings the scholars, unless they were rich enough to 'size' for coals in their own rooms, drew their forms round the common fire, which blazed on the spacious hearth, now concealed behind the panels of the northern wall— a place of much importance, if we may judge from the frequent references to it in the accounts, and full of memories, we may be

---

[1] The bequest of 'overworn clothing' to sizars, which is common in the wills of Fellows who died in College in the sixteenth and early seventeenth centuries, illustrates the homely relations which existed between tutor and pupil.

sure, of Cambridge days to many a squire and parson in after life. For this fireplace the College set up a 'mantil-tree' and made 'doggs of our owne stuffe' in 1574. 'A pare of fyre-irons to burn sea-cole for yᵉ hall' was got in 1572, and bellows in 1600. The Hall was the one comfortably furnished apartment in the College. At the lower end was a screen. The walls were not wainscoted, but hung with 'arresse', or 'clothes'—most likely painted—which from time to time were taken down, dusted, and 'ayered abroade'. The floor was 'tiled', probably with stone, and on occasions strewn with rushes. There was a long table for the Fellows' use, but the scholars took their meals at trestles, which were removed when the Hall was wanted for general purposes. The Master sat on a chair, the Fellows on forms (as they did until 1875). There was a 'cort cobbord', on which vessels of silver or pewter were placed; 'an oyster table'; and a 'desk which yᵉ schollers read upon', on which was laid 'the byble for yᵉ schollers to read in yᵉ hall' during meals, as the statutes directed. The most singular feature to modern eyes was the stocks, which stood by the screen at the entrance. Stocking was a usual punishment for the contumacious undergraduate or bachelor, and similar incentives to virtue existed in other college halls. By a decree of the Heads of Houses in 1571 it was enacted that any person *in statu pupillari* presuming to bathe in a river, pond, or any other water in the county of Cambridge should be flogged in the presence of all the members of his college and, if he were a Bachelor of Arts, should be set in the stocks for a whole day in the college hall and should pay a fine of 10s. towards the commons of all the members of the college before he was let out. To the alternative punishment of flogging, which it is said that Milton underwent at Christ's, the Jesus books possibly refer in a mysterious entry which occurs in the year 1582, when one of the Fellows, Mr Murgetrod, received the handsome sum of 5s. 10d. *pro puero vapulando*. But the largeness of the sum and the exceptional circumstance that the words are Latin suggest that *Puer Vapulans* may have been the title of a Latin play, of which Mr Murgetrod was author or stage director.

Plays, usually in Latin, were performed in College throughout the whole of this period; the first mention of them is in 1561, the last in 1622. The occasions for acting them were the 'breakings up' at Christmas, the Annunciation and the Commencement. One of the Fellows was always responsible for their management. In 1563 the *Adelphi* and the *Curculio* were acted; next year the *Eunucus;* in 1580 the *Bacchides*. There was a 'dialogg and shewe' at Christmas 1564, and Mr Forthe had a 'shewe' in 1568. In 1564 the Bursar paid the large sum of 6s. 'for a parasites cote and hose, for the stuffe and makinge of it'. 'Making a theatre' in the same year cost only 12d., but the stage cost as much as 23s. 2d. in 1577, and much larger sums were sometimes spent on the plays. In 1569 'ye Goodwife Linsey' receives 2s. 8d. for 'a platter and a sawser lost at the playes', which, as they weighed 4 lb, were evidently of pewter; in later years the College provided its own 'comodie pott'. The stage was usually in the Hall, but sometimes the plays were acted in the chapel. The occasion was commonly an opportunity for what would now be called a 'rag'. The Bursar frequently had to pay for broken windows; once the clock was 'broke'. On another occasion considerable damage was done by a torch, 'which burned in ye toppe of ye Hall'.

Of the diet of the Fellows and better-off scholars the Bursars' accounts do not give us all the information that we should like to have. For their private sizings they reckoned with the Steward, who only accounted to the Bursar for necessaries, such as stock-fish, salt-fish, salt, bread, beer, oatmeal. There was a fish-house in the kitchen and another in the cloister, in which the dry stock-fish was piled on layers of sedge in a high stack, the top of which was reached by a ladder. The College supplied its own poultry; there was a hen-house and a dove-house, and frequent payments were made to old men and boys for killing buzzards and polecats which threatened them. The College also kept swans, attended to by 'swanyards,' at Willingham and Basingbourn. It contracted with a warrener at Newmarket for the supply of 'conyes', at 10d. a couple from Michaelmas to Shrovetide. At the Feast of Jesus and on Audit day there are 'exceedings'; on the latter occasion we hear of powdered beef and 'dubbell Beare', and the College tenant at Shelford regularly supplied a boar. Tobacco at the Audit was first paid for in 1657. The dishes used at meals, it seems, were exclusively of pewter, but the salt cellars were of silver; wooden trenchers had apparently quite gone out of use. From time to time the College sent its old 'vessel', as the pewter service was called, to Sturbridge Fair to be exchanged for new.

Of the amusements of our Elizabethan predecessors at Jesus the Bursars have naturally less to tell. There was a 'tenis cort' in 1572, which was in or next to the portion of the nunnery cloister which then existed in the third or 'Pump' court on the north side of the Hall. In 1604 a new tennis-court was built, which cost the College £8 7s. 6d., 'besides a pretor collected amongst ye schollars'. A bowling-alley is mentioned in 1631. In 1582 the Graveley tenants brought hens to the Master and Fellows at Shrovetide, and it may be conjectured that they suffered the usual fate of Shrovetide hens. Bonfires were a recognized institution, for which Midsummer Day and, after 1605, 5 November were the principal occasions. So far was authority from condemning such performances that when Dr Whitaker, Master of St John's, was charged with lack of loyalty in celebrating the anniversary of the Queen's accession in his college, to prove the falsehood of the allegation he assured Lord Burghley that there were 'bone fiers in both courtes of the College'. At Jesus, among other occasions, there were bonfires for Queen Elizabeth's proclamation in 1558, for the peace with France in 1559, noticeably on Charles I's coronation day in 1648, and, even more curiously, in 1668 on the anniversary of his decapitation. Football was so popular at Cambridge in the days of Elizabeth and James I that we cannot doubt that it was played on Jesus Close. But on account of disturbances which took place at a match between 'certain schollers of Cambridge and divers of Chesterton', the Heads found it necessary to pass an edict against football matches, except within the precincts of the colleges, 'not permitting any stranger or scholars of other colleges or houses to play with them or in their company', which must have considerably detracted from the interest of the game. In the years 1594–1604 there existed a College boat, but it does not appear whether it was used for recreation. It had a canvas 'tilth' or awning, and besides oars had a 'conte', or punting pole, and a 'haylinge line'.

Stearn's, Cambridge

INTERIOR OF CHAPEL: THE CROSSING (1959)

Plate IV

INTERIOR OF CHAPEL: THE CHOIR (1928)

CHAPTER V

REBELLION AND COMMONWEALTH

THE Mastership of Roger Andrewes carries us over the first
seven years of the reign of Charles I, but may be regarded as
belonging wholly to that of his father. Save for the differences
between the Master and the Fellows, it was a time of absolute
quiescence in the history of the College. In the general forward
movement of the University Jesus had hardly held its place since
Ithell's death, and from the active controversies of the day its
resident members had generally held aloof. The religious attitude
of the society during the last half of the sixteenth century had
been sufficiently clear. Less Protestant than other colleges in the
reign of Edward VI, it had been more Roman in the days of
revived Romanism, and more Anglican in the long war waged
against the Cambridge Puritans by Parker, Whitgift, and Bancroft. With the exception of John Dod, no prominent exponent
of Genevan views was counted among the Fellows of Jesus.
None of them had drawn upon himself the censure of the Vice-
Chancellor or Heads for heterodox views expressed in the pulpit
of St Mary's. Among the rank and file of its students there were
a few, such as Francis Higginson and John Eliot, who, later in
life, were pressed into Nonconformity by the rigid rule of Laud.
But hitherto no intestine differences on questions of doctrine or
discipline had broken the quiet of the cloisters, and the shock of
the revolution of 1642 fell upon a college at unity with itself.

William Beale, D.D., who was appointed to the Mastership on
the resignation of Dr Andrewes, might, perhaps, under altered
conditions, have left a name for scholarly attainments as distinguished as that of either of his immediate predecessors. He had
been a Westminster scholar of Trinity, graduated as B.A. in
1609–10, and was chosen a Fellow of Jesus in 1611. He resigned

his Fellowship in 1625, and probably left Cambridge at the same time. His success as a tutor had been marked; his pupils, we are told, were very numerous, and many of them were sons of noblemen and gentlemen of rank. Hyde, afterwards Lord Clarendon, styles him his worthy and learned chaplain; Baker says he was one of the best administrators that the University ever had. He resigned the Mastership of Jesus when he was elected to that of St John's, early in 1634, but he did not cease to interest himself in the well-being of his old College, and liberally contributed to the cost of the new buildings there, put up in the Mastership of his successor, Dr Sterne. With Sterne, as we shall see, it was his lot to be intimately associated in the troublous days that presently befell the University.

It is the peculiar distinction of Jesus College that it has furnished to the Church of England not less than five Archbishops—Cranmer, Bancroft, Herring and Hutton of Canterbury, and Sterne of York. The eminence to which he attained after the Restoration is not, however, the chief ground on which a Jesus man should recall with veneration the name of Richard Sterne. Had he died obscurely in exile, as Dr Beale did, he would still deserve to be remembered as the greatest of the Masters of Jesus. His tenure of rule was limited to a space of scarcely eight years, but the energetic and reforming spirit which he applied to the work of his office made those years, independently of the dramatic incidents which coloured them, an epoch in the College history, and, in some sense, the beginning of its modern period.

Richard Sterne, a native of Mansfield, Notts, had been a scholar of Trinity, graduated B.A. there in 1614–15, was elected a Fellow of Corpus in 1620, and was admitted Master of Jesus 7 March 1633–4, on which day the Master and Fellows of Corpus brought him to his new College and were entertained by the society of Jesus. About the same time he became chaplain to Archbishop Laud, and, along with Dr Beale of St John's and Dr Cosin of Peterhouse, he became prominent in championing Laudian views of Church discipline at Cambridge. In 1635 Laud claimed as Metropolitan the right of visiting the University in matters ecclesiastical. The claim was disputed by the University, and, though the King in Council decided in favour of the Archbishop, the threatened visitation never took place. However, a report of 'Certain Disorders in Cambridge to be considered in my Visitation' was drawn up and sent to Laud by either Sterne or Cosin. It presents a curious and interesting picture of the lamentable neglect of decency and reverence into which the chapel services had fallen. Five colleges, of which Jesus was one, were excepted from its strictures, and of them the report merely says: 'They endeavour for order and have brought it to some good passe: Yet here for Apparel and fasting-night suppers are they faultie still'. Sterne attended Laud on the scaffold, and printed the address which he made to the people before his death.[1]

Among the first questions which claimed the attention of the new Master was that of the management of the College finances. In spite of alterations in the value of money and the increase in the annual income, the mode of distribution of the revenues prescribed by the statutes was rigidly adhered to in the audited accounts which were submitted to the Visitor. Since 1557 the practice appears to have grown up of carrying the over-plus of receipts after payment of the statutable charges to another account, which came to be known as 'the Dividend Paper'. This was never submitted to the Visitor. As it included all land and house rents other than those anciently reserved, as well as the fines on leases, the dividend naturally became a matter of far more consequence to the Fellows than their statutable emoluments. Hitherto there had been no recognized method of distributing the dividend money. An unscrupulous Master, such as Andrewes, might avail himself of his position as Bursar to appropriate the whole amount. Two months after he entered on office Sterne and the Fellows adopted the arrangement that the proceeds of fines should be divided into twenty parts, whereof two should go to the use of the College, two to the Master, and one to each of the Fellows. At the same time they sensibly agreed to drop the practice of giving leases for lives.

[1] It is worth remarking that Thomas Carr, who was Strafford's chaplain and attended him on the scaffold, was a Fellow of Jesus (admitted Fellow in 1612.)

Though the settlement on the dividend question was, no doubt, a practical one, it contained in it the seeds of evil. To the Fellows of early times, who received only a small stipend of fixed amount, the value of a Fellowship consisted mainly in the right to occupy College rooms and the allowance for commons. Their pecuniary income was derived almost entirely from pupils. Residence in College was therefore a practical necessity, and, indeed, was strictly required by the statutes, except in special cases approved by the Master. The arrangement of 1634, while it indefinitely increased the value of a Fellowship, left no provision for augmenting the stipends of the official lecturers. The Head Lector, the Greek Lector, and the two Sublectors continued to exist and to draw the pittances which the statutes allowed them, augmented by the groats contributed by their auditors, but it was inevitable that their offices should become practical sinecures. In course of time the official staff was reduced to a single Lector, and one of his principal duties was to deliver a ridiculous Latin speech once a year in the College Hall. Scribbled specimens of such orations may be found among the lumber of the Library—weary exhibitions of pedantic humour, crammed with tags from Juvenal and Virgil, jests on the founder's cocks displayed in the Hall windows, remonstrances against the 'boatus' which, it seems, undergraduates raised during chapel service, exhortations to early rising, and such domestic matters. The last stage of degeneration was reached when the sole function left to the 'Praelector' was that of presenting for degrees, when it was his duty to vouch for the *doctrina* of candidates with whose intellectual furnishing his office gave him no concern.

The increased value of a Fellowship, especially in relation to the emoluments of a tutor, also tended to encourage non-residence. From this date licences for Fellows 'to absent themselves', usually for a few months at a time, but in some cases for indefinite periods, are of constant occurrence in the register. Clerical Fellows divided their time between the College and their cures, and those attached to the study of civil law naturally found employment in London or in the service of the State abroad. Fellows who were absent, with permission, from Cambridge received both their statutable stipend and their dividend during the period of their non-residence.

During the neglectful days of the Mastership of Roger Andrewes the number of students had fallen to a low ebb. In the last five years of his rule, 1628–32, only forty-one admission fees were accounted for. In the year of Beale's accession, the admissions went up with a sudden bound to forty-two, and in the five years ending 1638 the total recorded was 119. In 1641 ninety residents were assessed to poll-tax. The number cannot be considered very high, for it was exceeded by Catharine Hall and Magdalene, and was less than half the total credited to Emmanuel. But since the last addition to the chamber space of the College, in 1568, the standard of comfort had greatly advanced. In particular the large number of Fellow-Commoners attracted to the College by Beale and Sterne made some extension of chamber room an imperative necessity. In 1637 the College decided to proceed with the erection of a range of buildings on the north side of the entrance court, facing the gate-tower and the small school-house block. The building operations went on for three years, and when they were brought to a conclusion in January 1641–2, the total sum expended on them was found to be £1,544. As the College had apparently no reserve fund, special measures had to be taken for raising so large a sum. It was agreed that for five years following the Audit of 1639 a sum of £40 should annually be set aside for the new building, £36 in each year from the dividends of the Master and Fellows, and the remainder from the chest. One hundred pounds was obtained on loan, and the remainder was contributed by the piety of various members of the College, whose names, with the amount of their donations, are recorded in the Form for Commemoration of Benefactors.

The meagre details of expenditure included in the Bursars' accounts of the first thirty years of the seventeenth century under the head of *Templum* point to the continued neglect of the chapel and its services. A dawning regard for ritual is suggested by a payment for nine Latin service-books in the first year of Beale's Mastership. Hitherto the Latin version of the Common Prayer-Book, which had been specially sanctioned for use in College chapels, had been almost entirely neglected at Cambridge, owing to the prejudice of the Puritan party. Laud had brought it into use at Oxford, and its introduction at Jesus may be set down to his influence. It was left to Sterne to carry into full effect Laud's views as to church appointments and ceremonial. His first step, taken in 1634, six months after he became Master, was to introduce an organ into the chapel. Its builder, Robert Dallam, received £200 from the College. An organist was appointed, with a salary which was provided by a quarterly tax of 12d., levied on all whose names were on the College books, except sizars, who, in lieu of payment, were required to blow the organ in turn. Wax-tapers were provided by a similar tax of 6d. Two years later the College paid a sum of £37 16s. 9d. for 'ye raile, floore, freeze, hangings, etc., about the altar, together with ye Letany desk', the last of which, a double stool of characteristic Jacobean workmanship, remains in use to the present day. New plate for the Communion Service was provided in 1639.

Had it been possible for the Master and Fellows, as they sat at their 'audit chear' in the founder's chamber on 12 January 1641-2, to exclude from their thoughts the troubles brewing in the political world, they must have regarded their position and prospects with considerable complacency. They had that day closed the New Building account; the College had acquired a range of chambers fairer to outward view and more commodious than the old cloister buildings, and Sherman says that it was free from debt; the number of its students was at least as large as it had ever been within living memory; the Fellows were at harmony among themselves, and shared the Master's satisfaction in the restoration to the chapel services of that beauty and reverence which had been wanting since the changes of 1558. But it is not hazardous to guess that their talk was of other and less cheerful matters. Eight days before their Audit meeting the King had made his abortive attempt to arrest the Five Members; the final rupture with Parliament and the King's departure for York was the latest piece of intelligence that had reached them from London. The national question was already involved in one personal to themselves. The committee which the House of Commons, in its last session, had empowered to consider abuses in religion and civil government at the universities had singled out Jesus as the first object of its inquiries at Cambridge, and the Master and Fellows had been compelled to bring up their statutes and account-books to be examined by the committee, sitting in London. And, though trouble on that account was perhaps for the moment over-past, a deeper anxiety must have occupied their thoughts in connexion with the recent order of the Commons requiring Heads of Colleges to displace the Communion table from the east end of their chapels, to take away the rails and level the chancel, to remove crucifixes, tapers, and basons from the Communion table—to undo, in fact, all that the society of Jesus had been at such pains to effect in the improvement of the chapel services.

Trouble deepened as the year 1642 advanced. There was plague in the town in the summer, and the College contributed to the relief of the 'visited'. On 29 June the King addressed a letter to the Vice-Chancellor, requesting the University and colleges to contribute money for his defence. On 24 July he followed it up with a request that the colleges would send him their plate. To both applications Jesus College gave a prompt and favourable answer. On 29 July it passed an order that 1,201 ounces of plate —the pieces being specified in a list—should be delivered to Mr John Poley for the King's use, and on 29 August it obtained a loan from a friend of the Master's, at Newstead in Nottingham-shire, with the same object. The plate, with that contributed by other colleges, was safely conveyed to the King at Nottingham, in spite of the vigilance of Cromwell, who lay in wait for it with a disorderly band of peasants on the road between Cambridge and Huntingdon.

Retribution was swift to overtake the Heads who were chiefly responsible for sending the plate. The story of Dr Sterne's treat-ment is told in Walker's *Sufferings of the Clergy*:

Together with Dr *Beale* Master of St *John's*, and Dr *Martin*, Master of *Queens*, he was seized by Cromwell (who had with some Parties of Soldiers surrounded the several Chapels, whilst the Scholars were at Prayers) and carried in Triumph to *London*. . . . In the Villages, as they passed from *Cambridge* to *London*, the People were called by some of their Agents to come and Abuse and Revile them: They were also led leisurely through the midst of Bartholomew Fair; as they passed along they were entertained with Exclamations, Reproaches, Scorns and Curses; and it was a great Providence, considering the Prejudice which the People had to them, that they found no worse Usage. After their Confinement (in the Tower), tho' they often Petitioned to be heard, yet they could never obtain either a Trial, or their Liberty. They had been a full Year under Restraint in other Prisons, when they were at length, *Friday August* 11, 1643, by order of the Parliament, sent on board the Ship; the name of which was the *Prosperous Saylor*, then lying at *Wapping*. . . . Being come on Shipboard, they were instantly put under Hatches, where the Decks were so Low, that they could not stand upright; and yet were denied *Stools to sit on*, or so much as a *Burthen of Straw to ly on*. Into this *Little Ease*, in a small Ship, they crowd no less than 80 *Prisoners of Quality*; and that they might stifle one another, having no more Breath than what they suck'd from one another's Mouth, most maliciously and (Certainly) to a *Murtherous Intent*, they stop up all the *small Augur-Holes*, and all other inlets which might relieve them with Fresh Air.

In December 1642, the Fellows of the three colleges joined in a petition to the House of Commons for the release of the imprisoned Masters, but the House took no further notice of it than to order the latter to be transferred from the Tower to the custody of 'the Keeper of Lord Peters's House in Aldersgate Street, to be there kept until the pleasure of this House be further known'. Dr Sterne was allowed to perform the last offices of piety to his old friend, Archbishop Laud, on the scaffold at Tower Hill, and soon afterwards regained his liberty. He seems to have been in trouble again in 1650-1, the year of Worcester fight, for the Audit accounts of that year have an enigmatical item: 'To Bailies for apprehending Dr Sterne, £1'. In the following year there is a charge for 'the Butler's journey to Dr Sterne', who was then, possibly, at Stevenage, where, until the Restoration, he maintained himself by keeping a school. Dr Beale, less happy than his successor in the Lodge at Jesus, did not live to see the triumph of the cause for which he suffered. He died at Madrid in 1651. Baker says that to prevent his body from falling into the hands of the Inquisitors it was buried in quicklime beneath the floor of the chamber in which he died.

Sterne was not at once deprived of the Mastership when he was arrested, and the Fellows continued to pay his dues to Mrs Sterne until they were themselves dispossessed. On 23 February 1642–3 they agreed:

> Intuitu periculorum undique impendentium omnes socii veniam absentiae concessam habent usque ad festum Michaelis.

On 7 November 1643 it was agreed by the President and nine Fellows to extend this leave of absence until Michaelmas 1644.

It was a bitter constraint that rendered these resolutions necessary. During the year 1643 Cambridge was converted by Cromwell into an armed camp, and no scholar was allowed to pass outside the town unless a townsman vouched that he was a 'confider'. A breast-work was raised at the eastern end of Jesus Lane, and Jesus Grove—'no idolatrous one', says Fuller—was cut down.

> Multitudes of soldiers [says the *Querela Cantabrigiensis*], were quarter'd in those Glorious and Ancient Structures which the Devout and Royal Founders design'd for *Sanctuaries of Learning and Piety*: but were made by them mere *Spittals* and *Bawdy Houses* for sick and debauch'd Soldiers. To this must be added that they Tore and Defac'd the Buildings, Pull'd down and Burn'd the Wainscote of the Chambers, the Bedsteds, Chairs, Stools, and Shelves for Books.

The following entries in the Bursars' book suggest conditions of life which must have been intolerable to the quiet scholar:

> 1643–44—To soldiers y^t came to be billetted, Oct. 20, 1643, 2^s 6^d.
>   For mending windows, locks, bedsteads, etc., broken by
>   ye souldiers billetted in ye College, 18^s.
> 1644–45—To three troopers out three days in Bedfordshire, 6^s.

After the resolution passed in November 1643, the majority of the Fellows quitted the College. But before they went they took down and concealed the organ, and buried the College plate—such of it as had not gone to the King—in the Master's orchard. Throughout the year following nothing but formal business was transacted. The register only notices two admissions, and only three undergraduates had licence *ad respondendum quaestioni*.

In the last days of the same year the notorious William Dowsing came to Cambridge armed with power to put into execution the ordinance of Parliament for the reformation of churches and chapels. The curious diary kept by this ignorant enthusiast informs us of the extent of his depredations. He visited Jesus on 28 December, and, in the presence of one of the Fellows, Mr Boyleston, 'digg'd up the Steps there and brake downe Superstitions of Saints and Angels, 120 at the least'. Mr Boyleston may have been an unwilling witness of the desecration, but the fact that he was one of the two Fellows who were not 'outed' by the Earl of Manchester in the following year raises a presumption that he was an assenting party. The 'superstitions' which were broken down were evidently in the windows. The Audit Book this year mentions payments amounting in all to £10 16s. 0d. for mending windows in the chapel, and there is another item of £3 6s. 6d. 'for levelling yᵉ chapel, tiles, lime, sand and labourers' wages'. During the levelling the workmen discovered the coffin lid of Berta Rosata, which now lies in the south transept, but presumably was then in the chancel.

On 22 January 1643-4, the Houses of Parliament passed an Ordinance for Regulating the University of Cambridge which empowered the Earl of Manchester to endeavour the reformation of the University, and to eject such Masters or Fellows of colleges as were scandalous in their lives or doctrines, or opposed the proceedings of Parliament. The Earl came to Cambridge in February, and notified the Masters and scholars of each college to be in residence on 10 March next ensuing, then to answer such things as should be demanded by him. Stephen Hall, the President of Jesus, seems to have ignored the summons. The Audit Book disappeared, and was not produced for inspection. The Sequestrators were obliged to force the locks of the Treasury, and of the College plate three pieces only were discoverable. For this contumacy—though the assigned reason was his refusal to take the Covenant—the President was ejected on 15 March. This was the first ejection by Parliamentary order at Cambridge. Hall was also imprisoned for more than three years in the Compter in South-wark. On 12 April the Earl came in person to the chapel, and in presence of all the Fellows then resident declared Thomas Young to be Master of the College in the room of Dr Sterne, put him in the Master's stall, and delivered to him the statutes of the College. The new Master signed a declaration in the register that he would promote piety and learning in the College agreeably to the late Solemn National League and Covenant. Probably only two Fellows were present at the induction, for the remainder, fourteen in number, were all ejected before the year was ended. The two who made their peace and apparently accepted the Covenant were John Boyleston and Thomas Allen. Of these renegades Sherman, who was a furious Royalist, somewhat obscurely remarks: 'The one [i.e. Boyleston] stood behind a curtain to witness the evils which others endured with firmness and courage; the other, afflicted to behold the exequies of his Alma Mater, made his own life a filial offering at her grave and, to escape the hands of wicked rebels, laid violent hands upon himself'. Neither of them retained his Fellowship after Michaelmas 1645. Boyleston retired to a living in Derbyshire, overlived the Restoration, and died a Canon of Lichfield. Seven of the vacant Fellowships were filled up by the Earl of Manchester between 3 October 1644 and 5 May 1645, and a few more in succeeding years. But until the Restoration the number of Fellows was never greater than twelve.

In a volume of old letters and documents preserved at the College there is an account of some of its Fellow-Commoners written by a Mr Thomas Cannon, who was a Fellow from 1609 to 1637. Among them are several who served with distinction in the Civil Wars on the side either of King or Parliament. Among Parliamentary officers may be mentioned Colonel Ralph Welden, who commanded a brigade at the siege of Bristol in 1645, and was afterwards Parliamentary Governor of Plymouth; Colonel Edward Aldrich, Governor of Aylesbury; and Sir Richard Onslow, a prominent member of the Long Parliament, and Colonel at the siege of Basing House. On the King's side were Lord Charles Goring, who, with his brother, the better-known Lord George Goring, commanded in the royal cavalry; he fought at Newbury, and afterwards became Earl of Norwich; Sir John Watts, Governor for the King of Chirk Castle, and one of the prisoners taken at the siege of Colchester; and Sir William Boteler, killed at Cropredy Bridge.

Except the three mentioned in Cannon's list, it would be difficult to point to any Jesus man of eminence on the Parliamentary side. The men who had come under the influence of Beale when he was tutor were, with scarcely an exception, devoted Royalists. Some of the more remarkable of them deserve a brief mention here. Sir John Bramston (adm. 1593) became Chief Justice of the King's Bench in 1635; against his private opinion he concurred with the other judges in pronouncing the legality of ship-money, and was consequently threatened by the Commons with impeachment. Christopher Hatton (adm. 1619–20) came of a family many of whose members were educated at Jesus. He was a member of the Long Parliament, joined the King at Oxford, was raised to the peerage as Baron Hatton of Kirby in 1643, and after the Restoration was Governor of Guernsey. He had bright parts, says Roger North, and professed to be religious, for he published *Hatton's Psalms*, with a prayer suitable to each; nevertheless, he deserted his family, and 'diverted himself with players and such idle people'. Sir Richard Fanshawe, who was Hatton's cousin (adm. 1623), was secretary to Prince Charles, and generally in attendance on him during the Civil War. At the Restoration he was elected M.P. for the University and in 1663 was appointed Ambassador to Spain. His poetical translations of Horace, Guarini's *Pastor Fido*, and the *Lusiad* deserve a high place in the literature of his time. Peter Vowel (adm. 1622) was a notability of another kind; he was 'schoolmaster at Islington', and executed in 1654 for complicity in Gerard's plot against the Protector.

Among the clergy who suffered in the Rebellion there were not less than five Jesus men who then or later were bishops: Thomas Westfield (Fellow in 1598), Bishop of Bristol, 1642; Griffith Williams (adm. 1599), Bishop of Ossory, 1641; John Owen (originally of Christ's, Fellow of Jesus in 1599), Bishop of St Asaph, 1629; Humphrey Henchman (adm. 1608, migrated next year to Christ's), Bishop of Salisbury, 1660, and of London, 1663; Robert Morgan (adm. 1624), Bishop of Bangor, 1666.

Thomas Young had been approved for the Mastership by the Assembly of Divines at Westminster, of which he was himself a member. He had been Milton's tutor before the poet went to St Paul's School, and a friendly correspondence had been kept up between them in later years. He had won credit by his book, *Dies Dominica* (1639), on the observance of the Sabbath, but it was his activity in controversial theology which commended him to the Assembly. 'Presbyterianorum Smectymnianorum Primipilus' is Sherman's contemptuous description of him, referring to the leading part which he took in the work published under the assumed name, Smectymnuus, a name made up of the initials of the five contributing divines, T and Y standing for Thomas Young. The book, which was an answer to Bishop Hall's defence of the liturgy and episcopalian government entitled *An Humble Remonstrance to the High Court of Parliament*, is best remembered now for the reason that Milton championed the cause of his former teacher in the *Apology for Smectymnuus*. Young was a Scotchman, and had not graduated at either of the English Universities. Such a man might seem to the divines eminently calculated to carry out that reformation, 'as well of the statutes as of the members of the College', of which the Earl of Manchester gave warning in the mandate for his admission. Singularly little is to be gathered of his career as Master. So much is evident, that he did not attempt any very striking changes. In spite of his anti-episcopalian bias, he was a King's man, and even when Charles was a prisoner in the hands of the Parliament there were sanctioned bonfires in the cloister-court on his coronation day. His reputation as a minister in the eastern counties, where he held the living of Stowmarket, attracted to the College considerable numbers of the sons of Puritan families in that quarter. In spite of the disturbance of the Civil War the College rapidly regained its numbers. In the five years ending 1649 ninety-two admissions were accounted for.

In October 1649 the Parliament ordered the Committee for Reforming the Universities to call upon all Heads and Fellows of colleges to subscribe the Engagement, whereby they pledged themselves to be faithful to the Commonwealth of England, as established, without a King or House of Lords. The Thomas Young fell under the general suspicion with which the Government looked upon the Presbyterian ministers after the Battle of Dunbar and, as he took no notice of the summons to subscribe, he was ejected from the Mastership on 14 November 1650, and in his place the Committee appointed Mr John Worthington, a Fellow of Emmanuel. Four of the Fellows, Bantoft, Whitfield, Tilney, and Yarburgh, were dispossessed for the same reason and about the same time.

One of the two Fellows appointed in the vacant places was John Sherman of Queens'. The historian of Jesus College deserves something more than a passing recognition in a history which is in part based on his labours. He was a native of Dedham in Essex. From one branch of his family, which emigrated in the seventeenth century to the American plantations, sprang the celebrated General Sherman. The fact that Sherman subscribed the Engagement casts a shadow of suspicion on the fervid royalism which colours his *Historia*. His partisanship is indeed a serious deduction from the value of his work, so far as it relates to his own times. Conveniently forgetting the manner of his own acquisition of a Fellowship, he passes over the interesting Commonwealth period with a sneering mention of Young and Worthington as intruded into the Mastership 'authoritate, si Dis placet, Parliamentaria'. He writes a pompous Latin which savours of the College exercise; but in questions of fact he may generally be relied on. His materials were derived from a diligent examination of College and nunnery documents, as well as from printed sources, and for the times immediately preceding his own he drew on the recollections of older residents of the College. He became a Canon and Archdeacon of Salisbury, died in 1671, and was buried in the chancel of the College chapel. His *Historia*, dedicated to Dr Boldero, was carried down approximately to the year of his death. A printed edition, containing, however, only a portion of Sherman's work, was brought out in 1840 by J. O. Halliwell, afterwards better known as the Shakespearean scholar, Halliwell-Phillipps; but it teems with errors, and has little value.

It was in a happy hour that the Commissioners, looking around them for a successor to the ejected Young, made choice of John Worthington. At this distance of time his chief title to remembrance is that he was one of the group of Cambridge Platonists, and the editor of the works of 'the incomparable' Joseph Mede and of John Smith's *Select Discourses*. To his contemporaries he was endeared by the lovable qualities of his character, qualities discernible by us in his letters and diary (published by the Chetham Society). They may be expressed in the eulogium which Archbishop Tillotson pronounced in his funeral sermon:

> His whole Demeanour was Pious and Grave; and yet not blemish'd with any Moroseness or fond Affectation. And as his Knowledge was great, so was his Humility. He was a zealous and sincere Friend where he profess'd Kindness. . . . He was universally inoffensive, kind and obliging, even to those that differ'd from him: And, to set off these Virtues, there was added to them, in a very eminent degree, *the Ornament of a meek and quiet Spirit, which in the sight of God is of great Price.* Especially in Debates and Controversies of Religion he was not apt to be passionate and contentious. . . . But that which was most singularly Eminent in him was the Publickness of his Spirit, and his great Zeal and Industry to be profitable and useful to the World, especially in those things which tended to the promoting of Learning and Piety.

The new Master, indeed, had none of the intractability of his Presbyterian predecessor and, as he had received episcopal Orders, his appointment was regarded with some degree of favour by the exiled Churchmen. Though his predecessor had been 'outed' for declining the Engagement, it seems that Worthington was not asked to accept it, nor had he taken the Covenant. He had been moved to deep sorrow by the death of King Charles and, preaching on the occasion, he chose for his texts, 'The beauty of Israel is slain. How are the mighty fallen!' and 'Behold and see if there be any sorrow like unto our sorrow'. Of his appointment at Jesus Worthington writes: 'When I came hither first it was not my seeking, and I could have left it as willingly for Dr Sterne, if he could have brought himself in. He desired of me to accept of it, and procured the Fellows to desire me.' Sundry symptoms show that old grudges presently died away under the Master's gentle influence. In 1651 'widow Welsh', inspired, no doubt, by some of the old society, became the means of restoring the lost Audit Book. Next year, through the agency of a certain Mr Buck, one of the Esquire Bedels, the buried plate was brought to light. In the same year the organ was discovered; the time had not yet come when it could be replaced in the chapel, but the 'discovery' looks as though it had a delicate reference to Worthington's devotion to music.

The year 1660, of course, brought the restoration of the old society, or rather the remnant of it spared by death or matrimony. Of the fourteen ejected Fellows three only were reinstated, the President, Stephen Hall, being one of them. Two of the three died, and the third resigned his place within two years from their restoration. Had the number of the restored been greater it might have gone hard with some of the intruded Fellows; but as there were only twelve of the latter, the statutable number of Fellowships would not be exceeded by the inclusion of them all. But institution by the Visitor must, of course, be a condition of the retention of their places, for during the interregnum the College had been empowered by order of the House of Commons (7 November 1645) to elect and admit Fellows without presenting any names to the Bishop of Ely, who was then a prisoner in the Tower. 'It was suspected that there would have been a refusall of some.' But Matthew Wren, the restored Bishop of Ely, 'was very fair and civill towards them, and dispatched them without the usuall height of the fees, and persuaded them to studiousness and peace, against all animosities, etc.' The unanimity with which the intruded Fellows submitted themselves, and the readiness of the bishop to accept their submission, show that they had not committed themselves to any opinions hostile to episcopacy. Some of them—Sherman being of the number—were perfervid Churchmen and Royalists, and made no secret of their attitude in the interval between Cromwell's death and the proclamation of Charles. At the Commencement in July 1660, before Worthington had left the lodge, a Johnian prevaricator, in his speech, styled the 'Jesuits' papists, with double reference to their name and religious leanings. A Jesus prevaricator, on the following day, retorted with an ingenious play on the familiar nickname of the Johnians, 'Cum sus audet contendere cum Jesuitis, tum certe "*Suis* et ipsa Roma viribus ruit." ' [1]

Justice could not be complete without the restoration of the Mastership to Sterne; but before he returned to the College it was well understood that he was destined for the bishopric of Carlisle. Worthington's friends hoped that after a formal cession of his office he might be reappointed to it by the Visitor. But Bishop Wren had already decided on giving it to Dr Pearson. With unruffled serenity Worthington withdrew with his young wife to his poor vicarage at Fen Ditton, 'standing bleek and alone, and therefore obnoxious to the cold weather and the violence of disbanded soldiers, of which there have been some late proofs'. At Ditton he hoped that he might still be able to do service to the University, though his disposition was inclined rather to devotional retirement, 'about which I did love to talk with worthy Mr Thristcross, who knew Mr Ferrar and Little Gedding'. There is a charming interchange of courtesies in the letters which passed between him and Dr Sterne on the subject of the return of the latter to the lodge, and when Dr and Mrs Sterne arrived there they were entertained by the out-going Master with an elaborate musical performance in their honour.

Worthington died in 1671 at Hackney, where he was at the time lecturer in the parish church. His only son, John, was admitted a pensioner of the College in 1680. He declined the oaths at the Revolution and, dying in 1737, left by will a sum of £800 to the Master and Fellows for the purpose of founding a new Fellowship. This portion of the will remained unadministered until 1766, and in that year the College declined the benefaction on the ground that it was insufficient for the maintenance of a Fellow on the conditions required by the statutes.

Sterne became Archbishop of York in 1664 and died in 1683. In 1671 he gave to the College an annual rent-charge of £40, to make provision for four scholars, two of them born in that part

[1] The speech of the Jesus prevaricator is printed in *The Hutton Correspondence* (Surtees Society's publications).

of Yorkshire which is in the diocese of York, the other two born in Nottinghamshire, and of them one in Sterne's native town, Mansfield. The Archbishop's great-grandson, Laurence Sterne, was a scholar on this foundation.

CHAPTER VI

RESTORATION DAYS

DR WORTHINGTON left the lodge on 3 November 1660 to take up his abode at Ditton, and on 4 December following he notes in his diary: 'This day Dr Pearson was admitted Master of Jesus College'. The selection of so great a scholar for the Mastership is creditable to the discernment of the restored Visitor, Bishop Wren. Undoubtedly Pearson's is the greatest name in the list of Masters of Jesus, but his Cambridge career is connected not so much with Jesus as with King's, where he was a Fellow, or with Trinity, to the Mastership of which he was translated by royal mandate in April 1662. To his famous *Exposition of the Creed* (published in 1659) he principally owed his nomination to the Mastership of Jesus. 'His extensive knowledge, personal integrity and prudence', the Bishop's letter to the Fellows says, 'will be a model to the whole society.' During the few months in which he held the Mastership he acted as a delegate at the Savoy Conference, was selected to revise the Prayer-Book, and was made Lady Margaret's Reader in Divinity. There is no portrait of him at Jesus, and his only monument there is the inscription which he caused to be placed in the chapel on the grave of his old friend Stephen Hall, the sturdy President of 1644.

Even more ephemeral than Pearson's tenure of the Mastership was that of his successor, Dr Joseph Beaumont. His history is bound up with that of Peterhouse, of which college he was a Fellow from 1636 until his ejection in 1644, and to it he returned as Master in April 1663. He was admitted Master of Jesus on 19 April 1662. He owed the preferment to both Masterships to his father-in-law, Bishop Wren. 'Vir Musis charissimus', Sherman says of him, and though his poetry soon lost its vogue, he deserves a place among the lesser poetic lights of the seventeenth century. His colossal production, *Psyche*, is of the same pattern of versified philosophy as More's *Song of the Soul*; but in prose he assailed the tenets of More and the Latitudinarians. In the twelve months of his Mastership he took in hand the restoration of the chapel and its services to the conditions existing previous to 1643. Nothing seems to have been done to the fabric, but 'the Cherubims' were 'cleared' and set up; evidently they had been hidden in anticipation of Dowsing's raid. Some of the old Communion plate, dug up from the Master's orchard, was refashioned, and additions were made to it. The organ was put back in its place, and, somewhat later, the celebrated organ-builder, Thamar, was engaged to tune and repair it.

Only one of the Fellows refused the declaration which the Act of Uniformity imposed on all Heads, Fellows, and other office-holders in the universities. The single stickler for conscience was Edmund Hough (elected February 1655–6). The grounds of his objection are not clear. Sherman says that he was 'ecclesiae filius', and after his ejection he conformed, and died Vicar of Halifax, Yorkshire; but, says Calamy, 'he carried it in a very friendly manner to the Dissenters'.

Hough was the tutor under whom John Strype, the ecclesiastical historian, was admitted, 29 March 1662. Strype, or Strijp, as his name is written in the register, came of a Protestant refugee family, whose original home was in the Spanish Netherlands. Educated at St Paul's School, he was attracted to Jesus by one of the exhibitions there in the gift of the Dean and Chapter of St Paul's. After the expulsion of his tutor Strype's family thought the College 'too superstishus' for his continuance there, and he migrated in 1663 to Catharine Hall. His short connexion with Jesus would not need commemoration were it not that to it we are indebted for an extremely interesting account of undergraduate life in the College, contained in a letter which he wrote to his mother in London soon after his first coming to Cambridge.

> Do not wonder [he writes], so much at our Commons: they are more than many Colleges have. Trinity itself (where Herring and Davies are), which is the famousest College in the University, have

but three half-pence. We have roast meat, dinner and supper,
throughout the week; and such meat as you know I had not use to
care for; and that is Veal; but now I have learnt to eat it. Sometimes,
neverthelesse, we have boiled meat, with pottage; and beef and
mutton, which I am glad of; except Fridays and Saturdays, and sometimes Wednesdays; which days we have fish at dinner, and tansy or
pudding for supper. Our parts then are slender enough. But there is
this remedy: we may retire unto the Butteries, and there take a
half-pennie loafe and butter or cheese; or else to the Kitchen, and
take there what the Cook hath. But for my part, I am sure, I never
visited the Kitchen yet, since I have been here, and the Butteries but
seldom after meals; unlesse for a Ciza, that is for a Farthing-worth of
Small-beer; so that lesse than a Peny in Beer doth serve me a whole
Day. Neverthelesse, sometimes we have Exceedings; then we have
two or three Dishes (but that is very rare); otherwise never but one;
so that a Cake and a Cheese would be very welcome to me; and a
Neat's tongue, or some such thing, if it would not require too much
money. If you do intend to send me anything, do not send it yet,
until you hear further of me when I would have them sent; and that
is, when I have got me a Chamber; for as yet, I am in a Chamber that
doth not at all please me. I have thoughts of one, which is a very
handsome one, and one pair of stairs high, and that looketh into the
Master's garden. The price is but 20s. per annum, ten whereof a
Knight's son, and lately admitted into this College, doth pay;
though he did not come till about Midsummer, so that I shall have
but 10s. to pay a year; besides my income, which may be about
40s. or thereabouts. . . . My breakings out are now all gone. Indeed
I was afraid at my first coming it would have proved the Itch; but
I am fairly rid on it; but I fear I shall get it, let me do what I can; for
there are many here that have it cruelly. Some of them take strong
purges that would kill a horse, weeks together for it, to get it away,
and are hardly rid of it. At my first Coming I laid alone; but since,
my Tutor desired me to let a very clear lad lay with me, and an
Alderman's son of Colchester, which I could not deny, being newly
come; he hath laid with me now for almost a fortnight, and will do
till he can provide himself with a Chamber. I have been with all my
Acquaintance, who have entreated me very courteously, especially
Jonathan Houghton. I went to his Chamber the Friday night I first
came, and there he made me stay and sup with him, and would have
had me laid with him that night, and was extraordinary kind to me.

> ... We go twice a day to Chapel; in the morning about 7, and in the
> evening about 5. After we come from Chapel in the morning, which
> is towards 8, we go to the Butteries for our breakfast, which is
> usually five Farthings; an half penny loaf and butter, and a cize of
> beer. But sometimes I go to an honest House near the College, and
> have a pint of milk boiled for my breakfast.

Since the time of Duport Jesus had been ruled by a succession
of Masters, each of whom had been distinguished for scholarship.
In the appointments of Pearson and Beaumont, Bishop Wren had
respected the high tradition which for seventy years had been
associated with the office; but personal and political considerations
guided him in the choice of Beaumont's successor. Dr Edmund
Boldero, who was admitted Master on 27 May 1663, had been
prominent as a 'sufferer' in the Royalist cause, and when it came
to the turn of the faithful to reap their reward he was not the
man to allow his claims to be overlooked. He was of Wren's
own college, Pembroke; had been extruded from his Fellowship
there in 1644, and had afterwards been kept in London by the
Parliament, at excessive charges to himself. After his liberation
he had taken service in Scotland as a captain under Montrose,
and 'between the ladder and the rope had narrowly escaped
hanging'. Later he is heard of at Bury St Edmund's, where he
kept a Church of England conventicle, using the Common
Prayer. At the Restoration he became Bishop Wren's chaplain.
Gilbert Wakefield's story of the manner in which he obtained the
Mastership is palpably an invention, but, for all that, may reflect
something of the character of the soldier-divine.

> On a vacancy of the mastership, Boldero, without any pretensions to
> the appointment, in *plain English*, plucks up his spirits, or, in Homer's
> language, 'speaks to his magnanimous mind', and presents his peti-
> tion to the Bishop. 'Who are you?' says his Lordship. 'I know
> nothing of you; I never heard of you before.' 'My Lord, I have
> suffered long and severely for my attachment to our royal master,
> as well as your Lordship has. I believe your Lordship and I have
> been *in all the gaols in England*.' 'What does the fellow mean? Man! I
> never was confined in any prison but the Tower.' 'And, my Lord,'
> said Boldero, 'I have been in all the rest myself.' The Bishop's

heart relented, and he good-naturedly admitted the claim of his petitioner.

Walker, writing in 1714, says of Boldero: 'He is well remembered at this Day for a Man of an *honest good Meaning*, tho' he would often be very unfortunate in expressing it'. Under his sway, though perhaps the cause lay rather in the general abandonment of ideals which accompanied the Restoration than in the Master's example, there can be no doubt that the College started on the downward plane of indolent dilettantism, which passed for refinement in the combination-rooms of Cambridge when the enthusiasms of the war-time had passed away. John North, who was admitted as a 'Nobleman' at Jesus in February 1660, and became a Fellow in September 1666, found there a society in which his habitual sobriety was deemed extraordinary. 'After dinner, and in evenings, he kept company with the fellows and fellow-commoners in the garden; but not for long, for he could not be pleased with such insipid pastime as bowls, or less material discourse, such as town tales, or punning, and the like.' At length 'he declined the parlour, and consorted rather with the younger gentlemen than the grave, and, as he thought, perhaps, empty seniors of the College'. His dislike for the society of the Fellows was met by a corresponding 'morosity' on their part, and North at last sacrificed his Fellowship and migrated to Trinity, where he found better company, especially that of Newton and Barrow.

Dr North was a good, if not a great, scholar, and a lover of books even more than a scholar. He became Regius Professor of Greek in 1672, when he was only twenty-eight, succeeded Barrow in the Mastership of Trinity in 1677, and died in 1683. For our knowledge of his life and character we are indebted to his biography, which in its entertaining discursiveness is more than a biography, written by his younger brother, the well-known Roger North. Roger was admitted as a Fellow-Commoner at Jesus in October 1667, under the tuition of his brother, the Doctor, and he gossips pleasantly enough of his own undergraduate days in his *Autobiography*.

At Cambridge I lived a year, in which time nothing extraordinary happened to me, unless it were that I was forced to live in the quality of a nobleman, with a very strait allowance. I was not capable to conduct myself, but had a brother who was in the place of tutor, and provided all things for me. Besides the first cost of a gown which was not over rich, few of ordinary quality spent less than I did. And it chiefly lay in not going in company, for I had not confidence, nor money, and very seldom on my own account made or received a visit. . . . I did most extremely envy the common scholars for the joy they had at football, and lament my own condition, that was tied up by quality from mixing with them, and enjoying the freedom of rambling that they had. And not having either money or assurance to mix with my equals, who were wild and extravagant enough, was obliged to walk with grave seniors, and to know no other diversion. . . . As to study there, I followed my own appetite, which was to natural philosophy, which they call physics, and particularly Descartes, whose works I dare say I read over three times before I understood him. . . . And at that time new philosophy was a sort of heresy, and my brother cared not to encourage me much in it.

The old books on physics he could not 'thresh at', but he found delight in mathematics, especially in Barrow's *Euclid*. Algebra he 'was not a match for', and logic he did not touch upon. In after life he showed his regard for his old College by ordering that the original manuscript of his *Examen*, a book of memoirs of the reign of Charles II, much valued by Lord Macaulay, should be deposited in its Library, where it still remains. In 1730, more than sixty years after his own admission, he sent his second son, Montagu, to Jesus, and there is extant a series of sensible, fatherly letters (printed by Dr Jessopp in his edition of the *Autobiography*), which he addressed to the young scholar at Cambridge. They have much of the easy, conversational grace which characterizes his *Examen* and *Memoirs*, and in their tone and the unconstrained relations which they show between father and son they are nearer akin to modern habits of mind than to the Restoration days when the writer was a freshman. Undergraduate life had greatly changed since then, as he reminds his son. The days were past when two or three undergraduates shared a chamber with their tutor. Montagu had a chamber, 'I cannot say too good, but much too big for you, for it held Doctor North and myself. My study was up a little stair by the bedside, and his by the chimney. The greatest inconvenience is the sun's heat in summer afternoons, and then we retired to the bedchamber.' Roger's little study, in a garret at the west end of the Hall, remains much as he may have left it, the only unaltered study in the College. Some amateur hand, possibly his, has adorned its wainscot with roughly-executed paintings, among them the two crowing cocks whose answering labels, ἐγὼ εἰμὶ ἀλέκτωρ and οὕτως καὶ ἐγώ, every Jesus man is familiar with.

In 1665 Cambridge suffered from a dreadful outbreak of plague. Several College servants at Jesus received charitable allowances when they were 'visited', but it does not appear that there were any fatal cases within the College precincts. On 7 August all the Fellows had leave of absence until the cessation of the epidemic, but three of them voluntarily remained at their posts. In the summer of the following year the pestilence returned with increased fatality. On 25 June a meeting of the society was called, evidently in haste, for the conclusions were entered not in the register, but on a vacant leaf of the Plate Book. The Fellows were allowed to remain away from the College until the following November, or later if necessary. In case it should be unsafe for any of them to remain, careful persons were to be brought in to secure the College. Meals were to be taken in the Buttery.

John Flamsteed, the chief of Jesus men of science, was admitted a sizar on 21 December 1670. He was then twenty-four years of age, had already contributed astronomical papers to the *Philosophical Transactions* of the Royal Society, and was known to Newton and Barrow. While at Jesus he commenced, with a seven-foot telescope and a wooden quadrant of eighteen inches radius, those observations which, protracted through a laborious lifetime, bore fruit in his *British Catalogue*, 'one of the proudest productions of the Royal Observatory at Greenwich'. He was appointed to the new office of Astronomer Royal in 1675, but the tenuity of his stipend compelled him throughout life to take private pupils and labour as a country parson. His life was embittered and his fame in his lifetime dimmed by a professional quarrel with Newton, by whom, not without reason, he conceived himself to have been neglected and disparaged. But later times have done ampler justice to the great observer whose labours consecrated Flamsteed Hill for all time as the omphalos of English astronomy.

The Restoration period is remarkable for the number of scholarship endowments which it brought to the College. The first, in 1671, was the already mentioned foundation of the four Sterne scholarships. In 1675 two more, for boys from Sevenoaks School, were given by Lady Boswell, relict of Sir William Boswell, formerly Fellow, and Ambassador at the Hague in the reign of Charles I. In 1677 Dr Henry Brunsell, Prebendary of Ely, founded three exhibitions; and in 1682 John Somervile bequeathed a scholarship for a boy educated at Loughborough School. But the most important was the noble foundation of the Rustat scholarships in 1671.

Tobias Rustat, the founder, was the son of Robert Rustat, Rector of Skeffington, Leicestershire, who was admitted at Jesus in the year 1580. The family took its name apparently from the lordship of Rustadt in Saxony. Tobias had not received a University education; indeed, he had received very little education of any kind; 'a very simple, ignorant, but honest and loyal creature' Evelyn calls him. He was born in 1606, and in his younger days had accompanied the Earl of Denbigh's son, Viscount Fielding, on an embassy to the Venetian Court. From the 'italianate' morals of Venice, notorious in the early seventeenth century for their corrupting influence on English travellers, he remained conspicuously free. A companion in this embassy describes him as 'a sober person and religious; he was the most diligent attending servant in the whole family, early and late, very exact and complete and in his place; which hath since often brought to my mind that of Solomon, The hand of the diligent maketh rich, *Proverbs* 10, *4th verse*'. The source of his wealth was a fortunate investment—the purchase from the needy King of the reversion of the place of Yeoman of the Robes to the young Prince of

Wales, afterwards Charles II. He attended on the Prince during
the Civil War, and was with him and the Queen at Paris after
1645. He acted as a confidential courier between the exiled Court
and the Royalists in England, and was personally engaged in the
Kentish rising in July 1648. In the skirmish at Nonsuch which
ended this enterprise he was the means of saving the life of the
young Duke of Buckingham. He shared the poverty and dis-
tresses of the Royalists at Paris and the Hague, and obtained his
reward at the Restoration when, his reversion having fallen, he
got the place of Yeoman of the Robes, and was made besides
keeper of the royal palace of Hampton Court. Within a few
years he grew very rich, 'by his wonderful frugality', as Evelyn
says. He survived the Stuart dynasty, and received an allowance
in the reign of William III among other old household servants of
Charles II. He died, 'a bachelour', on 15 March 1693-4, at the
age of eighty-seven, and, at his own desire, was buried in the
College chapel. The College gratefully commemorated its benefactor by putting up in his memory a large monument of white
marble, which, among a variety of armorial and other devices,
has his portrait in medallion. The inscription beneath, of his own
composition, says:

> The greatest part of the estate he gathered by God's blessing, the
> King's favour and his Industry, he disposed in his Lifetime in
> Workes of Charity; and found the more he bestowed on Churches,
> Hospitalls, Universities and Colledges, and upon Poor Widows and
> Orphans of Orthodox Ministers, the more he had at the year's end.

A list of his many benefactions, amounting in the total to
£10,695, is among the documents in the College muniment-
room. Among them are gifts of £1,000 each to the University
Library at Cambridge and to St John's College (Laud's college)
at Oxford; and of £1,020 for the purchase of a fee farm at Non-
Eaton for pensions to widows of orthodox clergymen, to be
nominated by the Master and Fellows of Jesus.

Rustat's directions as regards his scholarship foundation were
precise, and were embodied in statutes framed by himself and
approved by the Visitor. The scholars were to be 'sonnes of

Clergymen already dead who had taken yᵉ Holy Order of Priesthood according to yᵉ Rights and Usages of yᵉ Church of England'. An alteration of the statutes in 1861 extended the benefits of the foundation to the sons of living clergymen. The number of scholars was to be nine, and their stipend £15 each. By subsequent additions to the original foundation the Rustat Scholarship Fund was largely increased. The scholars on the Rustat foundation are still distinguished by a special gown of cloth prescribed by the founder, though very few of them have worn it in recent years.

Dr Boldero deserves to be had in remembrance chiefly on account of his services and benefactions to the College Library; as the Latin inscription over its entrance informs us, 'he constructed anew the bookcases, bestowed much pains in arranging the classes, and, to complete his good services, bequeathed all his books to the Library'. The long, low room in which it is contained is not the least venerable and interesting part of a College rich above its fellows in the charms of antiquity. The open roof of oak remains exactly as we may suppose it was finished by Bishop Alcock, and the seal of his workmanship is yet to be seen in the cocks sculptured on the doorcase and painted in the windows which look into the cloister. Each window has two lights, and in each light is a cock standing on a globe, the Bishop's rebus. Beneath the cocks is inscribed in Latin the designation of the class of books which adjoins each window, *Phisica*, *Lex Civilis*, and so forth; and labels issuing from the cocks' beaks contain texts from the Vulgate or the Fathers appropriate to the subject of the books in the class. For example, the class of the Canon Law has for its pair of texts the two passages from the Psalms, *Legem statuit ei in via quam elegit* (Ps. xxiv. 12) and *Legem pone mihi domine viam iustificacionum tuarum* (Ps. cxix. 33). A feature of the room until recently was a human skeleton contained in a wooden case; probably it dates from the later years of the seventeenth century, when the study of anatomy began to attract attention in the University. It has been banished (one hopes only temporarily) to another part of the College.

Sherman says that the Library was scantily furnished before the year 1600, and it probably contained few books when Boldero took it in hand.[1] It received considerable bequests both of money and books in the latter half of the seventeenth century. Its principal endowment proceeds from a bequest of William Grimbaldston, M.D., in 1725. It contains a good collection of monastic manuscripts, most of them given by Thomas Man, Fellow in 1685. Man successively held the livings of Helmsley (near to Rievaux Abbey) and Northallerton (in the gift of the Dean and Chapter of Durham), and seems to have had exceptional opportunities for picking up books from the libraries of Yorkshire and Durham religious houses. A catalogue of the manuscript has been printed by Dr M. R. James (Cambridge University Press, 1895).

Dr Boldero died on 5 July 1679, and was succeeded by Dr Humphry Gower. But Gower's tenure of office was of the shortest, for he resigned on December of the same year on election to the Mastership of his old college, St John's. He was a man of doggedly tenacious character, as he showed in 1693, when he resisted a mandamus to eject the non-juring Fellows of St John's. The strictness of his rule at that college made him unpopular with the undergraduates, one of whom, Abraham De la Pryme, has handed down the irreverent jest made on his appointment there:

> Our master, they say, is a mighty high proud man. . . . He came from Jesus College to be master here, and he was so sevear that he was commonly called the divel of Jesus; and when he was made master here some unlucky scholars broke this jest upon him—that now the divel was entered into the heard of swine; for us Johnians are abusively called hoggs.

Dr William Saywell, who filled the place vacated by Dr Gower, was, like him, a Johnian (Fellow in 1666). He had some reputation in his day as a controversial theologian, and championed the cause of the Church against Baxter. His Mastership,

---

[1] The books in the Library were originally chained, according to the usual practice of the Middle Ages, as is shown by the rivets remaining on many of them, and by entries in the accounts—e.g. 1557-8, 'to the smithe for nailes and cheyning bokes in the librarye, 5d.'. Twelve books were chained in the chapel in 1579-80.

which ended with his death on 9 June 1701, was altogether uneventful. The evil days of James II passed, on the whole, quietly
enough in our College history, but brought trouble to one of the
junior Fellows, Edward Spence. In a sermon preached before the
University on 5 November 1686 he imprudently reflected on
the Roman Church. For this he was prosecuted at the instance
of Joshua Basset, Fellow of Caius and a suspected Papist, who next
year was thrust by the King into the Mastership of Sidney.
Spence had to make a public recantation in the Senate House, and
the disgrace seems to have affected the poor man's wits. He died
lunatic, but a Fellow to the last, in 1735. The entire society
acquiesced in the Revolution of 1688. Nevertheless, among
the rank and file of the College there were a few adherents
of the fallen Stuarts, the most noteworthy among whom were
Laurence Howell (adm. 1681) and Nathaniel Spinckes (adm.
1672). Howell, a learned but vitriolic controversialist, was sentenced to whipping, fine and imprisonment for a seditious libel
on George I; the whipping was remitted in consideration of the
fact that he was a clergyman, but he died in Newgate Prison in
1720. Spinckes, a man of high character, warm charity and wide
learning, was author of *The Sick Man Visited*, a work which went
through many editions in the early part of the eighteenth century.
He was consecrated bishop in 1713 by Dr Hickes, the non-juring
Bishop of Thetford, and died in 1727. On the accession of
George I only one of the Fellows, Samuel Townsend (elected in
1707), refused the oaths and was deprived of his Fellowship. Not
until the crisis of the French Revolution do we hear of another
ejection from a Fellowship at Jesus on political grounds.

   The religious battle-cries which had been the vital breath of the
University since Reformation days died away after 1688 in controversial bickerings which were of small concern to the nation
at large. Triumphant orthodoxy henceforth kept the doors of the
University barred equally against the Papist and the Protestant
Dissenter, and Churchmanship lost its energy when it had removed its antagonists. None the less it remained sleeplessly on
guard against the intrusions of heterodoxy, and the case of
Whiston, who, for suspected Arianism, was banished from

Cambridge and deprived of his professorship in 1710, shows how little Whig doctrines of toleration found favour in the University. In the last decade of the seventeenth century Quakers were the object of almost as much suspicion as Romanists; indeed, the Quaker was regarded as the ally of the Pope, if he were not a Papist in disguise. To the authorities of Jesus the sect was the more obnoxious because its meetings were held at the house of a shoemaker, named Brazier, in Jesus Lane, and if, as seems probable, this house was on the site of the present Friends' Meeting House, the objectionable conventicle was on the verge of the College Close. Severe measures, then, were deemed necessary when it was discovered that an undergraduate of the College was frequenting the Quaker meetings, and the following recantation was exacted from him and entered, with his signature, in the register on 14 February 1698–9:

Whereas I, Roger Kelsall, have been guilty of very great offences to ye dishonour of God and ye Xtian Religion, to ye Disgrace and Scandall of ye College and University, by frequenting ye Quakers' meetings and countenancing y^t dangerous Sect, and publickly maintaining their erroneous principles, and also by reviling ye Holy Sacraments of Baptism and ye Lord's Supper, and accusing ye Rites and Ceremonies of ye Church of England of Superstition, and further for refusing to act according to my Duty and Station in ye Colledge: for all wch I deserve to be severely censured: I do here in ye presence of God, and you all, solemnly profess and declare that I am heartily sorry for ye same, and beg pardon of God and you for ye Scandall I have given you: And do sincerely promise (by God's assistance) to avoid ye like miscarriages for ye time to come, and in all things to comport myself as becomes a Schollar and a Christian.

The poor boy speedily forgot his abjuration. The next entry, dated 4 March, tells us that Roger Kelsall, having secretly withdrawn from College, and having thrown in his lot with the Quakers—*Quassatores*, as the Latin has it—and having publicly professed their insane doctrines, is, by unanimous consent of the President and Fellows, pronounced expelled.

The College made no addition to its buildings in the latter part of the seventeenth century, and the alterations were few and unimportant. Sherman, the historian, and another Fellow, Charles Gibson, each left by will the sum of £100 for the adornment of the chapel. These bequests enabled the College in 1675 to pave the chancel with black and white marble, and to carry out some minor repairs. In 1684 the east end of the chapel within the rails was wainscoted at the expense of the Master, Dr Saywell, and the President, Dr Cooke. In 1692 the Parlour was altered. It was approached in those days by the 'Parlour staircase'—now popularly called 'Cow Lane'—in the angle of the cloister court. Very little is heard of it before the Restoration, but not long after that event it began to be fitted up in a modern style of comfort. The Fellows as late as 1666 still sat on forms there, but six leather chairs had been bought for it in 1665, and others followed soon afterwards. We first hear of a carpet there in 1682: 'an apple-roster for ye Parlo^r' was got in 1691.

CHAPTER VII

BETWEEN THE REVOLUTIONS

THE long Mastership of Dr Charles Ashton (1701–52) occupied
almost exactly the first half of the eighteenth century. Among
the admissions of that period are to be found the names of several
men who attained eminence in their day. Foremost among them
is Laurence Sterne, and in the list are included two Archbishops
of Canterbury, Herring and Hutton, and the honoured names of
David Hartley and John Jortin, both of them Fellows of the
College. We have learnt, not without reason, to look upon the
early Georgian period as one of intellectual stagnation at the
universities, when the nation looked for stimulus and suggestion
anywhere rather than to its historic centres of learning. It might
be supposed, from the fact that Jesus still bred pupils of such distinction, that it was less affected than other colleges by the
sterility of the times, and still faithfully performed its task as a
place of education as well as of sound learning.

All the evidence we possess contradicts such a flattering conclusion. Scarcely even in the dark days of Edward VI and Mary,
when learning was discounted and bankruptcy and dissolution
imminent, had the College descended to so low a position in
numbers and perhaps in reputation. The drop in numbers was
in sympathy with a corresponding decline in the University
generally. The useful tables in Bass Mullinger's *History of the
University of Cambridge* (included in the series of Epochs of Church
History) show that the number of admissions to the B.A. degree
at Cambridge reached a maximum of 290 in 1623, declining
afterwards during the Civil War, and rising again in 1672 to 255.
After the latter year there was a long and steady decline until the
minimum was reached about the middle of the eighteenth century; between 1750 and 1775 the number of B.A. degrees only

once reached 100. At Jesus the fall in numbers was even more accentuated than in other colleges. The following figures for three separate periods, each of five years, illustrate the progressive decline. The numbers are of admissions to the three classes of Fellow-Commoners, pensioners and sizars, of B.A. degrees taken, and of testimonials for Holy Orders. The first period is shared between the Masterships of Dr Boldero and Dr Saywell, the second is of the first, and the third of the last, years of Dr Ashton's Mastership.

	Fellow-Com-moners.	Pen-sioners.	Sizars.	Total Admis-sions.	B.A.	Testi-monials.
1676/7–1680/1	7	43	64	114	69	62
1702/3–1706/7	12	34	44	90	67	71
1747/8–1751/2	2	8	19	29	14	30

The figures for the last period bring to light two features which reflect on the efficiency of the College as a place of general education even more unfavourably than the drop in the number of admissions. In the first place, only one-half of its few students qualified for a degree, and, secondly, practically every undergraduate was a candidate for Orders, and obtained the College testimonial whether he graduated or not. Never was the sway of the Church more undisputed in the universities, and especially at Jesus, than in the first half of the eighteenth century. The Nonconformist had no place in the College at all; but it would seem that in denying him entrance it in effect shut its doors also on many a worthy bidden guest, and gave the stamp of its approval to such as had not

> learned aught the least
> That to the faithful herdsman's art belongs.

Another circumstance will be noted, that the class of pensioners—'volunteers', as Fuller calls them—had become all but extinct. The gentleman or merchant who was able to pay for his son's education either did not send him to the University, or had no confidence that he would get what he paid for at Jesus.

Rustat's foundation kept up a thin circulation of undergraduate blood which saved the College from absolute deliquium; but the oft-recurring description of the applicant for admission as *clerici defuncti filius* is an indication that the typical undergraduate at Jesus came of a class which was held in those days in low social esteem, and from the most indigent members of it.

Yet in the first years at least of Ashton's Mastership the Fellows of Jesus were men furnished with ability and, in one field, entitled to respect for scholarship. It was for Jesus the day of patristic theology—a study, indeed, of unquestioned value and importance, but one which was outside the curriculum of the ordinary undergraduate and, in the low esteem in which theological learning was generally held at Cambridge, attracted far less attention in the period with which we are dealing than in the preceding or following centuries. But no Jesus Fellow won himself a prominent place in the new studies of mathematics and physics which for a century after Newton's death practically monopolized the arena of the Cambridge schools. In Humanities no Jesus Fellow followed where Bentley showed the way. No civil lawyer went out from Jesus, as in the seventeenth century, equipped for the service of the State. The tutor at Jesus was not greatly concerned in the subjects which were, or should have been, of most living interest to his pupil. The old intimacy in daily life, too, was disappearing. John North 'lay with his tutor'—in the same bed, it would seem—when he was a freshman and, when he was a Fellow, shared a bedroom with his Fellow-Commoner brother. His nephew Montagu, a pensioner, had, as we have seen, a chamber to himself, and much too big for him. From Reneu's letters we learn that one tutor, Grigg, in the first decade of the century, kept up something of the old friendly relations, and at least 'sat' with his pupil. But 'don' and undergraduate drifted apart when the Fellow shut himself up in a solitary study, or hovered between Cambridge and a country incumbency. The tie must have been altogether snapped when it became the practice to allot the freshman to two or three tutors, as was the rule in the middle of the century.

Dr Ashton, Saywell's successor in the Mastership, was of

Queens' College; had been elected to a Fellowship there in 1687; afterwards became chaplain to Symon Patrick, Bishop of Ely, and by him was selected for the Mastership of Jesus. If learning, virtue, and amiability were the only necessary qualifications for the headship of a College, the bishop was justified in his appointment. But it was Dr Ashton's misfortune that his unquestioned merits were obscured by an insuperable diffidence. In College he led a very retired and studious life, only quitting Cambridge when a chapter meeting required his presence at Ely. His manuscript volumes of commentary and annotated books in the College Library attest the range and profundity of his learning, but he could never be prevailed upon to publish anything in his own name. After his death one of the Fellows, Frederick Keller, brought out an edition of Justin Martyr's *Apologies* from Dr Ashton's manuscript notes; another Fellow, Dr Warren, was assisted by him in the preparation of an edition of the Commentary of Hierocles; a century later a third Fellow, Dr H. A. Woodham, availed himself of Ashton's materials in the preparation of an edition of Tertullian.

On the vacancy in the Lady Margaret Professorship occasioned by the death of Dr Gower in 1711, Ashton was strongly urged by his friends in the University to put himself forward as a candidate.[1] 'Why should you be still wanting to yourself? Shake off that hurtfull shynesse', wrote his friend, Charles Roderick, Provost of King's. But Ashton was proof against solicitation. The crisis of his life came at the election to the Regius Professorship of Divinity in 1717. Theological learning, it was acknowledged, was at a low ebb in the University. There was but one man whose qualifications for the chair could compare with Ashton's, and that man was Bentley. Bentley, indeed, as Master of Trinity was disqualified from holding the Professorship by a clause in the statute of foundation expressly prohibiting the Professor from holding any office in Trinity, to which college the Professorship is attached. But the University was sufficiently acquainted with the

---

[1] There are several letters, addressed to Dr Ashton, on the subject of this election and that to the Regius Professorship in 1717 in a volume of *Old Letters and Documents*, which is in the College Library.

audacity of Bentley's character to feel assured that he would override the statute in his own interest if he had the opportunity. Strong pressure was put on Ashton to allow himself to be nominated. Dr Laney, Master of Pembroke, wrote to him: 'It is you, and you only, that can rescue the University from disgrace or slavery in this election; for if Dr B. should carry his point, nobody out of Trinity College must ever hereafter expect any of the three [Regius] professorships.' 'I know you want neither the profit nor the honour of the place', wrote Sherlock from the Temple, 'but the University wants you. Should you refuse it at this time I shall never expect to see the credit of the chair retriev'd.' While Ashton hesitated Bentley acted with unscrupulous vigour. Dr Grigg, Master of Clare, was Vice-Chancellor and ex-officio an elector to the professorship. He had been a Fellow of Jesus, and was under obligations to Dr Ashton, which it was not convenient to forget. Of the other six electors one only, the President of Queens', was Bentley's supporter; the remainder—viz. the two senior Fellows of Trinity, and the Heads of King's, St John's, and Christ's—were known to be his uncompromising opponents. Through the agency of the Chancellor, the Duke of Somerset, Bentley prevailed on Grigg to absent himself from Cambridge, and to nominate Bentley himself as his deputy. Armed with the Vice-Chancellor's powers, he then summoned a meeting of the electors at a time when the two senior Fellows of his college were unable to attend and, in accordance with the statute, their places were taken by the next two in seniority, who, as it happened, were favourable to his cause. The remaining three electors, finding the result of the meeting a foregone conclusion, did not present themselves, and so, to the amazement of the University, Bentley was chosen Professor without opposition.

Ashton, as a Tory, had political as well as personal grounds for disliking the great Aristarchus, and on his side Bentley did not refrain from expressing his contempt for his timid opponent. 'Tradition reports', says Bishop Monk, 'that on occasion of some meeting where, after a question had been long discussed, Dr Ashton observed that "it was not quite clear to him", the Master of Trinity briskly demanded, "Are we, then, to wait until your

mud has subsided?'' But Ashton was generous enough to recognize his enemy's greatness in scholarship, and expressed strong
disapproval of an ill-natured attack upon him made by a Fellow
of Jesus, Styan Thirlby, in the preface of his edition of Justin
Martyr, published in 1720.

The letters of young William Reneu to the historian Strype,
preserved among the Baumgartner Papers in the University
Library, give us a remarkable picture of men and manners at
Jesus in the reign of Queen Anne. Reneu, like Strype, was the
son of a Huguenot settled in London, and from his eighth to his
thirteenth year he boarded with Strype at his parsonage in Essex.
Reneu was admitted a sizar on 26 June 1705, at the age of sixteen, and came up as a freshman in the following October. On
9 October the boy writes his first impressions of the College.
'The lads' are up to the ears in division about High Church and
Low Church, Whig and Tory. His tutor, the same William Grigg
who afterwards became Master of Clare and lent himself to Bentley's designs on the Regius Professorship, is learned and kind; he
sits with Reneu and advises him as to reading—'Terence, or other
good classical authors'. Mr Grigg lectures daily at 8 a.m. on
Logic and Greek Testament, and three times a week on Mathematics. In his second year Reneu is reading the Tusculan Questions and Homer, besides English books, and also attends Mr
Grigg's lectures on Clarke's Physics. For exercise he has the choice
of shooting, hunting, coursing, and football.[1] He is advised to
'smoak very much,' but only, as he explains to Strype, for the
benefit of his sore eyes, and he will take care to conceal it from
his father, who had as lieve see him dead as with a pipe in his

---

[1] 'As for camping-balls, that bubble-boy hath a shop in every college in
Cambridge', says Roger North, writing to his son Montagu at Jesus in 1730.
Roger remembered how in his own undergraduate days he had looked with
envy on the scholars' games at football, in which his dignity as a Fellow-
Commoner did not allow him to participate. The game ceased to be played at
Cambridge before the end of the century. Dr Corrie, in his diary, 10 *December*,
1838, remarks that, passing by Parker's Piece on that day, he 'saw some forty
gownsmen playing at football. The *novelty* and liveliness of the scene was very
amusing.' Wakefield mentions among the amusements of his undergraduate
days (1772–6) fishing and cricket. This is the earliest mention of cricket at
Jesus.

mouth. In January 1708-9 he takes his degree and is 'capped' by the Vice-Chancellor. As a B.A. he hopes to live handsomely on £60 per annum, but presently finds this an underestimate, and complains that his father is a little hard upon him in making him find himself in clothes and all other conveniences and necessaries out of an allowance of £50 per annum and his scholarship which he rates at £10 more.[1] 'I wish he don't hinder me of ye Fellowship I expect by forcing me to live so close in college, for fellows expect to be treated now and then by youngsters that expect to be members of ye society.' A southern Fellowship—Reneu is a southern man—may drop any day; speculating on which probability old Mr Reneu sends the Master half a chest of Florence, and as much to Mr Grigg, 'which, you may be sure, won't be to my disadvantage'. This ingenuous avowal possibly called to Strype's recollection the Act of Elizabeth (1589), given in his *Annals*, which prohibited bribery and treating in elections to Fellowships and scholarships. In November 1710 the long-expected contingency presents itself. A southern Fellow is desperately ill. Mr Allix,[2] one of the Fellows, is about to post to London, to make what interest he can with the Bishop of Ely for his brother. Reneu's tutor advises him to be as quick in his motions as Allix—'there's nothing like striking while ye Iron is hot'. Reneu will start for London as soon as he hears of the gentleman's death; will Strype call with him on the Bishop? Reneu senior even goes to the Bishop before it is certain that the man is dead. It is disappointing that Strype's influence with the Bishop 'had not ye good effect you and I expected'; indeed, he gave 'all ye trouble he possibly could'. Nevertheless, the Fellowship is secured, and 'all ye fellows respect me for coming of so well, and I don't doubt I shall live very comfortably among y^m'. Next year Reneu is considering the advisability of 'putting on a Cassock', as there is a small college living which will be vacant in

[1] Montagu North, who was a pensioner, had an allowance of £80 per annum, and was expected to pay his tailor's and milliner's bills out of it.

[2] Peter Allix, D.D., was the son of a Huguenot divine; was originally of Queens', where he graduated B.A.; was appointed to the Bishop of Ely's Fellowship at Jesus in 1704-5; became Dean of Gloucester, 1729, and of Ely, 1730. His brother never became a Fellow of Jesus.

six months; 'it is just £20 per annum, and a place where there are no Criticks, so yᵗ a young man need not be much concerned, tho' his sermons are not extraordinary'. The career of this self-helpful young man was cut short by death in 1721.

The lives of the two archbishops, Thomas Herring and Matthew Hutton, show a degree of parallelism which is really extraordinary. They were born in the same year, 1693, and entered at Jesus in 1710, Herring one day before Hutton, which small priority of time Herring maintained in the successive steps which led each to Canterbury. They were both of them Whigs and Latitudinarians, and Dr Ashton and the Fellows were High Church Tories. Seeing no hope of preferment in their own College, they migrated, Herring to Corpus, Hutton to Christ's; at their adopted colleges they were elected to Fellowships, Herring in 1716, Hutton the next year. Herring was promoted successively to the sees of Bangor in 1737, York in 1743, and Canterbury in 1747, and Hutton directly followed him in each of them. Herring died in 1757, and Hutton after holding the Primacy for one year only, in 1758.

John Jortin's *Life of Erasmus* has long been superseded, and scarcely justifies the reputation which it conferred on its author in his lifetime; but his *Contributions to Ecclesiastical History* contain matter which is still valuable, and have the recommendation of clear criticism and a vivid style. He was the son of a Huguenot refugee, Renatus Jordain, and after education at the Charterhouse entered at Jesus in 1715, and was elected Fellow in 1721. While he was an undergraduate he was selected by his tutor, Styan Thirlby, to translate some passages from Eustathius for the notes to Pope's Homer, and presumed to make some corrections in Pope's work, which the poet silently adopted.

David Hartley, the father of associationism in psychology, a native of Halifax, was admitted in April 1722, and became a Fellow in 1726. In the following year he received college testimonials for ordination, but gave up the intention of taking Orders and became a physician. He vacated his Fellowship by marriage in 1730. His *Observations on Man*, published in 1749, shared with the writings of Locke, Hume, and Paley the distinction of becoming a text-book in the schools at Cambridge, and gave a strong impetus to rationalism in the University. Nowhere was his influence more strongly felt than in his own College. In the last quarter of the eighteenth century, as we shall presently show, Jesus College, which till then had always walked in the most decorous paths of Anglican orthodoxy, under such guides as Tyrwhitt and Frend manifested decided tendencies towards extreme Latitudinarianism. Coleridge, in his undergraduate days, warmed with the ardour of the French Revolution, ranked Hartley with Milton, Newton, and, more significantly, with Dr Priestley, among 'coadjutors of God'.

> He, of mortal kind
> Wisest, he first who mark'd the ideal tribe
> Up the fine fibres through the sentient brain.

One portrait of Archbishop Sterne which hangs in the College derives interest from the inscription on the frame recording that it was the gift of his great-grandson Laurence Sterne, an alumnus of the College. 'I well remember', says Tristram Shandy, 'when my father went up along with me to enter my name at Jesus College in * * * *, it was a matter of just wonder with my worthy tutor and two or three fellows of that learned society that a man who knew not so much as the names of his tools'— in logic, be it understood—'should be able to work after that fashion with them.' The day so well remembered was, in fact, 6 July 1733, and Tristram's tutor was Mr Charles Cannon, who died in the following year; and, curiously enough, the register is convicted of a carelessness almost as reprehensible as Susannah's in the matter of the freshman's Christian name, which in the first instance was 'Nicodemus'd' into Henry. Sterne was nearly twenty when he was admitted, and no father accompanied him to Cambridge; for Roger Sterne, 'lieutenant in Handaside's regiment', had died two years before. The poor sizar had, however, a friend and patron in his uncle, Jaques Sterne, a Canon of York, who had himself been a scholar of Jesus. Before his admission Laurence had doubtless been promised a Sterne scholarship, and though he did not possess the necessary qualification of being a native of

Yorkshire or of Nottinghamshire, the College overlooked that circumstance in consideration of his kindred to the founder, and elected him at the end of his first year's residence. He did not, however, matriculate in the University until March 1735. Of his undergraduate career we know hardly anything. He incurred debts which long embarrassed him; but of ordinary misdemeanours, such as required admonition *coram magistro et sociis*, none are laid to his charge in the College records. In the little society at Jesus he formed one acquaintance which proved lasting. This was with an unwholesomely minded youth named John Hall, afterwards Hall-Stephenson, two years Sterne's junior in standing, who figures as Eugenius in *Tristram Shandy*, and was claimed by Sterne as a relation. In later life he published some 'lean and flashy' books of verse, called *Crazy Tales*, in a style of humour labelled 'Shandean', and presided over a club of 'Demoniacks', Sterne being one of them, at Crazy Castle, as he called his seat at Skelton. College tradition long told how the two friends 'used to study together under a large wallnutt-tree in the inner [? outer] court, where one of 'em wrote underneath these lines:

> This shou'd be the Tree of Knowledge,
> As it stands in so very wise a Colledge.'

The ancient tree thus associated with the memory of Laurence Sterne was in his day one of the sights of Cambridge. We hear of it as early as 1592, when it seems that there was an arbour under or near it. In 1710 the space which its branches covered measured 96 feet across from side to side. It is said to have overshadowed every room in the court, and perhaps for that reason was cut down about the end of the eighteenth century.

Something of the Shandean influence may have rested on the two minor poets, Francis Fawkes and Thomas Nevile, who entered the College about a year after Sterne took his B.A. degree, and within six months of each other. Fawkes, a jovial Kentish parson, translated Theocritus with the assistance of Jortin, and afterwards versified Apollonius Rhodius, Anacreon and Bion. He is remembered, if at all, for his song, 'The Brown Jug'.

Nevile, who was elected to a Fellowship in 1746, published *Imitations of Horace, Juvenal, and Persius.* He was also the reputed author of *The Capitade*, a scurrilous attack on the Heads of Houses at Cambridge, first printed in the London *Evening Post*, 1 November 1750. The only creditable feature in this discreditable performance was that he respected the Head of his own College, the venerable Dr Ashton:

> Ashton the wise, the learn'd, the ag'd, the good,
> Whose soul unmov'd Temptation hath withstood;
> Heedless of courts and courtiers to his trust
> He steadfast lives, nor dares to be unjust;
> Gen'rous, sincere, free as when life began,
> He rests a college monarch, yet a worthy man.

Religion, except in outward forms, or as matter for doctrinal controversy, slumbered at Cambridge through all the long years of Ashton's Mastership. Methodism was, indeed, astir in the country, but as yet no answering breath of religious emotion had stirred the dull waters of Cambridge formalism. The name of Henry Venn among the admissions of 1742, when he migrated to Jesus after three months' residence at St John's, is, however, a premonition of the great movement of Cambridge evangelicalism, prolonged far into the next century by Venn's pupil and friend, Charles Simeon. But Venn, the son of a High Church clergyman, did not adopt evangelical views until after he had taken his degree and had removed to a London curacy. He was elected to a Fellowship at Queens' in 1749, and published his *Complete Duty of Man* in 1763.

In 1752, when Dr Ashton died, Bishop Gooch appointed in his place Philip Yonge, D.D., a Fellow of Trinity and at the time of his appointment Public Orator and a Canon of Westminster. He resigned the Mastership in 1758 on his promotion to the bishopric of Bristol, was translated to Norwich in 1761, and died in 1783. The six years of his reign at Jesus were altogether unremarkable. The total of admissions showed no sign of recovery, and there was the same extraordinary disproportion as in Ashton's last years between the numbers of those who received college testimonials for ordination and of those who attained the B.A. degree.

In the year 1747–8 begins the series of Tripos lists contained in the University calendar. The first Jesus name of any distinction which occurs in them is that of Samuel Hallifax, who is set down as third Wrangler in 1754. But he owed his place in the list to the prerogative possessed in those days by the Vice-Chancellor —Dr Yonge held the office in 1745—of placing one nominee where he pleased in the order of merit, and Hallifax did not actually take the Tripos examination at all. He was, however, Senior Chancellor's Medallist in 1754 and Members' Prizeman in 1756. Elected to a Fellowship in 1756, he resigned it in 1760 and migrated to Trinity Hall, where he was a successful tutor. He held the two Arabic professorships simultaneously and, being a gentleman of happy versatility of talent, resigned them both for the chair of Civil Law. He became successively Bishop of Gloucester in 1781 and of St Asaph in 1789. Thomas Castley, a Westmorland man, was Senior Wrangler and second Chancellor's Medallist in 1755, the first Medallist being another Jesus man, East Apthorp, a native of New England, afterwards a Prebendary of St Paul's. Of a more remarkable man than any of these, Robert Tyrwhitt, lowest Wrangler in 1757, something will be said in the next chapter.

John Lakin, who held the Mastership for a twelvemonth in 1562–3, William Beale, who held it for a like period in 1633–4, John Reston and John Duport were the only Fellows of Jesus who had so far been advanced to the Headship. Dr Lynford Caryl, who succeeded Bishop Yonge, had been admitted a sizar of the College in 1723, was a Fellow from 1733 to 1750, and acted as Bursar for some part of that time. He resigned his Fellowship on being appointed a Prebendary of Canterbury and in the following year became Registrary of the University. He was all that a Bursar and Registrary should be—accurate, industrious, and methodical. At Canterbury he arranged the chapter documents, which had been previously left in inextricable disorder, and he rendered the same service to the Jesus muniments. He arranged and catalogued the College and nunnery records, made a systematic transcript

of the register, continued down to his own time the biographical
notes in Sherman's *Historia*, and revived the 'Conclusion Book',
which had been begun but discontinued after a few months' trial
at the commencement of Dr Yonge's Mastership. After 1758 the
entries in the register are confined to purely formal matters, and
the more important business of the College is contained in the
'Conclusion Book', which is written entirely in English. Dr
Caryl had a reputation for unimpeachable integrity; was esteemed
without an equal in the prudent and dexterous management of
University elections; was distinguished by a solemnity of manner
and precision in expression about which Gilbert Wakefield has
some anecdotes; wrote in a very clear and beautiful hand, and
was evidently fond of penmanship. Of more vivifying qualities
of mind and character which he may have possessed we are
uninformed.

The admissions to the College fell to their lowest point
about the time of Dr Caryl's appointment. In the five years
ending 1764 only twenty-three undergraduates of all classes
entered the College; sixteen B.A. degrees were taken, and college
testimonials were given in eighteen instances. From this time to
the end of the century there was a slight progressive increase in
numbers. In the period 1790–4 the entries were forty-one, B.A.
degrees nineteen, and not fewer than twenty-nine members of
the College obtained testimonials for orders.

Of the languid years during which Dr Caryl presided over
Jesus little need be said. Gilbert Wakefield (adm. 1772), in his
autobiographic *Memoirs*, gives us no favourable impression of the
efficiency of the teaching staff in his undergraduate days. Yet
Wakefield was quite disposed to regard its shortcomings with
leniency, and his loyalty to the College amounted to enthusiasm.
Things were not quite so bad as Gibbon had found them, twenty
years before, at Magdalen, Oxford. Indeed, Wakefield expresses
devout gratitude that his father (a Jesus man himself) was not prevailed upon to enter him at Christ Church, Oxford, where orthodox theology, High Church politics, and passive obedience sat
enthroned and spread a stupefying influence around them. His
tutors, he says, were placid, amiable men of respectable abilities,

but deficient in activity and zeal. He found college lectures in algebra and logic odious beyond conception, and could not prevail upon himself to open Euclid, 'the old carpenter'. He had no private tutor to direct his studies until a few months before his degree, when a Mr Mounsey, lately elected a Fellow of the College from Peterhouse, took a friendly interest in him. Under his direction Wakefield, though to the last 'a mean proficient in the higher parts of algebra and fluxions', made such progress in his mathematical studies that he was placed second in the list of Wranglers in the Tripos of 1776. From his perfunctory mathematical work he turned with enthusiasm to classics. He competed unsuccessfully for the newly-established Browne Medals in 1775, but gained the second Chancellor's Medal in 1776, and the second Members' Prize in 1777 and 1778. He was elected to a Fellowship in April, 1776, and vacated it by marriage three years later.

Wakefield's *Memoirs* give a measure of the man's garrulous inconsequence and vanity. Alike in politics, religion and scholarship, he showed himself altogether lacking in discretion. In 1799 he was imprisoned in Dorchester gaol for expressing a treasonable wish that the French Revolutionists would invade and conquer England. In 1797 he published an ill-judged attack on Porson's edition of the *Hecuba*, which provoked Porson's retort, 'What's Hecuba to him, or he to Hecuba?' It is not a little remarkable that, at the time when Cambridge scholarship had attained in Porson's work its highest perfection of exactness, the 'incurably inaccurate' productions of Wakefield should have passed as creditable specimens of criticism. Yet his edition of Lucretius (1796-7) imposed on scholars far more competent than himself, and held its ground until it was displaced by Lachmann's great work on the same author. Wakefield's reputation for scholarship received its *coup-de-grâce* in the preface to Professor Munro's edition of Lucretius.

Though the old practice of lodging Fellows and their pupils, two or more, in a single room was given up about the beginning of the period reviewed in this chapter, the deplenishment of the College rendered any extension of chamber space unnecessary.

The alterations in the buildings made at this time had for their object either their embellishment, according to prevalent fashions in architecture and decoration, or the comfort of their occupants. In external appearance the most important change was that made in the years 1718–20, when the entire front of the College was heightened. This was effected by adding a third storey to the west wing of the lodge, and by converting the garrets in the highest floor of the old school-house range westward of the gate into chambers covered by a low-pitched roof. The cost of the addition to the lodge was £266, part of which was defrayed out of a legacy of £100 given by Dr Charles Proby. 'The remaining summ', writes Dr Ashton, 'I paid out of my own money, chusing to have that for my share in the expense of a work so much for ye use and ornament of ye College.' The alterations in the range westward of the gate, including the wainscoting of the chambers, were paid for by subscriptions obtained from members of the College. The effect of these changes, which Dr Ashton contemplated with such satisfaction, was to ruin the picturesque front shown in Loggan's design. Alcock's graceful gate-tower was three parts buried in the mass right and left of it; the dormer windows, breaking the roof-slope at irregular intervals, were ruled out; and all the windows, except those on the ground-floor, which were out of sight from the approach to the College, were regularly sashed in the approved Italian fashion.[1] Some sacrifice to uniformity was permitted on the side next the court, where the windows on the highest floor were made to correspond with those in the older buildings.

Alterations to the Hall were taken in hand in 1703, when it was paved with freestone and wainscoted (in deal) after an 'Italian' design. A new bell-turret was at the same time put up. Then, too, the piers of red brick and stone which flank the iron gate at the end of 'the Chimney' next Jesus Lane were built. Previously the gate had been a wooden one set in an arch in the boundary wall of the College. The chapel, fortunately, suffered from nothing worse than neglect. Its size and the uncompromising character

[1] In the muniment room there is a paper of *Accounts of the New Building* of 1719. They show that the windows were sashed then, and in 1791.

of its Gothicism made its adaptation to eighteenth-century models
of elegance an undertaking beyond the resources of the society.
The task of classicizing it was reserved to a more opulent generation and a Unitarian benefactor. Almost the only items connected
with it which can be gleaned from the Accounts and the Conclusion Book in the period 1701–81 relate to the stipend of the
clock-keeper and to the organ. In 1764 the society agreed to dis-
continue the salary paid to the organist, and the organ speedily
fell into disrepair. Cole has a note about it in his manuscripts:

> I was told, Mar. 4, 1776, by a Domestick of the College that tho'
> they have a very good Organ in the Chapel, to which the Singing
> men used to resort on Surplice Nights, and always made use of in
> my Time of being in the University, that it is now laid aside as a
> useless Piece of Lumber and Expence. I suppose the Revenue appro-
> priated to it is now applied to other more profitable uses.

The last stage in the history of this organ—the same which
was hidden to escape destruction at the hands of Dowsing and so
graciously restored to Dr Worthington—was reached in 1790,
when it was agreed by the society 'to make a present of the
remains of our Organ to the Parish of All Saints in Cambridge'.

Plate V

Stearn's, Cambridge

THE HALL (1959)

Plate VI

THE CLOISTER: FIFTEENTH-
CENTURY DOORWAYS (*above*)

DOORWAY AND PASSAGE
LEADING TO CLOISTER (*below*)

Country

ORIEL WINDOW IN HALL (*abo*

STALL-END IN CHAPEL (*belo*

CHAPTER VIII

THE JESUS UNITARIANS

DR ASHTON'S long rule had preserved at Jesus half-way into the eighteenth century the creeds and prejudices of the close of the seventeenth. He lived to witness the final downfall of the exiled royal family, to whose principles, we are told, if not to their persons, he was devotedly attached; and he had seen latitudinarianism—notably in the persons of his pupils, Herring and Hutton—enthroned in the high places of the Church. But in the studies and in the parlour of the College High Church Anglicanism held its ground as firmly as in the days of Bancroft and Richard Sterne. Deism, Socinianism, Methodism, had successively invaded the world and the University, but had altogether failed to find an entrance to the cloisters of Jesus. Ashton's death in 1752 led to a complete detachment from the old ideas. The change did not come at once; but during the Masterships of Yonge and Caryl the seeds which fructified in the French Revolution period were germinating in the minds of certain undergraduates who became Fellows of the College in the generation which succeeded Ashton. Under their influence the formerly sleepy society became one of the most active in the University. The neglectful tutors of the earlier time were replaced by men of warm sympathies, apt to impress their character and views on their pupils. Religious enthusiasm awoke, and in some cases took an extreme form.[1] The interest of the Fellows was transferred from books to life, and, as a consequence, the minds of their pupils were less chained to the old routine of studies. At no period in its history had the College a more brilliant set of undergraduates than in the last

---

[1] The Rev. Thomas Philip Foley—'Handsome Foley', as he was called—was Fellow from 1780 to 1790; he became a devoted adherent of Joanna Southcote, and acted as her secretary. See Gunning's *Reminiscences*, vol. i, pp. 62–71.

decade of the eighteenth century, when it included among them such men as William Otter, E. D. Clarke, Robert Malthus, and S. T. Coleridge.

Some of the merit of infusing this new life was due to the two men who successively held the Mastership in the last years of the century. Richard Beadon, Master from 1781 to 1789, was educated at Blundell's School, Tiverton, and at St John's (adm. 1754). He was eighth Wrangler and senior Chancellor's Medallist in 1758, became Fellow and tutor of his college, and in 1768 was elected Public Orator. After he became Master of Jesus he was placed in charge of Prince Frederick William, afterwards Duke of Gloucester and Chancellor of the University, then an undergraduate at Trinity. His portrait presents a handsome, prosperous-looking man, with an air of cheerful activity which is in marked contrast with the pinched and mortified features of Dr Ashton and the severely repressive countenance of Dr Caryl. Beadon was, no doubt, a courtier, and his attentions to the young Prince won him the favour of the King, who made him Bishop of Gloucester in 1789, and translated him to Bath and Wells in 1802. Nevertheless, he was an excellent Master and Vice-Chancellor, and left a name for kindness and hospitality. The fame and popularity which he had won as a tutor was an attraction to young men of ability, and he was the first Master since the Revolution who seems to have had a genuine liking and sympathy for the undergraduate. His successor, William Pearce (1789–1820) had been, like him, a Fellow and tutor of St John's; graduated in 1767 as third Wrangler and second Chancellor's Medallist; became Public Orator in 1778; and was successively Master of the Temple (1787–97), and Dean of Ely (1797–1820). The inscription on his monument in the chapel proclaims him as a champion of the King, the Church, and Christian verity—a character perhaps earned by the part which he played in the Frend dispute. His action in that matter was, perhaps, arbitrary, but arbitrary measures had some measure of justification in 1793. Moreover, the proceedings were initiated, not by the Master, but by some of the Fellows in his absence; and it is to his credit that, having ranged himself against Frend in the College issue, he abstained from taking part, as a Head, in the trial before the Vice-Chancellor's Court. Whatever may be thought at this distance of time of his action, it may be observed that, but for some petulant remarks of Frend himself, there was no suggestion either in the College or outside it that it was dictated by any but conscientious motives, and it is certain that the tension of the time caused no break in the friendly relations between him and the Fellows, whichever side they took in the dispute. He had the reputation of being a wit and one of the best talkers in the University. The stories that are told of his relations with Coleridge show that he could be severe on occasions; but there was a compliment in his severity, and Coleridge was flattered by thinking that the Master saw something in him that was not of the common run.

But if Beadon and Pearce did a good deal to popularize the College and to increase its academic efficiency, the real credit of inspiring it with wider aims, and with ambitions that did not stop at the Tripos or wither in a College living, belongs to the two Unitarians, Tyrwhitt and Frend. Cambridge Unitarianism was no sudden growth. The doctrine of the Trinity, more than any other, had occupied the field of religious controversy in the University ever since the commencement of the eighteenth century, when Whiston, for sentiments labelled Arian, but really a fantastic evolution of his own, had been expelled from the University and deprived of the Lucasian Professorship of Mathematics (1710). He subsequently left the communion of the Church and joined the General Baptists. But, as a rule, the earlier leaders of the Unitarian attack on the orthodox position remained within the fold of the Church. Dr Samuel Clarke (of Caius), who succeeded Whiston as the leader of the Arians, was Rector of St James's, Westminster; he advised his followers to disregard the difficulties of subscription, and to remain within the Church 'to leaven the mass'. Among his principal lieutenants was John Jackson, admitted at Jesus in 1702, sometimes called the 'Chronologist', from his valuable work, *Chronological Antiquities*, published in 1752. Though after ordination he refused further subscription, and thereby forfeited a prebendal stall at Salisbury, he performed his duties as a parish priest to the last. In the last quarter of the

century the gulf which divided Cambridge Arians from the
Church gradually widened. *Ex hypothesi*, every graduate, as he
had subscribed the Articles at his degree, was a member of
the Church of England; but many renounced the connection.
Nowhere was the revolt against subscription more marked than at
Jesus. John Braithwaite, Fellow from 1754 to 1789, refused all
College livings from scruples connected with the Articles. Gilbert
Wakefield bitterly reprobated his own disingenuousness in accept-
ing deacon's orders in spite of his Arian convictions, and, from an
objection to renewing his subscription, he never took the M.A.
degree. Tyrwhitt proposed a Grace in 1771 for the abolition of
subscription at the B.A. degree; the attempt was not successful,
but it led in the following year to the substitution, in place of
subscription, of a declaration on the part of the candidate that he
was *bona-fide* a member of the Church of England. Dr Thomas
Edwards, Fellow in 1783-5, proposed a Grace in 1787 to abolish
the declaration; he was author of a work on *The Limits and Importance of Free Inquiry in Matters of Religion*. Frend actively
supported Edwards's proposal, renounced his Orders, and severed
his connection with the Church.

Robert Tyrwhitt was born in 1735, and was twenty-two years
the senior of Frend. He was admitted in 1753, graduated in 1757,
being lowest in the wranglers of his year, was elected to a Fellowship in November, 1759, and immediately after was appointed
Praelector Graecus by the College. He was ordained a month
after he became a Fellow, but never took a cure. His deep religious feeling, devotion to learning, and amiable character gave
him a strong attractive power in his College and the University.
Wakefield, though he denies that he was seduced by Tyrwhitt
from the paths of orthodoxy, allows that his character for sincerity in the search for religious truth aroused the interest of the
undergraduates of his time. Tyrwhitt was first drawn to adopt
Unitarian views by the study of Dr Clarke's works. In 1777 he
resigned his Fellowship for religious motives and gave up attending chapel. He devoted himself to the study of Hebrew, and
in 1784 joined a Unitarian society for promoting knowledge of
the Scriptures. Later, however, he seceded from the London

Unitarian society on the ground that in one of its publications it had used language which he deemed offensive with regard to the belief in the Second Person of the Trinity. His habits were simple, and by his brother's death he came into property which made him a comparatively wealthy man; a large part of his income was spent in private charity, and during his lifetime he bestowed £1,200 upon the College. Dying, at the age of eighty, in 1817, he left £4,000 by will to the University for the promotion of Hebrew study, with which sum the scholarships known by his name were founded. A Latin inscription of singular beauty on his grave in the chapel records that within the walls of the College, which he had loved above all things, and in his lifetime had adorned with amplest gifts, he had lived for more than sixty years: 'Vitam umbratilem excoluit et literarum sacrarum studio et quieti deditus secretum iter peregit.' The gentle wisdom of his character is brought into relief by the contrast with the untempered zeal of Frend.

William Frend was originally of Christ's. He was second Wrangler and second Smith's Prizeman in 1780; migrated to Jesus, on the advice of Dr Caryl, in the same year, and was forthwith elected to a scholarship, and in the following year to a Fellowship. He was ordained in 1780, became Vicar of Madingley, and was zealous in the performance of his parish duties. At the same time he held the position of College tutor with conspicuous success. Among his pupils were Edward Otter, second Wrangler in 1786, and his brother William, fourth Wrangler in 1790, Malthus and E. D. Clarke. As all of these men became respected and orthodox clergymen, we may credit Frend's statement that he never employed his position as tutor to influence the minds of his pupils in the direction of his own religious views. In 1787 he became a convert to Unitarianism, resigned his living, and published an Address to the Inhabitants of Cambridge advocating his new creed. For this, in the following year, he was removed by Dr Beadon from the tutorship, an office which was worth £150 a year. He appealed to the Visitor, but without success. On the advice of his friends he travelled for a time on the Continent. Returning to Cambridge, he devoted himself to the study of Hebrew, and translated the historical books of the Old Testament for Dr Priestley's new translation of the Scriptures. His relations with the rest of the society were so far friendly. 'Mr Frend's company', writes Coleridge in January 1792, 'is by no means invidious. On the contrary, Pearce himself is very intimate with him.' Among the Fellows there were some who were his warm friends and supporters, though they did not share his views, nor allow their partizanship to interrupt relations with those who took the other side of the dispute. Among his opponents there were some men whose political views were narrow, but they were at least not more illiberal than the great majority of Cambridge residents outside Trinity. The religious motives on which they based their attack were perhaps mingled with some personal resentment at the unconcealed contempt with which Frend regarded the clerical 'don'. But Gunning and Coleridge—both of them passionate partizans of Frend—are witnesses that some of his opponents among the Fellows—Mathew, the President, and Plampin, one of the tutors, especially—were honourable and kindly gentlemen. Moreover, the view which the majority of the Fellows took of Frend's celebrated pamphlet was that which would have been taken in 1793 by the whole of the clergy and nine-tenths of the educated laity. And Frend's intimacy with Priestley, whose house had been burnt by the Birmingham mob in 1791, made him trebly suspect. It was whispered that there was a Jacobin party in the University, who had opened a treasonable correspondence with the National Convention, and that their names and letters were in the hands of the Government. Five persons were said to be concerned in it, and it was generally supposed that Frend was one of them; Dr Edwards, of Jesus, was said to be another. The supposed plot was a mere fiction, and perhaps nobody very seriously believed in it; Gunning says that he once dined with a party at which the five conspirators, for the first time in their lives, found themselves in the same room together. Yet a man of less suspicious antecedents than Frend's would have found it dangerous to express views more moderate than his at a time when nervous alarms of sedition agitated the Government and country. On the last day of 1792 Tom Paine's effigy was burnt by the mob on the Market Hill at Cambridge. Before that, on December 15, at a large meeting in the Town Hall, it was resolved, among other things, 'to bring to punishment all such who shall distribute or bring to the public eye any pamphlets or papers containing opinions or sentiments tending to promote disaffection and encourage sedition'. Within two months of this warning (16 February 1793) the publication was announced of Frend's pamphlet, *Peace and Union recommended to the Associated Bodies of Republicans and Anti-Republicans*.

The political contents of this pamphlet were such as no sane judgment could have held to be dangerous. Frend was not, *de parti pris*, a Republican, nor a believer in the political perfectibility which was preached by the French Revolutionists. Reform of Parliament, Triennial Elections, Abolition of the Game Laws, Political Education of the Electorate, etc., were his harmless recommendations, and they were urged in temperate language. But it must be admitted that in speaking of religious matters he used language which, if only on grounds of taste, was highly discreditable. In speaking of the most solemn rites, not only those of the English Church, but such as are common to all Christian sects, he expressed himself with a flippancy and irreverence which even his friends could not defend.

On 22 February, a week after the publication of the pamphlet, the resident Fellows met and passed the following resolution:

Resolved, that a pamphlet entitled Peace and Union, lately published by W. Frend, M.A., Fellow of this college, appears to us to have been written with the evil intent of prejudicing the clergy in the eyes of the laity, of degrading in the publick esteem the doctrines and rites of the Established Church, and of disturbing the harmony of Society. And that, as we feel it to be our particular duty to disavow principles calculated to mislead the minds of young men entrusted to our care, a copy of the said pamphlet be sent both to the Vice-Chancellor of the University, and to the Visitor of the College, inclosed in a letter to each, expressing our disapprobation of the opinions therein delivered, and humbly requesting them to take such measures as in their judgment may appear most proper for the effectual suppression of their dangerous tendency.

Five Fellows signed this resolution. Outside the College action was taken by twenty-seven members of the University, who met on 4 March at the lodge of the Vice-Chancellor, Dr Milner, President of Queens', and entered into resolutions to prosecute the author. For the present it will be convenient to follow the course of events in the College; later we shall return to the proceedings in the Vice-Chancellor's Court. The Master, after taking legal advice, summoned a meeting of the Fellows on 3 April. Ten Fellows, not counting Frend, were present. After the meeting had gone on for about an hour Frend was called into the parlour by the porter, and the Master, in the presence of the Fellows, showing him the pamphlet, asked him whether he avowed himself the author of it. Frend, acting on legal advice, declined either to admit or to deny the authorship, and demanded a written accusation stating the passages in the pamphlet referred to and the statutes against which he had offended. He was asked to withdraw, and late in the evening was called in again and informed that the meeting declined to deliver a written charge, and that, if he would not proceed on his defence, the meeting would proceed without it. His reply was that he would proceed as soon as the conditions for which he had already asked were complied with. Next morning he was again summoned to the parlour. He demanded to see the proceedings of the meeting of the previous day, and was informed that this would not be allowed. He urged that he had a material objection to propose, but the Master declined to hear him, saying that, if he had anything to say in his defence, it should have been said yesterday. He then read from a written paper the following resolution:

> It is the opinion of this meeting that Mr Frend be removed from the college, that is, from the precincts of the college, and from residence in it, till he shall produce such proofs of good behaviour as shall be satisfactory to the master and major part of the fellows, and that he may be allowed a month from this time to settle his affairs in college.

The Master and six Fellows agreed to this resolution; four Fellows voted against it. Against the decision of the majority Frend appealed on 17 April to the Visitor, requesting his interposition on the grounds that no exceptionable passages in the pamphlet nor any statutes of the College against which he had offended had been pointed out; that he had had no opportunity of vindicating himself from the charges; that it did not appear from the statutes of the College that the Master and six Fellows, or any other number less than the majority of all the Fellows, were competent to inflict any punishment on a Fellow; and that the sentence of removal from the College was not warranted by the statutes. The Master and five Fellows in their reply addressed to the Bishop alleged that their disapprobation was not based on detached passages, but on the general tenor and tendency of the composition. In answer to the objection that no laws of the College against which Frend had offended had been pointed out, they claimed that the College, *quatenus* a college, had an inherent right, independently of any express or particular statute, to take cognizance of and to punish offences *contra bonos mores* committed by its members. To the objection that a majority of all the Fellows was required for the infliction of punishment on any of their number they answered that their sentence was virtually passed by a majority of all the Fellows, inasmuch as a majority of those present at the meeting had concurred in it. They admitted that the sentence of removal from the College was not expressly marked out in the statutes, but pointed out that they conferred a power of total expulsion, and claimed that the necessary authority which the College possessed in all cases of discipline entitled it to pronounce the lighter sentence, whether specifically described in the statutes or not. The answer of the Master and the five Fellows shows that they were quite aware that there was nothing within the four corners of the statutes to warrant the punishment on which they had determined. In support of their position they point out that temporary amotion was a punishment well known and frequent in the practice of all colleges; but the obvious answer to this was that Frend's amotion was not intended to be temporary, and that, if the temporary removal of a Fellow existed at all as a practice, it was at those colleges whose statutes sanctioned it, which was not the case at Jesus.

Frend's appeal was supported by a protest on the part of three of the dissident Fellows, Newton, Whitehead, and Edward Otter. A long correspondence followed, resulting in the dismissal of the appeal by the Visitor and in the confirmation of the sentence of the College. Up to this time Frend had been generally resident in College. On 26 July, at a meeting of the Master and all the resident Fellows, it was agreed:

> That if Mr Frend does not quit the college according to the sentence, no time should be lost in enforcing the sentence in the manner pointed out by Sir William Scott, in an opinion given by him on this occasion.

The Master and two Fellows signed this conclusion; in consequence of it the Master wrote to Frend, who happened then to be absent from the College, informing him that on and after 2 August admission to the College would be denied him. Frend, in his printed account of the proceedings against him, describes how the sentence was enforced.

> On that day [August 2] Mr Frend returned to College, and about twelve o'clock received an intimation in writing from the master that the College servants were prohibited from supplying him in future with necessaries. Between three and four he went, according to a previous engagement, into the town to dinner, and soon heard that, immediately upon his going out, the College gates were all shut. About seven he went down to the College, found the great gate shut, rang the bell and, on the porter's opening the gate, walked in, and in a tone of authority reprimanded the porter for shutting the gates at so unreasonable an hour. From thence he went to the lodge to expostulate with the master on the absurdity of these proceedings, and, not finding him at home, left a note, desiring the master to declare whether the gates were shut by his order or not. After having thus shown his perfect contempt of the master's orders, he returned to his friend's house, and spent only one morning afterwards in College. On the twenty-seventh of September, indeed, he intended to revisit the College, but found that Mr Plampin, from the malignity of whose zeal nothing else could be expected, had taken the precaution to order the gates to be shut, and an iron chain to be kept across the great door.

Though they excluded Frend from the College, the victorious party did not venture to propose that he should be deprived of the emoluments of his Fellowship, which he retained for many years, and only resigned on his marriage in 1808. On leaving the University he went to London, where he became secretary and actuary of the Rock Assurance Company. He lived there in good society, actively co-operated with Burdett, Horne Tooke, and other Radical leaders, and died, long after the generation who had fought over his case were in their graves, in 1841.

Something has still to be said of the proceedings against Frend in the Vice-Chancellor's Court, which terminated some time before his expulsion from the College. The 'promoter' of the indictment was Dr Kipling of St John's, who at the time was acting as deputy for the Regius Professor of Divinity, Dr Watson, Bishop of Llandaff. His qualifications for the professoriate were scanty, and his dubious Latinity and pompous bearing exposed him to the jibes and flouts of all the wits in the University. Throughout the proceedings Frend poured contempt and scorn on the poor man. A dramatic incident in the trial was when a certain Grace of 1603, on which Kipling based his case, was found on examination to have no existence in the Registrary's copy of the University Grace-Book. It was unfortunate for Frend that the Vice-Chancellor of the year was the celebrated Dr Isaac Milner, President of Queens'. The party in the University opposed to Frend was composed largely of the Methodists, or 'Saints', as they were then called, and among them Milner figured as light and leader. With very questionable propriety he had permitted the meeting of the twenty-seven, at which the prosecution was resolved on, to take place in Queens' lodge, and though he was not actually present at that meeting, he had from the first shown a decided bias against Frend. In the address which he made to the undergraduates when he delivered judgment in the Senate House he took credit to himself for never having been suspected of being fond of possessing offices or dignities. But it was pretty well understood that he desired to stand well with the Ministry, and after the trial he took pains to impress on Pitt that the expulsion of Frend had caused the downfall of Jacobinism in the University.

The Vice-Chancellor's Court met for the first time on 3 May and was continued by adjournments until 30 May, when Frend was called upon to retract and confess his error. When the form of recantation was handed to him and he was asked to subscribe it, he replied melodramatically that he would sooner cut off his hand than sign it. Thereupon the Vice-Chancellor, with the assent of the majority of the Heads of colleges, who constituted the court, pronounced sentence of banishment from the University. On the day following the trial Frend gave notice of his intention to appeal against the decision, and a new court of delegates was shortly afterwards appointed to hear his objections. Both this court and that of the King's Bench, to which Frend subsequently carried the case, upheld the original sentence. It is the defect of academic decrees that the power is often lacking to enforce them. Thus it happened that Frend was present in the Senate House at the Commencement, after the confirmation of the sentence, when Dr Kipling, 'in a violent declamation in bad Latin, addressed a formal prayer to the Supreme Being on the success of his late labours', and in the course of his harangue alluded to Frend as *exsul et extorris*, though he was actually at the doctor's elbow.

A scene in the Senate House during Frend's trial serves to introduce one of the most famous of the sons of Jesus, Samuel Taylor Coleridge. Gunning, in his *Reminiscences*, is our authority for the story, and it shall be told in his words:

The Undergraduates were unanimous in favour of Mr Frend, and every satirical remark reflecting upon the conduct and motives of his prosecutors was vociferously applauded. At length the Court desired the Proctors to interfere. Mr Farish, the Senior Proctor, having marked one man who had particularly distinguished himself by applauding, and noted his position in the gallery, selected him as a fit subject for punishment. He went into the gallery, and having previously ascertained the exact situation of the culprit, he touched a person, whom he supposed to be the same, on the shoulder, and asked him his name and college. The person thus addressed assured him that he had been perfectly quiet. Farish replied: 'I have been watching you for a long time, and have seen you repeatedly clapping your hands.' 'I wish this were possible,' said the man, and, turning round,

exhibited an arm so deformed that his hands could not by any pos-
sibility be brought together; this exculpation was received with
repeated rounds of applause, which continued for some minutes.
The name of the young man was Charnock, and his College Clare
Hall; the real culprit was S. T. Coleridge of Jesus College, who,
having observed that the Proctor had noticed him, and was coming
into the gallery, turned round to the person who was standing
behind him, and made an offer of exchanging places, which was
gladly accepted by the unsuspecting man. Coleridge immediately
retreated, and, mixing with the crowd, entirely escaped suspicion.
This conduct on the part of Coleridge was severely censured by the
Undergraduates, as it was quite clear that, to escape punishment
himself, he would have subjected an innocent man to rustication or
expulsion.

Gunning's anecdote has to be corrected in one respect. A
writer in the *Athenaeum* says that the version of the story given
in after-life by Coleridge himself was that Charnock, like Coleridge, felt strongly in favour of the accused, and it had been
previously agreed between them that Coleridge should be most
violent in opposition to the Vice-Chancellor, and that if his conduct excited observation, when the Proctor was sent up he should
slip away, and leave Charnock to take his place and bear the brunt
of the affray.

In order of time Coleridge's admission at Jesus (5 February) 1791
comes after that of some of the men who are reserved to the next
chapter. He is mentioned here because of his connexion with the
Jesus Unitarians. Until he reached the age of twenty-six it must
be remembered that his professed creed was Unitarianism, to
which he was converted by Frend. There was a time in his life,
not long after he left the University, when he announced himself
to preach in the Unitarian Chapel at Bath as 'the Rev. S. T.
Coleridge, of Jesus College, Cambridge', and, to mark his sever-
ance from the 'gentlemen in black', so much reprobated in Frend's
tract, performed that office in blue coat and white waistcoat. It
was the overwhelming influence of the French Revolution that
gave the bent to his early views on politics and religion, quite
independently of such a minor consideration as the selection of

his College; a youth of his precocious and susceptible nature might as well have been a Unitarian at Queens' or an anti-Pittite at St John's. But he could hardly have lighted in 1791 on a College where he would have found so much encouragement in the expression of his enthusiasms as Jesus, or where the interchange of ideas on the great topics of the day was so unfettered. The ordinary restrictions on frank communication between 'don' and undergraduate did not exist in the case of Frend and Edwards, neither of whom held College office. If young Coleridge took colouring from their sides, he also gave them of his own. In one of his letters to Southey, written in 1794, he describes a tea-party at the house of Dr Edwards, at which the great Pantisocratic scheme was maintained by himself in a discussion which lasted six hours and left the doctor convinced of the impregnability of the system.

Coleridge was, no doubt, attracted to Jesus by the hope of getting a Rustat Scholarship and, in fact, he was admitted to one in his first term of residence, November 1791. The annual value of a Rustat Scholarship was then about £14, and a gratuity of £15 was allowed to scholars who 'appeared' at the Rustat examination in Easter week. Coleridge received this gratuity three times. At first he seriously devoted himself to the prescribed studies of the day. In his second term he gained the College prize for a Latin Declamation on the subject of 'Posthumous Fame'. It is still extant in a book in the Library, in a hand-writing apparently that of Coleridge. It is a very perfunctory performance, and the sentiments which it expresses—Cromwell is compared to Catiline and to men who, like Eratosthenes, *gloriam super ruinas et incendia ponunt*—are very unlike Coleridge's notions of a year or two later. In his first year he won the Browne Medal for a Greek Ode, the subject being the 'Slave Trade'. In his second year he competed again, but unsuccessfully, with an Ode on the 'Praise of Astronomy'. He thought this second ode better than the other; there is a translation of it by Southey. In the same year he was a competitor for the Craven Scholarship. Out of about eighteen candidates, he was one of four selected, among the four being Butler, afterwards Headmaster of Harrow, and Keate, afterwards Headmaster of Eton. Coleridge was unsuccessful, and the failure damped his ardour. There was then no Classical Tripos; to obtain a Chancellor's Medal it was necessary that a candidate should have obtained honours in mathematics, and for mathematics Coleridge had neither aptitude nor inclination. So faded all visions of University honours and a College Fellowship, on which at one time, we are told, Coleridge had set his heart. The last record of his academic success is that of his election to a Foundation Scholarship at Jesus in 1793.

But long before this expiring flicker in the way of academic distinction, Coleridge had turned his thoughts to altogether different matters. He devoured books insatiably, and seems to have haunted the College Library. Metaphysics, poetry, travel, medicine, but chiefly politics and religion, all interested him by turns. He told Cottle that he believed that by his constant recommendations he had sold a whole edition of some books, particularly among freshmen at Cambridge, whom he advised to purchase three works—Simpson's Euclid, Hartley *On Man*, and Bowles's Poems. Under the inspiration of Bowles he wrote a good deal of poetry himself, some pieces of which appeared in the *Cambridge Intelligencer*, a newly established Radical paper, edited by a remarkable man, Benjamin Flower, with whom Coleridge made acquaintance. Among the poems of his College days may be remembered 'A Wish written in Jesus Wood, 10 February 1792', and the too-celebrated 'Monologue to a Young Jackass on Jesus Piece'. Another little piece, written apparently late in his Cambridge career, deserves notice for the circumstances of its composition—it was scribbled in a prayer-book in the College Chapel —as well as for the grave, regretful tone in which he refers in it to his neglected 'hours of youth'. There is another reference to the same subject in his 'Lines on an Autumnal Evening', written about the same time, where he alludes to the period

> when from the Muses' calm abode
> I came, with Learning's meed not unbestowed;
> Whenas she twined a laurel round my brow,
> And met my kiss, and half returned my vow.

The best picture of Coleridge in his College rooms is to be
seen in a letter to the *Gentleman's Magazine*, written in 1834, just
after the poet's death, by his old school and undergraduate friend,
C. V. Le Grice:

> He was very studious, but his reading was desultory and capricious.
> He took little exercise for the sake of exercise; but he was ready at
> any time to unbend his mind in conversation, and for the sake of this
> his room (the ground-floor room on the right-hand of the staircase
> facing the great gate) was a constant rendezvous of conversation-
> loving friends. What evenings have I spent in those rooms! What
> little suppers, or sizings, as they were called, have I enjoyed, when
> Æschylus and Plato and Thucydides were pushed aside with a pile
> of lexicons, etc., to discuss the pamphlets of the day. Ever and anon
> a pamphlet issued from the pen of Burke. There was no need of
> having the book before us. Coleridge had read it in the morning,
> and in the evening he would repeat whole pages *verbatim*. Frend's
> trial was then in progress. Pamphlets swarmed from the press.
> Coleridge had read them all; and in the evening, with our negus, we
> had them *viva-voce* gloriously.

When Coleridge returned to College in October 1793, it was
to find that Frend had been excluded from it. Possibly that circumstance may have brought to a climax the dissatisfaction with
his position at Cambridge which had for some time been growing
in his breast. But there were other and more ordinary reasons
for that feeling. He had lost all ambition of obtaining University
honours, and he had landed himself seriously in debt—Gillman
says that it was by giving *carte blanche* to a tradesman for the
furnishing of his rooms, but his family ascribed it to dissipated
habits and, though Coleridge deeply and honestly resented their
suspicions, his admissions in later life show that they were not
entirely baseless. 'At Jesus', he writes, 'the heaviest of my offences
consisted in the folly of assuming the show of vices from which
I was all but free, and which, in the comparatively few exceptions,
left loathing and self-disgust in my mind'; and he argues the comparatively venial character of his transgressions from the fact that
his 'extravagations' did not lose him the esteem of a single fellow-
collegiate. Whatever the cause, shortly after the beginning of

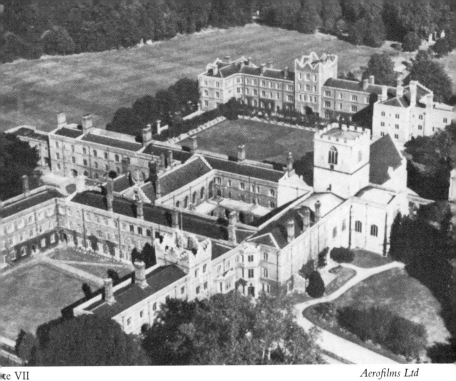

Aerofilms Ltd

Above: AERIAL VIEW OF THE COLLEGE (1947)

Below: THE 1638 RANGE (1959)

Country Life

Plate VIII

Above: ACKERMANN'S VIEW OF THE COLLEGE (1814)

Below: THE CLOISTERS AND CHAPEL (1959)

Stearn's, Cambrid

the October term it was discovered that Coleridge had vanished
from College without leaving a trace. The Rustat Book shows
that he resided only five weeks in that term. He was heavily
indebted to his tutor and, as weeks went by without news of
his whereabouts, the College was compelled to pass an order
(19 December 1793): 'Agreed, that if Coleridge, who has left College without leave, should not return within a month from this
day, and pay his debts to his tutor, or give reasonable security that
they should be paid, his name be taken off the Boards.' Just a
fortnight before the College passed this resolution its truant
scholar had enlisted in the 15th Dragoons in the assumed name of
Silas Tomkins Comberbacke.

With his regimental experiences we have no concern here; it
is enough to say that they were altogether unhappy. It was a
profound relief to him when his elder brother, George, who had
acted as his guardian since his father's death, procured his discharge. This was in April 1794 and Coleridge at once returned to
Jesus. On the 10th of that month it is recorded in the register,
'Coleridge admonitus est per Magistrum in praesentia Sociorum.'
In a letter to his brother Coleridge says that Dr Pearce behaved
with great asperity, but the Fellows were disposed to leniency.
He was sentenced to a month's confinement to the precincts of
the College, and to translate the works of Demetrius Phalereus
into English. Dr Pearce probably understood Coleridge better
than the fellows did—at least, Coleridge saw an implied compliment in the latter part of his sentence. 'The Demetrius is dry,
and utterly untransferable to *modern* use, and yet from the Doctor's
words I suspect that he wishes it to be a publication, as he has more
than once sent to know how I go on, and pressed me to exert
erudition in some notes and to write a preface.'

The May term of 1794 seems to have been got through with
great decorum. Coleridge politely informed his less studious
friends that he must drop their acquaintance, and possibly he did
so. Among Jesus friends with whom he remained more or less
intimate were George Caldwell (senior Chancellor's Medallist in
1795), John Brooke, and William John Lushington ('a man of
Briarean intellect'), all of them men of his own year, who

afterwards became Fellows of the College. To prove the sincerity of his resolutions he began a new Greek ode, which aimed at correctness and perspicuity, not genius.

But when he came back to Cambridge in the following September he came sevenfold possessed with the demons of revolt. 'Since I quitted this room', he writes to Southey, 'what and how important events have been evolved. America! Southey! Miss Fricker! . . . Pantisocracy! Oh, I shall have such a scheme of it.' The wonderful Pantisocratic project, an ideal society which was to recall Astraea to earth in a colony on the banks of the Susquehannah, was the talk of the University. Small wonder that Dr Pearce and the Fellows were seriously uneasy about this new extravagance of their favoured prodigal, and their annoyance was increased by the publication in October of '*The Fall of Robespierre*, An Historical Drama, by S. T. Coleridge', dedicated to a fellow-student at Jesus, H. Martin, who paid for its publication. Southey had written two acts of the play, but 'it would be ridiculous to put two names to *such* a work', said Coleridge, who was under no delusion as to its literary merits, though he was willing to appropriate to himself the notoriety which its authorship conferred. Dr Pearce took him severely to task for its supposed Jacobinism, but Coleridge cut short the discussion by assuring the Master that he mistook the matter altogether; that he was neither Jacobin nor Democrat, but a Pantisocrat. The College which had condemned Frend's pamphlet was scarcely likely to condone Coleridge's poem. Possibly there were threatenings of another convening. But, if so, Coleridge anticipated judgment by taking himself off—this time for good. The Rustat Book shows that he resided nine weeks in this term. On 16 December we hear of him in London in the company of Holcroft, Godwin, and the editor of the *Morning Chronicle*. On 17 December he has heard that 'they are making a row about him at Jesus'; but, indeed, the College showed extraordinary patience in its treatment of him. All through the Lent term of 1795 it kept the door open for his return, and duly credited him with £2 11s. 6d., as his stipend in that term as a non-resident Rustat scholar. At last, on 6 April they were forced to the melancholy conclusion: 'Whereas

Coleridge is still in arrears with his Tutors, and has been absent for some time from College (where we know not), it is ordered by the Master and Fellows that his name be taken off the boards on the 14th day of June next, unless cause be shown to the contrary, or some one of the Fellows declares himself willing to be his Tutor before that time, and that his present Tutors do endeavour to inform him of this order.'

So closed Coleridge's career at Jesus. It was forty years before he again set foot in Cambridge—namely, in 1833, on the occasion of a meeting of the British Association. 'My emotions', he wrote, 'at revisiting the University were at first overwhelming. I could not speak for an hour; yet my feelings, on the whole, were very pleasurable.' It is pleasant to think that in later life Coleridge always spoke with kindly and grateful feelings of his old College, and even in younger days no expression of anger or disdain towards it ever escaped him. It was otherwise with his friend Southey, whose lines on 'The Chapel Bell', written in undergraduate days, fiercely attack the 'snuffling, snaffling Fellows' and 'Romish rites' of Balliol, Oxford. Of his Jesus days, when he allowed himself to recall them, Coleridge never spoke but with affection. 'In an inauspicious hour I left the friendly cloisters and happy grove of quiet, ever-honoured Jesus College, Cambridge'; so he writes in his *Biographia Literaria*. And in *The Friend* he cannot pass the name of Dr Jortin, the biographer of Erasmus, without an appended note describing him as 'one of the many illustrious nurselings of the College to which I deem it no small honour to have belonged—Jesus, Cambridge'.

CHAPTER IX

THREE FRIENDS

MALTHUS, William Otter, and E. D. Clarke had recently taken their B.A. degree when Coleridge came to Jesus as a freshman in 1791. It does not appear that he made their acquaintance; at least, they were not of his 'set'. They were, all of them, admitted under the tutorship of Frend, but they do not seem to have been touched with his Unitarian and revolutionary sympathies. The three were fast friends while they were at Jesus, and their intimacy lasted through life. Otter, surviving the others, wrote the *Life and Remains* of Clarke (1829) and the biographical sketch of Malthus prefixed to the 1836 edition of the *Principles of Political Economy*. He was brother of Edward Otter, second Wrangler in 1786, who was one of the minority of Fellows who supported Frend in 1793. William was fourth Wrangler in 1790, became a Fellow in 1796, and remained in residence as tutor until 1804. He was the first Principal of King's College, London (appointed in 1828), became Bishop of Chichester in 1830, and died in 1840.

Thomas Robert Malthus, who was the eldest of the three, was admitted at Jesus in 1784. Everything in his antecedent life should have predisposed him to advanced views in religion and politics. He received his first teaching from his father, who had some acquaintance with Rousseau and was an ardent admirer of Condorcet and Godwin. Afterwards he became a pupil of Gilbert Wakefield at a Dissenting school at Warrington, and it was on Wakefield's advice that he was sent to Jesus. But so far was he from adopting the views of Wakefield and Frend that, after leaving Cambridge, he took Orders, and for a time held a country curacy. He was ninth Wrangler in 1788 and succeeded to a Fellowship in June 1793, three months after the College had passed sentence of expulsion on Frend. A controversy with

Godwin led to the publication (in 1798) of his *Essay on Population*. With the object of collecting information he travelled in 1799 to Hamburg and Sweden in company with three Jesus friends, William Otter, Clarke, and Cripps, and he added notes to the last volume of Clarke's *Travels*. In 1801 he met William Pitt at a supper at Jesus College lodge, when the conversation was chiefly directed to poetry and foreign politics. Possibly Malthus's Essay came in for discussion also; at least, Pitt became a convert to the economical views of Malthus, and probably helped him to the Professorship of History and Political Economy which he obtained at Haileybury College in 1805. Malthus married and resigned his Fellowship in 1804.

The name of Edward Daniel Clarke, 'Viator celeberrimus', is now scarcely remembered outside the walls of the College of which he was so distinguished an ornament in the first two decades of the last century. He was admitted in the same year as William Otter (1786) at the early age of sixteen. Dr Beadon, then Master, procured for him the place of chapel clerk, and on the death of his father, which happened in his second term, he was elected to a Rustat Scholarship. His undergraduate studies were of the discursive kind which characterized much of his work in later life. For mathematics he, like Coleridge, had no taste, and in the then constitution and practice of the College there was nothing to encourage the study of classics. 'All the classical lectures', says Otter, 'which were given during the three years of his residence were confined to the two little tracts of Tacitus, *De Moribus Germanorum* and *De Vita Agricolae*, and the only occasions upon which he was called upon to revise his classical knowledge were the delivery of a Latin declamation in the chapel once a year, and the usual examination of the Rustat scholars at Easter, for which latter no great preparation was required.' He found relaxation from the perfunctory studies of the place in the subjects of history, antiquities, and especially in English poetry, his favourite author being Gray. 'Distinguished members of the College'—the 'dons' we may suppose them to have been—'were glad to relax their severer labours in light and tasteful discussions' with him on such topics. The story which tells of the balloon made by him in his third year shows either that he found special favour with the powers that were, or that undergraduates were more emancipated from the conventions of discipline a hundred years ago than they are today:

> This balloon, which was magnificent in its size and splendid in its decorations, was constructed and manœuvred, from first to last, entirely by himself. It was the contrivance of many anxious thoughts, and the labour of many weeks, to bring it to what he wished; and when at last it was completed to his satisfaction, and had been suspended for some days in the College Hall, of which it occupied the whole height, he announced a time for its ascension. There was nothing at that period very new in balloons[1] or very curious in the species which he had adopted; but by some means he had contrived to disseminate not only within the walls of his own College, but throughout the whole University, a prodigious curiosity respecting the fate of his experiment. On the day appointed a vast concourse of people was assembled, both within and around the College; and the balloon, having been brought to its station (the grass-plot within the cloisters) was happily launched by himself, amidst the applause of all ranks and degrees of gownsmen, who had crowded the roof as well as the area of the cloisters, and filled the contiguous apartments of the Master's lodge. The whole scene, in short, succeeded to his utmost wish; nor is it easy to forget the delight which flashed from his eye and the triumphant wave of his cap when the machine, with its little freight (a kitten), having cleared the College battlements, was seen soaring in full security over the towers of the great gate. Its course was followed on horseback by several persons, who had voluntarily undertaken to recover it; and all went home delighted with an exhibition upon which nobody would have ventured in such a place but himself.

Clarke's humble attainments in mathematics were rewarded by a place among the junior Optimes in the Tripos of 1790. For the time this inglorious result closed his connexion with the College. He became private tutor to a nephew of the Duke of Dorset, and in 1792 accompanied Lord Berwick (afterwards Ambassador

[1] Mr Astley, famous for his circus at Westminster Bridge, sent up two balloons from Emmanuel College Close in 1784, and in 1786 there was an ascent from the grounds of Trinity Hall.

at the Court of Naples), who was of Clarke's year at Jesus, on a
Continental tour, remaining abroad, with only a few weeks'
interval, until the summer of 1794. Afterwards he acted as tutor
in the families of various titled people, and travelled with his
pupils in Scotland and Wales. So it came about that he never met
Coleridge at Jesus. He was elected to a Fellowship in June 1795,
and returned to College as Bursar in 1798. To Clarke's restless
spirit the routine of College life was supremely distasteful. For
a time he took up the study of chemistry with some enthusiasm,
but he was delighted when an opportunity presented itself of
renewing his foreign travels. The funds for doing so were provided by a Fellow-Commoner of the College, John Martin Cripps,
who had lately succeeded to property near Clarke's home in
Sussex. He was warmly attached to Clarke and came to Cambridge with him in 1798 with the object of supplying, under his
tuition, the defects of a limited education. Starting in May 1799,
they were accompanied through North Germany and Sweden
by William Otter and Malthus, and afterwards prolonged their
tour through Russia to Palestine, Egypt, Turkey, and Greece,
returning to Cambridge in October, 1802.

> In the course of this tour [says Gunning], Clark wrote repeatedly to
> his Cambridge friends. His letters were always lively, and his des-
> criptions very graphic. The country he travelled through being
> little known, they excited the greatest attention. I recollect dining
> with Outram (the Public Orator), when a packet arrived from
> Clarke. The first letter began with these words: 'Here I am, eating
> strawberries within the Arctic Circle.' We were so intent on his
> dessert that we forgot our own.

The interest which his letters aroused was more than sustained
when he brought with him to Cambridge the collections, scientific
and archaeological, which he had formed during his travels. His
manuscripts, including an early Plato from Patmos, went to the
Bodleian Library at Oxford; his coins were sold to a private
collector; of the marbles some were secured by the British
Museum, others were presented to the University of Cambridge.
Among the latter was the celebrated Cistophorus from Eleusis,
which Clarke, with more enthusiasm than knowledge, affirmed

to be a 'Ceres'; it is now in the Fitzwilliam Museum. It excited extraordinary interest; artists and men of letters came from far to see it. 'As for our Master,' wrote Clarke, 'he pulls off his gown and dances round it.' The University conferred on Clarke the degree of LL.D., and on Cripps that of M.A. One monument of Clarke's Oriental travels survives to perpetuate his memory in his own College—the fine Oriental plane which is the chief feature of the Fellows' garden. As an inscription on a plate affixed to its trunk records, the seeds were brought from Thermopylae and planted there by Clarke himself in 1802.

Clarke settled down quietly in College to arrange his collections and to write the six volumes of his Travels, the first of which appeared in 1812. Some verses, addressed by him to Otter, describe his College rooms—on the first floor of the staircase opposite the Gate, Coleridge's staircase—hung with art treasures collected at home and abroad.

> Say, will your thoughts to Rhadegunda roam,
> And view the wanderer in his peaceful home?
> While Fancy, waking, paints the well-known scene:
> The walls monastic, and the college green;
> The chamber hung with painting's deathless dyes,
> Where breathing canvas bids old Shakespeare rise;
> The tints which Venice from a Titian drew,
> De Heem's warm touch and Herman's silver hue, etc.

By the supposed portrait of Shakespeare there hangs a tale. Clarke bought it for a guinea of a shoemaker, in whose shop he found it covered with dirt. He had it cleaned and, having persuaded himself that it was a portrait of Shakespeare by Mark Garrard, he put it in a magnificent frame and obtained permission to exhibit it in the University Library. Kerrich, the principal librarian, who was an authority on painting, pronounced it to be a portrait of an Elector Palatine; but so great was the influence of Clarke's name that on the first day of the exhibition upwards of 3,000 persons went to see it. Clarke wrote a small pamphlet to prove that it was an original Shakespeare. Finally, however, he made a present of it to the shoemaker of whom he purchased it.

In the summer of 1803 the threat of a French invasion produced a remarkable outburst of patriotic spirit throughout the nation, and volunteer corps for the defence of the country were enrolled in all parts of England. Cambridgeshire provided 2,886 volunteers, for whose equipment upwards of £6,000 was locally subscribed, the University contributing £1,000. A University corps, consisting of four companies of light infantry, including gownsmen of every rank and degree, was enrolled. The Heads and tutors allowed one hour each day for the purpose of drill, and a Grace was passed allowing the term to students of the University who might be absent on military service. At each of the crises, 1803, 1859, and 1899, Jesus answered the call to arms with enthusiasm, and 'dons and undergraduates vied with one another in making themselves efficient volunteers'. In 1803 the 'dons' set a particularly good example. Clergymen in those days were not allowed to bear arms, but Otter, the tutor, was on the committee, and twenty-one out of the 180 members of the corps came from Jesus. Clarke threw himself with characteristic impetuosity into the volunteering business. A letter of his, addressed to a College friend and dated 15 November, 1803, gives an interesting picture of the enthusiasm awakened in the University, and of the healthy unanimity which animated the College in this as well as other matters.

> I am just come from practising the light infantry manœuvres, over all the hedges and ditches, towards Madingley, wet, muddy, and oozing at every pore. Malthus left me this morning; but still new lions pour in—*n'importe!* The Bursar talks of building a new Combination Room; and certainly we must have a new table in the Hall —we have not room even for the members of the College, and still less for lions, who always occupy considerable space. . . . At present nothing is talked of in Cambridge but the drill—who shoulders best, and who trod down Beverley's heels in close marching. Yesterday we had a sort of sham fight on Parker's Piece, and they all allow we do better than the Town Volunteers. We paraded through the streets from Clare Hall to Parker's Piece with a full band of music. The corps is intended as a nursery of corps, to supply the nation with officers and drill-serjeants. We are all officers in turn. At present the corps consists of four companies of thirty

men in each, commanded by Captain Bircham as general, and by Thackery, myself, Johnson, and Dr Sill, with covering serjeants who succeed to our posts when we fall into the ranks.

In 1805 Clarke succeeded his friend Otter in the office of Senior Tutor, but vacated both that and his Fellowship by marriage in the following year. He was ordained in 1805 by his old friend, Dr Beadon, Bishop of Bath and Wells, and was instituted shortly after to the College living of Harlton. Harlton, like other College livings near Cambridge, had then no parsonage, and Clarke lived first in Cambridge, afterwards at Anstey Hall, Trumpington. In 1807 he began his celebrated courses of lectures on mineralogy, a subject in which he had always taken a great, if not profoundly scientific, interest, and to illustrate which he had made large collections during his travels. The study of science was then at an extremely low ebb in the University; mineralogy in particular was little known or studied. Scientific accuracy was not looked for, nor did Clarke pretend to it; but his hearers were charmed with the brilliance of his imagination and the eloquence of his digressions.[1] A contemporary *jeu d'esprit*, attributed to Smyth, Professor of History, plays on the discursiveness of Clarke's treatment of the subject. Some verses may be quoted:

> I sing of a Tutor renown'd
> Who went roving and raving for knowledge,
>   And gather'd it all the world round,
> And brought it in boxes to College;
>   And because Mathematics was clear—
> Too clear for our Metaphysicians—
>   Introduced Dr Gall, as I hear,
> To enlighten his academicians.
>
>   His pupils flock'd eagerly round,
> When they heard there was nothing to bore 'em;
>   But guess their surprise when they found
> A lot of old skulls placed before 'em.

[1] He got the name of 'Stone' Clarke, to distinguish him from 'Bone' Clark, the anatomy Professor, and 'Tone' Clarke, otherwise John Clarke (afterwards Clarke-Whitfield), Professor of Music.

Astonish'd, confused, and perplext,
They stared at their Lecturer able,
And the freshmen expected that next
Old Nick would pop up through the table.

*   *   *   *   *

And *Flaxman* was now at the door
To talk of the *Ceres* divine;
And Bircham to settle the corps,
And Caldwell to sell him bad wine.
In the court were five lions from town,
And a message came hot from the Master;
So that round about, upstairs and down,
The plot thicken'd faster and faster.

In 1808, by a Grace of the Senate, Clarke was made the first
Professor of Mineralogy. In 1817 he was elected University
Librarian—such was his popularity that no candidate for the office
appeared against him. He held both appointments until his death
in 1822. He was buried in the College chapel, and a monument
there erected by his fellow-collegians bears his medallion portrait.
His friend, Dr Pearce, had passed away two years before him.

No additions were made to the College buildings during the
Masterships of Dr Beadon and Dr Pearce, and such alterations as
were introduced had for their single object the domestic comfort
of the residents. From the Norman arcades in the chapel to the
Palladian embellishments of the days of Dr Ashton, Jesus College
in the middle of the eighteenth century presented a series of
architectural types more complete than any other College in the
University. For three quarters of a century after that time the
art of architectural design at Cambridge was practically dead and,
except as destroyers, the decadent successors of Gibbs and Hawks-
moor left little substantial evidence of their workmanship. What
they did at Jesus was chiefly directed to internal decoration and
fittings. About the year 1762 the Combination Room was wainscoted, in consequence of a gift of £100 from Lord Middleton;
the architect employed was 'the ingenious' Mr Essex. About the
same year the cloister court was 'beautified and rendered more

open and airy' by the same architect. This was effected by substituting plain arches rising from the ground for the square-headed Tudor windows, each of three lights, which in Loggan's design are shown in the walls enclosing the grass-plot. The same desire for additional light induced the Master and Fellows in 1801 to lengthen the windows of the Hall by lowering the sills to the level of the top of the panelling of the side walls. In the chapel the Perpendicular eastern window of the chancel was altered by Essex during Dr Beadon's Mastership.

More important work was undertaken after 1788, in consequence of a gift of £200 by Mr Tyrwhitt 'for defraying the expense of repairing and fitting up the Inside of the College Chapel'. Tyrwhitt had parted company with the Church, and had ceased to attend services in the College chapel several years before this time, and his benefaction is significant of his wide tolerance and the importance which he attached to a religious basis in college education. It is needless to say that the reparations were carried out without the slightest regard for architectural congruity or historical associations. But credit is due to Tyrwhitt for undertaking a work which the neglect of a century had made in some form absolutely necessary. The chapel, being unwarmed, must have suffered badly from damp, and was, no doubt, cold and draughty; the woodwork of stalls and chancel screen was battered and decayed; and if any justification had been thought necessary for veneering the old fabric with classical ornament, it already existed in the wainscoting of the east end of the chancel, which had been done in 1679. No details of the work carried out in consequence of Tyrwhitt's benefaction are given in the Audit Book; but it appears that in the years 1789–92 the College spent a sum of £817, including Tyrwhitt's gift, on the work in the chapel. The old stalls were entirely removed, and painted deal seats of an inferior 'Grecian' design were substituted for them. Portions of the old woodwork of the stalls and screen were sold to the carpenter employed by the College; some part was bought by the Rev. Robert Masters, the antiquary and historian of Corpus. It is interesting to know that he paid five and a half guineas for it. It was, fortunately, preserved in Landbeach

Church, of which he was rector. Nearly a century later, in 1878, the College repurchased a portion of it from the parish. A fine door of carved oak, which came from Landbeach and appears to have been brought thither from Jesus Chapel, is now in the south transept of Ely Cathedral. The pulpit and parts of the screen are still at Landbeach. The chancel walls were reduced to one uniform yellow colour, with a band of black at the base. The eastern arch of the tower was walled up, and on the side of it next the chancel a gallery was placed, containing a pew for the Master's family. They entered from the Master's garden through a classical doorway, still to be seen on the outer wall at the south-eastern angle of the tower. The fifteenth-century roof of the chancel and the fine arcade in the triforium of the tower were concealed by plain and flat plaster ceilings. Some years later, in 1815, in consequence of another gift of £400 by Mr Tyrwhitt, the outer walls, which in parts were much decayed and uneven in surface, were faced with Roman cement 'coloured and finished as stonework', and the battlements and mouldings were repaired in the same economical material. The general effect of these alterations was regarded at the time with much complacency; the chancel in particular was considered to have 'an air of great elegance and beauty'.

This 'restoration' of Jesus Chapel was one of the last efforts at Cambridge of the school of correctness and classicism. Almost before its completion the first gropings after Gothic began. A letter in the *Gentleman's Magazine* of September 1815 states that:

The Chapel is undergoing a thorough repair, and is tastefully painting in the chaste style of antient wainscoting, by a Gentleman who has evidenced much ability in this peculiar line of his profession, and, when completed, will present an elegant model of Gothick Architecture.

When the wainscot was removed for painting and repair, the beautiful thirteenth-century piscina in the chancel was discovered. It is indicative of an altered feeling with regard to the artistic legacies of the past that its beauty was at once recognized, and it was not covered up again. Mr Hustler, the Bursar, restored the

decayed portions at his own expense. He also filled the east
window with portraits and armorial bearings in painted glass.
Mr Hustler, as we shall see in the next chapter, was the forerunner
of the ecclesiological revival which was so warmly taken up at
Jesus in the middle years of last century.

The *Reminiscences* of Henry Gunning of Christ's, the well-
known Esquire Bedell, present a series of lifelike pictures of men
and manners at Cambridge in the period covered by the Masterships of Dr Beadon and Dr Pearce. That period of forty years
witnessed a complete revolution, not only in the manners of undergraduates and 'dons', but in the attitude of the University to
the outer world. The change was brought about partly by the
Napoleonic wars, but was due in a greater degree to improved
methods of communication. When Gunning came up as a freshman in 1784 it was still the fashion for Fellows of colleges to
reside throughout vacations; many of them never slept outside
the University for years together. 'The last of this class was Mr
Burrell, the Bursar of Catherine Hall, who used to take his daily
walk in what is called "The Grove", and who never travelled
further than the Senate House, except once during the long vaca-
tion, when the Master of the College prevailed upon him to walk
half-way to Grantchester.' Times had altered when Dr Farmer
of Emmanuel, entering the vestry of St Mary's on Ascension
Day, boasted that at three o'clock the same morning he had been
blowing his pipe with the Worshipful Company of Pewterers.
When such rapid locomotion became possible the old secluded
life and circumscription of thought came to an abrupt end. The
prescribed studies of the place went on in much the same grooves;
indeed, these grooves were narrowed by the absorbing attention
paid to mathematics in the schools. But the degree and the
University rewards which it brought ceased to be the be-all and
the end-all of the thoughts of the more intelligent undergraduates
and their teachers, and books were appreciated in proportion as
they explained life. In the middle of the century the Fellows of
Jesus were commenting on Hierocles and Justin Martyr; before
its end the subjects which engrossed them were political economy
and travel. Coleridge and Sterne were not ordinary under-

graduates, and Cambridge influences played, no doubt, a minor part in the moulding of their abnormal genius. But they both browsed among books at Jesus, and it is not without significance that Sterne found his mental pabulum in medieval Latinists, while Coleridge looked for it in Burke, Priestley, and Bowles.

In the outward tokens of civilization the town of Cambridge at the end of the eighteenth century had made little advance on the days of Elizabeth. Gunning speaks feelingly of the horrible discomforts of its unpaved and unlighted streets. The undergraduates, he says, when encountered in the dark, were scarcely less ferocious than the members of the 'Mohock and Sweating Clubs'. Yet townspeople feared that if the streets were lighted town-and-gown fights would recur, since in the darkness persons, not being able to recognize each other, more frequently passed without quarrelling. Gas was not introduced at Cambridge until 1823; four gas-lamps were put up at Jesus that year—one at each end of 'the Chimney,' one in the first court, and one in 'Pump' court. A poem written by E. D. Clarke in his undergraduate days speaks of

> the cold cloister at the midnight hour,
> When lamps dim glimmering cast a misty light,

the lamps in question being the lineal representatives of the 'great and little lanthorns' which served the cloister in Elizabethan times. Staircases, except by private enterprise, were not lighted at all, as appears from a story told by Gunning of one Castley, a Fellow of the College, nicknamed from his unprepossessing appearance 'Ghastly'.

Castley was a man of very penurious habits, of which the following may be taken as an illustration: John Brooke (a fellow), whose rooms were on the same staircase, proposed that they should furnish a lamp at their mutual charges, to prevent the recurrence of much inconvenience to which they had been subjected of an evening from the darkness of the staircase. Castley said he considered it a piece of needless extravagance; but after a time he agreed to the proposition, with the condition that he should be allowed to furnish the oil on alternate nights, for he thought the porter, whom Brooke had proposed to employ, would charge too much. This was agreed to. To Brooke's great surprise he frequently found the lamp on Castley's nights burning brightly at a late hour, whereas when the porter lighted it on his nights, it had burnt out much earlier. One evening, when Brooke was reading in his room, with his door *sported*, he heard *a very quiet step* on the landing-place; and, opening his door *gently*, he surprised Castley in the very act of puffing out the lamp, by which dexterous manœuvre, on alternate nights, he was enabled to shirk the expense of providing oil!

The dinner hour was about one o'clock. Wakefield deplored that, since his undergraduate days, the time had been made so late; in consequence, the practice of taking afternoon tea had fallen into neglect, and the labours of the day were considered to be ended at dinner-time. Suppers and sizing parties filled up the evening, a sizing party differing from a supper in this, that at the former each guest contributed his share to the common meal. At eight o'clock the 'sizing bell' rang to signify that the 'sizing bill' was ready. Most colleges had a 'club', which met on stated nights each week in the Combination Room. That at Jesus is frequently mentioned in Clarke's letters. Undergraduates were admitted to it, and card-games were played, but play for high points was discountenanced. Pipes and tobacco were regularly provided for College feasts until the end of the period, but by a College order the payment for pipes was discontinued in 1822.

The barber was still an important functionary. His shop was originally on the ground-floor of the staircase next the porter's lodge. Possibly it had been given up in 1788, when the College passed an order 'that no Barber or Hairdresser be permitted to remain in College on a Sunday after the ceasing of St Mary's bell in the morning'.

CHAPTER X

THE GOTHIC RENASCENCE

DR WILLIAM FRENCH, who was Dr Pearce's successor in the Mastership (1820), was originally of Caius, graduated there as second Wrangler in 1811, and soon after became Fellow and tutor of Pembroke, which college had already supplied Jesus with three Masters. He owed his appointment to his friendship with Bishop Sparke of Ely, in whose family he had been a private tutor, and through the good offices of the same patron he obtained an Ely canonry in 1832. His abilities were of a respectable order; he published new translations of the Proverbs (in 1831) and of the Psalms (in 1842), and by his business capacity he greatly improved the finances of the College. But he was lacking in the social gifts of his two predecessors, and his magisterial formality of manner was not calculated to attract or inspire. The twenty-nine years of his reign witnessed a gradual and melancholy decline from the high and palmy state which the College held when he became Master. Numbers fell heavily; discipline and morals sank to a very low ebb; and the inefficiency of the tutors and indolence of their pupils is indicated by the fact that in the whole period only two Jesus men were placed among the first ten Wranglers, and seven only gained a first class in the Classical Tripos.

At first everything promised well for the College under its new Head. Its numbers had increased with extraordinary rapidity under Dr Pearce—far more rapidly than those of the University generally. The total of admissions in the five years ending in 1821 was 168—four times as many as in the first five years of Dr Pearce's rule, seven times as many as they had been in 1760–4. And with increased numbers came a marked change in the social quality of the undergraduates; whereas the sizars admitted in 1817–21 had dwindled to eleven in all, the Fellow-Commoners had increased to thirty-five. The change was certainly not without its disadvantages. The class of Fellow-Commoners—'Empty Bottles', as they were nicknamed—had, says the *Gradus ad Cantabrigiam*, 'a kind of prescriptive right to idleness, and fashion has inspired it with an habitual contempt for discipline'.[1] That they gave a non-reading tone to the College there can be no doubt. Two-thirds of the undergraduates never attained the B.A. degree. The proportion of those who took Orders was at the same time very much reduced. In the eighteenth century, as we have seen, almost every undergraduate of the College applied for testimonial letters; in 1817–21 only one-third of them did so.

It was, of course, impossible for the College to find rooms within its walls for its overflowing numbers. A College order of 1812 is the first indication that students *in statu pupillari* were permitted to 'keep' in lodgings. In 1822 the Master and Fellows resolved that 'owing to the great Increase in the Numbers of Members of the College it would be highly desirable to add to the present Buildings', and contracted with a builder for the erection of twelve additional sets of rooms in Pump Court. No architect was employed, but the builder was instructed to copy the pattern of the adjoining building next the Hall. Staircase 'K' (which was 'L' until 1922) was the nondescript result of these conditions. If artistically unlovely, it certainly has the merit of being commodious.

The long rule of Dr French was illuminated by few names of eminence among the undergraduates of the College. The names of those few were for the most part absent from the honour lists. Their genius, in whatever shape it showed itself, was certainly not the outcome of any rigorous pressure into academic moulds.

Charles Austin (adm. 1819), 'whose fame would now be more in proportion to his extraordinary abilities had not his unparalleled success as an advocate tempted him, before his days, to retire from the toils of a career of whose rewards he had had enough,' deserves mention here, not so much for his triumphs in

---

[1] Felix Vaughan, of Jesus, who was a senior Optime in the Tripos of 1790, is said to have been the first Fellow-Commoner in the University who took a degree in honours.

later life at the Parliamentary Bar as for his association in undergraduate days with T. B. Macaulay. Sir G. O. Trevelyan is
witness for the vivid impression which he left on his contemporaries:

> With his vigour and fervour, his depth of knowledge and breadth
> of humour, his close reasoning illustrated by an expansive imagina-
> tion—set off, as those gifts were, by the advantage, at that period of
> life so irresistible, of some experience of the world at home and
> abroad—Austin was indeed a king among his fellows—

> 'Grave, sedate,
> And (if the looks may indicate the age),
> Our senior some few years: no keener wit,
> No intellect more subtle, none more bold,
> Was found in all our host.'

So writes Moultrie, and the testimony of his verse is borne out by
John Stuart Mill's prose. 'The impression he gave was that of bound-
less strength, together with talents, which, combined with such
apparent force of will and character, seemed capable of dominating
the world.' He certainly was the only man who ever succeeded in
dominating Macaulay. Brimming over with ideas that were soon to
be known by the name of Utilitarian, a panegyrist of American
institutions and an unsparing assailant of ecclesiastical endowments
and hereditary privileges, he effectually cured the young undergraduate of his Tory opinions, which were never more than skin
deep, and brought him nearer to Radicalism than he ever was before
or since. . . . . To this hour men may be found in remote parsonages
who mildly resent the fascination which Austin of Jesus exercised
over Macaulay of Trinity.

George Stovin Venables (adm. 1828) was fifth in the first class
of the Classical Tripos of 1832—the list of that year being made
illustrious by the names of Professor Lushington, Richard Shilleto,
and W. H. Thompson, who were placed above him. He also
won the Chancellor's Medal for English verse in 1831. He was
elected to a Fellowship and for a short time was tutor of the College. In 1836 he followed Austin to the Parliamentary Bar, and
his remarkable literary gifts found expression only in anonymous

journalism, notably in *The Times*, for which, during a long series of years, he wrote the 'Annual Summary of Events', and in the *Saturday Review*, which he helped to found. He will be better remembered as one of a group of literary giants of the Victorian era, and as the original from whom Thackeray is said to have drawn his character of George Warrington. Of him Leslie Stephen writes:

> In the company of such men as Mr Thackeray, Lord Houghton, Mr Spedding, Lord Tennyson, Mr Brookfield, and many others not less well known he would be the life and soul of the party, full of fun, revelling in anecdotes, breaking out into Homeric laughter over jokes, the sarcastic wit of which Swift would have been proud of, though he might have sneered at their freedom from envy, hatred, malice, and all uncharitableness.

Thomas Attwood Walmisley, who was Professor of Music from 1836 to 1856, migrated from Corpus to Jesus in 1834 and took the B.A. degree in 1838. He had taken the degree of Mus. Bac. before he came to the College and had been organist at Trinity and at St John's since 1833. His anthem, 'Ponder my words', was written for the reopening of Jesus College Chapel in 1849.

James Orchard Halliwell, afterwards Halliwell-Phillipps, the Shakespearian scholar, migrated to Jesus from Trinity in 1838. He gained a scholarship and was made librarian. He catalogued the manuscripts in the Library and edited, with singular careless-ness, Sherman's *Historia*. He projected the Cambridge Anti-quarian Society, and was its first secretary. Before his nineteenth birthday he was elected a Fellow of the Royal Society. He left Cambridge without a degree in 1840.

In 1821 the society took the first step towards a reformation of its statutes. Up to this time the College had been governed by the code of Bishop West as amended by the Commissioners of 1549 and 1559. One of West's statutes prescribed that there should not be at the same time two Fellows of the same county and that the number of Fellows should be equally divided between natives of the northern and the southern parts of England. These restrictions had not been strictly observed, and there are several instances in the seventeenth and eighteenth centuries of elections to Fellowships of persons who were not natives of England. Royal mandates or the Visitor's licence had been frequently employed to overcome the difficulties which arose. John North, in 1666, had been put by mandate into a northern Fellowship, though he was a southern man. 'It is strange', said the Visitor, Bishop Wren, 'that Mr North should be looked upon as a northern man, who had nothing north about him but his name.' King Charles I, by letters patent in 1635, relaxed the statute so far as restriction to county was concerned, but retained the distinction between north and south. With the consent of the Visitor and the approval of the King in Council a new statute was made, which extended the choice of Fellows to all British subjects.

In 1837 the society proceeded further in the path of reform by appointing a committee of its members to examine the College statutes, with the view of applying to the proper authorities for the abolition of such statutes as had fallen into desuetude, and for the re-formation of such as were not exactly observed. The result of this examination was a recension of the statutes generally, which obtained the sanction of the Visitor, Bishop Allen, and the Privy Council in 1841. Many of the provisions of the old statutes which time had rendered inoperative were allowed to remain, but some important changes in the constitution of the College were introduced. In the first place, six only of the Fellows were henceforth required to be in Orders. The Elizabethan statutes assigned twelve Fellows to the study of Theology, and four to that of Civil Law. Hitherto, by a convenient fiction, lay Fellows had been regarded as students of Civil Law, though since the seventeenth century few of them took degrees in it. Secondly, a new statute gave recognition to the principle of payment of 'dividends' to the Master and Fellows. The Elizabethan statutes allowed them only certain fixed payments, and until 1841 the only sanction for the payment of dividends was the College order passed in the days of Dr Sterne. The result of this and other changes introduced in the new statutes was a great simplification of the Bursar's accounts.

In other respects the statutes were adapted to altered methods of College instruction for University degrees. The old disputations, presided over by the Dean, gave place in the new code to lectures on Theology, Metaphysics, Philosophy, Logic, Mathematics, and Literae Humaniores. It is to be doubted whether the College really undertook teaching in all these subjects. It is equally to be doubted whether, under the conditions presented by the Tripos examination system, it was possible to exact a strict compliance with the new ordinance requiring the Lector Publicus to examine all questionists in order to determine their fitness *ad respondendum quaestioni*. A new statute, *De divinis officiis*, supplied a somewhat remarkable omission. The Elizabethan code provided for services in the chapel on Sundays and saints' days only, and on those days only were the Fellows required to attend. On ordinary week-days 'the boys'—the word is a survival from Stanley's statutes—were to assemble in the chapel once daily, and there to repeat the Apostles' Creed, the Ten Commandments, and the Lord's Prayer, in English or Latin, and on Fridays to chant the Litany.[1] The new statute provided for daily services, morning and evening, and for the celebration of the Eucharist at least once in each term, as well as at the three principal festivals.

Two benefactions received during Dr French's Mastership should be mentioned here. The Rev. Edward Otter, Fellow (nephew of the Bishop), gave the proceeds of his Fellowship for the years 1839 and 1840, amounting to £308, to found a prize 'for encouraging amongst the undergraduates application to Scriptural study'. In 1839 the College received a bequest of £6,000 from Mrs Sarah Jones for founding three by-Fellowships in memory of the Rev. Thomas Dummer Ley, formerly a member of the College. By the statutes of 1861 the endowment of the Ley by-Fellowships was applied to the maintenance of open scholarships.

The restoration of the chapel was the great achievement of Dr French's Mastership—a work with which the Master's name deserves to be associated, as he was one of the first to interest

---

[1] But see p. 92, where John Strype says they attended chapel twice daily.

himself in it. Almost his last appearance in the chapel was on the occasion of its reopening, on All Saints' Day, 1849, and his monument there is the triplet in the eastern wall, built at his expense and, after his death, filled by his widow with stained glass to his memory. Jesus was almost the first College to apply itself to that work of restoration which became so universal in the following generation, and which did so much to alter the face of Cambridge, by no means always on principles that were sound or with results that were satisfactory. In the forties of the last century restoration might well have been a very disastrous affair. So far the highest efforts of revived Gothicism at Cambridge had been Wilkins's erections at King's, Corpus, and Trinity, and Rickman's new buildings at St John's; and Sidney afforded a recent (1832) and melancholy illustration of the imprudence of translating an old building into a style supposed to be medieval. It was the extreme good fortune of Jesus that the scheme for restoring the chapel, first mooted about 1832, bore no fruit until 1845, and that the architect whom the society then called in to their assistance was Pugin.

Some experimental work had been started in the chapel in 1828; and, though now forgotten, it aroused much interest at the time and gave the first suggestion for the more extensive operations of 1845-9. In the summer of the year mentioned, Charles Green, the Dean, opened out the westernmost of the five lancets in the north wall of the chancel, which had hitherto been blocked, and discovered the blind half-arch which adjoins it, and at the same time removed the wainscoting of 1679. His letters to Dr French are the first indication of an awakened appreciation of the native beauties of the chapel and a consciousness of the degradation to which it had been subjected in recent times. The contrast between the Early English part and the eastern window —the work of Essex, recently embellished with stained glass by William Hustler—he describes as 'appauling' [sic]. 'I trust', he writes, 'we shall have great satisfaction when the work is completed. These parts of the chapel will be restored to their pristine beauty. We have not stirred a single stone without authority.'

Charles Green's restoration was carried no further at the time;

but interest in the subject was kept awake by two legacies, each of £100, from William Hustler and Joseph Studholme, Fellows, who died in 1832, their bequests being 'in aid of a fund for the restoration of the Chapel'. At the audit of December 1844 these sums, with accumulated interest, amounted to £260. Thereupon, 'in consideration of the many years which must elapse before this fund could be adequate to the object proposed, and of the very deep interest taken in the subject by many members of the College', the Master and Fellows resolved to commence the work at once. They voted a sum of £500 for the purpose, and issued an appeal to members of the College. This appeal was sent out by the Dean, the Rev. John Gibson, to whose consummate taste and judgment the successful accomplishment of the enterprise was in large measure due. With his name will always be associated that of the Rev. Osmond Fisher. Gibson and Fisher were then junior Fellows, filled with the enthusiasms inspired by the Oxford Movement, who saw in the embellishment of the chapel and its services the means of awakening the College from its spiritual torpor. Their views were not altogether in harmony with those of the older Laodicean members of the society, or with the pronounced Evangelicalism of Dr Corrie, who succeeded Dr French as Master. But they made a profound impression on many of the undergraduates and, for the time, gave the College a distinctly High Anglican impress—moderate indeed, but conspicuously contrasted with the indifferentism which then characterized Cambridge in religious matters. The introduction of an organ, a trained choir of boys, and Gregorian chanting, was then a singularity in college chapels, unknown except at King's and Trinity and, on Sundays and saints' days, at St John's.[1] Sermons, equally a novelty, were introduced as a regular usage in Dr Corrie's Mastership, when Osmond Fisher was Dean.

In association with the two Fellows above named, a principal part in the restoration was taken by a Fellow-Commoner of the College, Mr (afterwards Sir John) Sutton (adm. 1840). He did not read for a degree but, being an accomplished musician,

---

[1] Intoned services were first introduced by Osmond Fisher in the Hall while the chapel was under restoration.

acted as organist for some years and published a book of anthems
for use in the chapel. He started the choir school, and taught the
boys himself, in general subjects as well as in music, remaining
in residence during vacations for that purpose. He was much
under the influence of Pugin—like whom he became, at a later
time, a Roman Catholic—and it was on his advice that Pugin's
services were engaged by the College. Sutton himself paid for
the screen, the organ, and the lectern, as well as for Pugin's
designs for the roof and floor. Restoration actually began in 1846,
when the lath-and-plaster partition wall filling the eastern tower
arch was taken down. An organ chamber on the north side of
the choir was built on the foundations, discovered under the soil,
of a chapel of nunnery date. Two thirteenth-century arches,
which were found complete in the masonry of the wall next the
choir, were opened out. Two other arches, communicating with
the north transept, were likewise opened, but it was found necessary to fill them with heavy tracery in order to give stability to
the tower. In the southern wall of the choir two arches were discovered opposite and corresponding to those on the northern
side, and it was at first proposed to open them and re-erect on this
side the chapel which existed there in nunnery days. Want of
funds prevented this plan from being carried out, as it may be
hoped that it hereafter may be. Its execution would greatly add
to the dignity of the chapel.

The architect employed so far had been Anthony Salvin but,
as the College was not satisfied with his plans, he was asked to
withdraw, and after an interval, during which Gibson and his
colleagues took the work into their own hands, Pugin was
brought in to complete the restoration. In the north transept the
Norman triplet in the north wall was discovered and the wall
repaired. The floor concealing the triforium in the tower was
removed. The tower piers were strengthened, and the mouldings
were cleared and repaired. In the choir the great eastern window
and the upper part of the wall containing it were entirely removed.
It must be borne in mind that this window and wall had been so
frequently tampered with that Alcock's design had been already
destroyed. A series of three lancets with blank intervening panels

was placed in the wall, their form and arrangement being suggested by remains discovered in the masonry. Above them was added a cinquefoil window, designed by Pugin. The side walls were lowered to their original height, and a new roof, following the pitch of the first pointed roof, as indicated by the water-line on the tower, was raised on them. The timber of Alcock's low-pitched roof was employed in forming the visible parts of the new one. The stalls were designed chiefly by Gibson and Fisher with the help of Rattee. They took their suggestions from the stalls at St John's (see p. 27), from panelling at Histon, from the remains at Landbeach, and from two book-board ends which were preserved in the lodge. The screen, Gothic altar-table and the standard candlesticks were designed by Pugin. He also furnished the design for the floor, in which he introduced the marble of the pavement laid down in 1675, intermixed with encaustic tiles.

On All Saints' Day, 1849, the chapel was reopened with a full choral service, 'said and sung', as a contemporary account says, 'in the manner of our cathedral churches, as was the case originally in all college chapels in the University'. The outlay up to December 1848 was £3,189, of which sum £1,119 had been obtained by subscriptions, and the rest was contributed by the College.

From 1849 Onwards

PART TWO

From 1849 Onwards

CHAPTER XI

THE MID-VICTORIAN REVOLUTION

In December 1849 the Bishop of Ely appointed a new Master of Jesus, in succession to William French, who had died a few days after the reopening of the College chapel. His nominee was George John Elwes Corrie, thirtieth Master of the College and the first of the line to possess more than one Christian name. The son of a Lincolnshire country parson, he had been an undergraduate at St Catharine's and a Fellow there. Undistinguished as a scholar, he was a man of deep if narrow piety, a die-hard Tory and a die-hard Anglican, disliking all forms of Dissent, whether Papist or Protestant.

His views were in complete harmony with the statutes by which the College was governed at the time. There had been no fundamental change in them for centuries, except that in 1841 the number of Fellows required to be in Orders had been halved. When Corrie became Master, Jesus, like the other colleges, was a quasi-monastic community, practically confined to Anglicans, but not quite. It is commonly stated, even by professional historians, that no one but an Anglican could be admitted to either of the ancient English universities at that time. This statement is true of Oxford but not quite true of Cambridge, which had always been more liberal. Non-Anglicans could be admitted to the University and to any of its colleges as undergraduates if the Fellows were willing to admit them, and a Papist was in fact admitted at Jesus as early as 1803. A Protestant Nonconformist, Benjamin Leigh Smith, who afterwards became an Arctic explorer, was admitted to the College towards the end of Dr French's time, though it is true that he had to wait until 1857 before it became possible for him to take a degree. The number of Nonconformists who even applied for admission to any Cambridge college before that date must have been very small, because it was hardly worth their while to enter—at least, if they had any academical ambitions—seeing that Anglicans alone could take degrees and Anglicans alone could hold Scholarships, Fellowships, or any university or college office.

At least six of the sixteen Fellows of Jesus had to be in priests' orders; and all the Fellows, whether clerical or lay, had to be celibate. They were not compelled to do any work for the College. They need not even be in residence. The big majority in fact were non-residents, who usually went to Cambridge merely for the annual audit, when they drew their stipends and voted each other leave of absence until the next audit. Yet they held their Fellowships for life—unless they married, in which event they forfeited them automatically. The Fellows had no voice in the appointment of the Master, who was nominated (almost always from outside the College) by the Bishop of Ely, as was also one of the Fellows known as the Ely Fellow. When any other Fellowship fell vacant the existing Fellows had to submit two names to the Bishop of Ely, who appointed whichever of the two he wished. The Master had to be in priest's orders but, unlike the Fellows, could marry if he wished, though Dr Corrie remained a bachelor until he died at the age of ninety-two, still in office.

Chapel services were compulsory and were of course Anglican. Some of the undergraduates were apparently slack in their attendance during Corrie's early years, for in 1851 the Fellows passed a resolution 'that all resident students be required to attend divine service in chapel at least once a day on week-days and twice on Sundays, unless prevented by sickness or by some sufficient cause to be allowed beforehand by the Dean; that no week be counted for residence to any student in which he fails to comply with this order'. Further, if he thereby lost a term, he was not to be allowed to keep the next term either.

The restoration of the chapel had been begun and completed during the last few years of Dr French's Mastership, but the work of beautifying its interior was spread over the greater part of the Mastership of his successor. During the years 1850–8 coloured glass, from designs by Pugin, was inserted in all the choir windows, beginning with the three eastern lancets, the glass for which was copied from windows in Chartres Cathedral. The westernmost lancet in the north wall shows scenes from the life of St Radegund. The work of decoration was then suspended for a few years to allow the tower to be strengthened and refaced. In 1867 the wooden ceiling of the nave was painted in brilliant colours from a design by William Morris, who introduced into it the text of the hymn, *Vexilla regis prodeunt*, written for St Radegund by Venantius Fortunatus. During the next three years the floor of the nave and transepts was lowered to the level of the pier-bases, the transept roofs were painted in bright colours, and the nave walls were panelled. In 1873–7 all the windows in the ante-chapel were fitted with coloured glass designed by Edward Burne-Jones (except for a few small contributions by Ford Madox Brown) and executed by William Morris. These windows display Pre-Raphaelite work at its best, and together form one of the most striking and brilliant features of the chapel. Fortunately for the College, its chapel has been restored, repaired, and embellished for more than a century by dons, architects, and builders who have loved it.

Although it took nearly the first thirty years of Dr Corrie's reign to complete the embellishment of the chapel, the principles of the Oxford Movement continued to flourish in it, despite the Master's dislike of what people were beginning to call 'Ritualism'. The chapel was noted for its music from the time of its reopening, and the services were so 'high' (as it is called) for that age that they greatly offended the American Puritan, William Everett, who was an undergraduate at Trinity from 1859 to 1862. In his book, *On the Cam*, he records that Jesus Chapel 'is of church-like proportions and is considered, next to that of King's, the most beautiful in Cambridge. Gregorian chants are introduced into the services there. [They] are considered to belong peculiarly to the High Church ritual; and indeed the whole college is given to the study of divinity of the most Anglican or even Anglo-Catholic kind.' He is pained by the reflection that Emmanuel, the home of the Puritan Harvard, and Jesus, the college of the Puritan Apostle, John Eliot, now 'contend for the honour of being the most Puseyite college in Cambridge'.

The English Nonconformists, who had obtained political emancipation during the Mastership of Dr French, very soon determined to acquire academical emancipation also, and they had many friends in Parliament, both Nonconformists and Anglicans. Dr Corrie's opposition to their ambitions was already well known: long before he became Master of Jesus he had published his *Brief Historical Notes of the Interference of the Crown in the Affairs of the English Universities*—the very title of which breathed defiance to any Parliament that would not let sleeping dons lie. Yet before he died in 1885 the Anglican religious society of which he became head in 1849 had been torn from ecclesiastical control and its membership and official posts thrown open to men of all religions and none.

The first blow was struck within a few months of his installation, when Parliament appointed a Royal Commission to enquire into the state of the two ancient universities, with a view to reforming them. When the Commissioners sent a questionnaire to the heads of all the colleges, Dr Corrie showed his hand at once. 'My Lord and Gentlemen', he wrote in reply, 'I feel obliged by a sense of public duty to decline answering any of the questions which I had the honour to receive from you a short time ago. I have the honour to be Your faithful servant, G. E. Corrie'.

In the following year (1851) he became Vice-Chancellor of the University, and in his execution of that office he showed the same contempt for the Commissioners that he showed as Master of his College. His celebrated letter to the railway company when he heard that they proposed to run cheap excursion trains to Cambridge on Sundays was typical of his attitude towards all non-

THE MID-VICTORIAN REVOLUTION

academical authorities. 'Sir', he wrote, 'I am sorry to find that the Directors of the Eastern Counties Railway have made arrangements for conveying foreigners and others to Cambridge on *Sundays* at such fares as may be likely to tempt persons who, having no regard for Sunday themselves, would inflict their presence on this University on that day of rest. I should be obliged therefore by your making it known to the Directors that such arrangements as those contemplated by them are as distasteful to the authorities of the University as they must be offensive to Almighty God and to all right-minded Christians.'

The railway authorities nevertheless inaugurated their cheap Sunday trains, and the Royal Commissioners in 1856 issued a report, despite the non-co-operation and even active opposition of Jesus and other colleges. The most important outcome of the report was that religious tests were abolished for the degree of Bachelor of Arts. This was a useful concession to non-Anglicans but it left them quite unsatisfied, seeing that they were still excluded from the Master's degree and consequently from membership of the Senate and so from any voice in University affairs; and they were still unable to hold a college Fellowship or any university or college office.

Jesus College in particular remained obstinately Anglican. In the very year in which the B.A. degree was opened to Nonconformists, the Master and Fellows removed from the College books the name of a non-resident Master of Arts—appropriately enough, he was called Pope—'in consequence of his having joined the Romish mission in this country'. In 1861, taking advantage of limitations on the powers of the Commissioners, they revised the statutes in an even more rigidly Anglican direction than before. Fellows were in future to take an oath before admission to office to make sure that they were still Anglicans, and the Master was to be deposed if at any time he ceased to be an Anglican.

It was not to be expected, therefore, that the opening of the B.A. degree to non-Anglicans would lead to an increase in the size of Jesus College, where Nonconformists would clearly not get a very warm welcome. One might nevertheless have expected it and the College continued to decrease for some years. When Corrie became Master in 1849, Jesus had fifty-six undergraduates and was eleventh in size among the seventeen Cambridge colleges. Only fifty-four men, including Fellows, could be housed in College. There were twenty sets of rooms in First Court, sixteen in the Cloister, and eighteen in Pump Court, which then consisted only of two staircases adjoining the Hall. Ten years later the number of undergraduates had shrunk to thirty-two, and there were now sets of rooms lying empty. Perhaps as a result of that state of affairs, the Master was allowed to annex College rooms to the Lodge, and continued to do so as late as 1860. The same conversion of collegiate rooms to magisterial uses went on throughout the University, the total population of which had fallen by 300. The Crimean War was possibly in part the cause of the decline.

Both University and College began to grow again in the sixties, and in 1869 the University totalled 2,000 undergraduates, 100 of whom were at Jesus, which was now sixth in size among the colleges. The Fellows therefore decided to build a new range, containing twenty-four sets of rooms, from designs by the then famous Mr Alfred Waterhouse. It ran parallel to the seventeenth-century range, to the north of it, thus converting the small Pump Court into a larger Second Court. The foundation stone was laid in the summer of 1869 by the President, not by the Master. The latter was perhaps ill. He was more probably at Newton, in the extreme north of the Isle of Ely, of which parish he held the incumbency throughout his tenure of the Mastership of Jesus.

In the autumn the Fellows gave a dinner in Hall to all the workmen employed on the building. The President sat at high table, accompanied by the Dean, two other clerical Fellows, the contractor and his son, and the clerk of the works. Down below there were about seventy workmen, one of whom proposed a toast which, in 1869, must have sounded absurdly revolutionary: 'Eight hours' work, eight hours' play, eight hours' sleep, and eight shillings a day'.

The new range was completed in the autumn of 1870. The

Cambridge Chronicle account of it perhaps did not quite mean all it said. 'There is no particular feature in the architecture', it reported, 'and it is in keeping with the remainder of the College buildings. A feature worthy of notice is that every set has a separate gyp-room. A tower and turret', it continued, 'surmount the building in the centre, and there is an entrance to the cricket-ground by an iron gate with ornamental piers. . . . The high hedge which formerly obscured the eastern aspect of the college has been removed and the Master's paddock thrown into the cricket-ground. Entering [Second Court] by the back gate from the field, we come upon an admirable arrangement of new-built offices; in the place of the old offices is a shrubbery, which serves as a shroud to the new offices.'

One surmises that 'the old offices' were earth closets, and that 'the new offices' were the first water closets in the history of the College. These and their surrounding shrubs were demolished in 1922 to make way for a block of lavatories built between the 1870 and 1823 ranges in that year, together with the first bathrooms ever erected in the College. It did not occur to the newspaper reporter in 1870 as noteworthy that there was not one bathroom in all the twenty-four new sets of rooms.

The 1870 building is not generally considered beautiful; but it is worth noting that B. W. Downs, in his *Cambridge Past and Present*, pays it the compliment of calling it 'Waterhouse's least unsuccessful Cambridge building'.

The Waterhouse Building had scarcely been brought into use when, in 1871, an Act of Parliament carried the movement for reforming the University much farther by abolishing religious tests for all degrees except in Divinity, for all University and College offices, and for all Fellowships except those confined to clerics, and by abolishing compulsory chapel-attendance for non-Anglicans. Celibacy was, however, retained for all Fellows, clerical or lay. The University grew—how far as a result of this legislation one cannot be sure—from just over 2,000 undergraduates in 1870 to nearly 3,000 in 1885. Jesus College grew even more rapidly—from just over 100 undergraduates in 1870 to more than double that number in 1880. From 1875 to 1881 it was the third largest college in the University, being exceeded only by Trinity and St John's.

This increase in numbers led in 1875 to the building of a Lecture Room (afterwards used also as an overflow Hall), with kitchen annexes under it, and the accommodation in Hall was increased by the addition of a new but unattractive entrance. This replaced the two staircases by which the Hall had until then been entered—one from the Cloisters, the other from Pump Court. The Fellows were in the same year provided with chairs to sit on at high table instead of forms. The undergraduates continued to sit on forms, but by way of compensation their feet were now protected from the cold stone floor by a wooden floor laid over it. The oriel window in Hall was at the same time embellished with coats of arms (some genuine, others bogus) of men who had been members of the College and of a few others who were mistakenly supposed to have been members. Other coats of arms, both genuine and bogus, were to be added to the College buildings at various dates down to 1930.

In 1877 another reforming Royal Commission was appointed and the Commissioners asked heads of Colleges to state what they considered to be the chief wants of the University. They received a characteristic reply from Dr Corrie. 'I trust', he wrote, 'that the Commissioners will excuse me for stating my opinion that the present chief want of the University is exemption from the disturbing power of Royal or Parliamentary Commissioners.'

The Commissioners, however, disregarded his opinion and in 1882 produced the statutes which completed the academical revolution begun in 1850. By this new code the Master and Fellows were to have the unrestricted right of election to all Fellowships, without reference to the Bishop of Ely. The Master was no longer to be appointed by the Bishop but to be elected by the Fellows. All Fellows were now free to marry if they wished. All religious tests were abolished and no Fellow need now be in Orders, except the Dean. Chapel services, on the other hand, were still to be Anglican and they remained compulsory for Anglican undergraduates until 1918, when the compulsion was allowed to lapse. The Bishop of Ely kept his traditional position as Visitor to the College, with power to act if the Master or Fellows failed to observe the statutes. Jesus, like the other colleges, was now required to pay a specified proportion of its income to University funds. Stipendiary Fellowships for non-residents were to come to an end when those who held them in 1882 died.

According to legend, Dr Corrie assured the Fellows of Jesus of his confidence that none of them would take advantage of the new statute allowing them to marry. All the resident Fellows but one, however, married within a year, some of them within a fortnight of the passing of the new statutes. The one survivor, J. C. Watt, remained a bachelor until his death in 1931. The sinecure non-residents, being under the old statutes, could only continue to draw their dividends so long as they remained un-married and possessed incomes under a stated amount. An out-standing example of this class of Fellow was Thomas King, who was non-resident from 1871 until he died thirty-two years later. Apart from his attendance at the annual audit, he passed his working hours inspecting schools in Cornwall.

For fear lest all the dons might in future get married and live far from the College, two houses for married men were built in the Close in 1885, so that there should be at least two Fellows in residence. These were named East House and North House. As a result of the social revolution of the mid-twentieth century, which made domestic servants very difficult to get, neither of the two houses was used after 1933 for the purpose for which it was built. East House was converted into bursarial and other offices. North House was converted into a tutorial office and several sets of rooms and was renamed Q Staircase, though its original name is still used at times.

Simultaneously with East House and North House, a new block of thirty-six sets of rooms, designed by Carpenter and Ingelow, was built between the Cloister and Midsummer Common, thus making a new Chapel Court. It was adorned with very feebly designed and executed coats of arms and with more vigorous statues of the patrons of the College—the Blessed Virgin Mary with the Child Jesus, St John the Evangelist, and the Glorious

Virgin St Radegund. The statues of St John and St Radegund usually pass unnoticed, being effectively obscured by the over-elaborate carving and crocketing of the niches in which they stand; but the Virgin and Child became more prominent in 1930, when Morley Horder provided the statue with a plainer and very effective background. The statue of St Radegund, who in her time performed miracles on behalf of oarsmen, looks appropriately towards the College boat-house, which had been built in 1883. Before that date, the boat club had housed its boats in hired premises. A clock turret was added to the boat-house in 1885.

The Carpenter Building had several drawbacks. One of these was that, like all its predecessors, it had no bathrooms—a defect which has never yet been remedied. A second was that it had a great deal of waste space within its walls. This was remedied in 1950-3, as will be seen later. A third defect is that the aggressive redness of the brick used in the building has never toned down. Sir Arthur Quiller-Couch, a Fellow of the College from 1912 to 1944, used to assert that this defect could easily be put right by painting the building with a solution of cow-dung, which would cause moss to grow all over it. The experiment was tried on a part of the building, but no moss appeared.

Dr Corrie's Mastership came to an end with his death in September 1885, when he was ninety-two years of age. He had resolutely opposed every change in the University and College and had lost every fight. As D. A. Winstanley says, 'the last ditch was his spiritual home'. Nevertheless, he has been judged too harshly. He cannot be blamed for having been born too late into the world, and he was something much more than the narrow-minded bigot that he has been called. Some of his apparent narrow-mindedness was no more than a disguise for a sense of humour that was too subtle for many of his contemporaries. His contention that all Fellows of colleges should be unmarried would find few defenders today, but many would assert that a consider-able number of the Fellowships at every college should be reserved for men living in college throughout term.

CHAPTER XII

DR CORRIE'S UNDERGRADUATES

THE Carpenter Building had been erected, says the College Conclusion Book in 1883, 'having regard to the large increase in late
years in the number of students resident in the University, of
whom a considerable number seek admission to this college each
year'; but by the time the new building was occupied the undergraduate population of the College had fallen by one-third—
from 216 in 1880 to 147 in 1884. It was no longer third in size
among the seventeen colleges. After Dr Corrie's death it fell to
tenth place.

There can be little doubt that the decline in numbers was due
to over-emphasis on rowing at Jesus during Corrie's later years,
coupled with the rowdiness and idleness of many of the rowing
men and the acquiescence of the Dean, E. H. Morgan. Even
H. A. Morgan (Tutor and afterwards Master), who had been an
ardent supporter of the boat club for many years, was moved to
say, 'The College is becoming nothing but a boat club, and it
will do it much good if the boat comes down'.

Organized rowing began at Cambridge in 1827. When Dr
Corrie became Master of Jesus the College boat was only ninth
on the river, and during the next seven years it sank to the
twenty-ninth place. Perhaps this decline was due to lack of discipline. In 1853, for instance, the boat club minute-book states
that during the May Races 'the crew and coxswain and secretary
partook of a supper of the most varied description'. In 1858,
when there were only thirty-nine undergraduates in the College,
the second May boat had to row with two empty thwarts. The
first boat's position on the river stayed in double figures until
1870, when it began to rise and made its first appearance at
Henley Regatta. The undergraduate population of the College

had also risen to three figures by this time, but it is risky to say which was cause and which was effect. In 1875 the first boat finished Head of the River for the first time in its history. It stayed there for the rest of Dr Corrie's Mastership—eleven years in all— even though the population of the College shrank considerably during his last four years. During the latter part of the eleven years the boat stayed Head partly through the efforts of old rowing men who came back merely to row in the May Races— a malpractice (shared by other colleges) which the University Boat Club soon afterwards ruled out of order.

It was ironical that this golden age of Jesus rowing, during which the College won the Grand Challenge Cup at Henley twice, should occur during Corrie's Mastership, for he was a strong opponent of the sport. When he was still at St Catharine's he had told the undergraduates there that 'so much evil was connected with boat racing' that he could not encourage it. His attitude remained unchanged when he became Master of Jesus. When P. M. Thornton in the early 'sixties asked him to support track athletics he replied, 'I will gladly support you in athletics, as I have done with cricket, but you must not ask me for support to rowing, an occupation to which I can give no countenance, owing to the bedizened women on the bank'.

The eighteen-seventies, with their increased number of undergraduates in both University and College, saw a great expansion, not merely in rowing, but in athletic activities of every kind. Before Corrie's Mastership there were only two inter-Varsity events—cricket, which dated from 1827, and rowing, which dated from 1829 but did not become an annual event until 1856. Rackets and real tennis were added in the 'fifties, shooting and track athletics in the 'sixties. In the 'seventies no fewer than five others were added—Rugby football, Association football, cycling, golf, and polo. The only other inter-Varsity contest added in Dr Corrie's time was lawn tennis, which had to wait until 1881, being long considered a woman's game.

The 'seventies saw the foundation of a number of social clubs and cultural societies in the College. The first of these was a club for the leading athletes, founded in 1874 and misleadingly called the Rhadegunds. Next, in 1877, came a social club, the Natives, founded (as its name suggests) for eating oysters. Another club with a misleading name was the Cranmer Society, which was a debating society founded in 1879. A Musical Society was founded in the same year. It gave concerts from time to time in the Guildhall; and of one of these, given in 1885, we read that 'considering that it was attended by 1,269 persons, we may consider it to have been a decided success'.

Until 1884 each of the College sports clubs had to raise and manage its own funds. In the autumn of that year the Jesus College Amalgamated Clubs came into existence, with a committee which allocated funds to each constituent club from a sum raised by a uniform levy on every undergraduate in the College. It was not until after the War of 1939–45 that non-sporting clubs, such as the Musical and Literary Societies, were admitted to membership of the Amalgamation.

Some interesting sidelights on life at the College during the decade 1860–70 are given in the reminiscences of three Jesus men.

Percy Thornton, the father of Cambridge track athletics, who was in residence from 1860 to 1864, tells us that in his time (astonishing as it seems now) not merely dons but also undergraduates were allowed to keep dogs in College. Thornton kept two dogs. One of these, a bulldog, unfortunately fought the Dean's bulldog, and he was therefore told that his dogs must leave College at once. Rather than be separated from them he went into lodgings in Malcolm Street with them.

A. L. Francis, who entered the College in 1866, says that in his time 'the hours kept were primitive; chapel at 7.30, I think, lectures from ten till one, afternoon chapel 4.30, dinner in Hall at 5—an ungodly hour. We had the long evenings to ourselves for work or play. Dr Corrie, Black Morgan, Red Morgan and his gyp, Moses—these were the most important personages in our lives.'

Arthur Gray, afterwards Master, entered the College in 1870. 'There were never more than four resident Fellows in my undergraduate days', he says, 'and sometimes only two; and the Master had a living near Wisbech, to which he was conscientiously bound for the more part of the year. . . . Cook and butler were in those days tradesmen, independent of the College, except that the College bargained with the cook to supply dinner in Hall at a fixed rate. . . . The Hall in those days had a stone floor and, not being heated, was deadly cold; each man had a pewter hot-water dish before him whereon his plate was laid. Frozen gravy, and caterpillars supplied with the vegetables, were principal constituents in our diet. Oppressed humanity found vent in a round robin, addressed to the Master and Fellows, and we all signed it. It began, "We, your petitioners, undergraduates of Jesus College", and ended, "Your petitioners will ever pray". Praying brought no discoverable results.' (As Winstanley says, 'College authorities are not apt to be deeply stirred by undergraduate complaints of the hall dinner, being so accustomed to them'.)

Arthur Gray is probably referring here to a petition which he is known to have signed in 1871, asking for 'properly cooked meat from the usual joints of recognized animals'. If he was not himself the author of that phrase it is at least very much in his style.

During the thirty-six years of Dr Corrie's Mastership 1290 men were admitted to the College. It is interesting to find that 391 of these (i.e. just over 30 per cent.) were sons of the clergy.

Before Corrie's time there had been five classes of undergraduates—Noblemen, Fellow-Commoners (both of which classes dined at high table), Scholars, Pensioners (called Commoners at Oxford), and Sizars, who performed menial duties in return for their keep. During Corrie's time only two classes appear in the admission register—Fellow-Commoners and Pensioners. The last Sizar had been admitted in 1838. Sizars now survived only at Trinity and St John's, and there they had been relieved of their menial duties. The number of Fellow-Commoners admitted at Jesus in Dr Corrie's time was only twelve. These were senior men and serious scholars, unlike the wealthy, riotous, idle Fellow-Commoners who had in former centuries frequented all colleges. The last of the twelve Fellow-Commoners was admitted in 1865.

No one was admitted to the College in Dr Corrie's time or before as a Scholar. Entrance Scholarships, awarded after a joint examination by a group of colleges, date only from the very late nineteenth century.[1] Before then, Scholarships were awarded after examinations held by each college separately during the Easter Term for men already in residence. At Jesus at the beginning of Dr Corrie's time there were fifty-one Scholarships, fifteen of which were open. There were also fourteen Rustat Scholarships, worth about £35 each per annum, for clergymen's orphans. The existence of these Scholarships no doubt accounts for the large number of sons of the clergy who applied for admission to the College. The other Scholarships, ranging in value from £75 (two only) to £2 a year, were tied to men from particular counties or particular schools, such as Loughborough, Sevenoaks, Tonbridge, and Doncaster.

The *Cambridge University Calendar* for 1850 estimates the average annual expense for an undergraduate at £61; but this excludes matriculation fees, examination fees, degree fees, maintenance during vacations, travelling, clothing, drinks and sizings in Hall, entertaining, Professorial lectures, and private tuition, as 'supervision' was called at that time. It is obvious therefore that even the better Scholarships did not nearly cover the cost of a Cambridge education.

Arthur Gray tells us that a son of the butler at Jesus in his time became an undergraduate at another college. We find from the *Alumni Cantabrigienses* that the same butler had an elder son who was admitted at Emmanuel and became a clerical schoolmaster. These two young men, however, were far from typical of their class. The talk of the 'continuous stream of poor boys' who are alleged to have entered the older universities before the twentieth century is humbug, if 'poor' is taken to mean working-class. The so-called 'poor boys' were poor only by contrast with the wealthy Fellow-Commoners. They were middle-class boys, whose parents were able to support them partly during term and wholly during vacations. The working-class boy at Cambridge before the twentieth century is as rare as a needle in a haystack. A change began with the Education Act of 1902, which empowered local education authorities to subsidize a few boys to go from the

[1] In the College admission register, the classification 'Scholar' appears for the first time in 1895.

elementary schools to secondary schools and a select few from secondary schools to universities; but there was a mere trickle of the latter class until the twenties and no large number until after the War of 1939–45.

It is interesting to see what schools Dr Corrie's 1,290 men came from.

The school of 48 of them is not stated in the admission register. Of the remaining 1,242, only 217 came from small local English schools, usually described as grammar schools. Private schools and private tutors sent 207. The remaining 818 (i.e. two-thirds of those whose schools are known) came from what are commonly called public schools or officially Headmasters' Conference Schools. Eleven of these came from foreign countries, 32 from British lands overseas (Australia 19, New Zealand 11, Canada 1, Mauritius 1), 16 from Scotland, 9 from Wales, and 3 from Ireland. The remainder came from English Public Schools. Those which sent ten or more were: Harrow 63, Eton 50, Uppingham 33, Haileybury 31, Marlborough 30, Shrewsbury 30, Repton 27, Rugby 26, St Edmund's Canterbury 24, King's College School Wimbledon 22, Winchester 22, Lancing 22, Tonbridge 21, Charterhouse 19, Radley 19, Rossall 18, Malvern 17, Brighton 15, Felsted 15, Clifton 14, Oundle 14, Christ's Hospital 13, Wellington 13, Durham 12, Sevenoaks 11, Blackheath Proprietary School 11, Merchant Taylors 10, Bradfield 10. George Fairbairn, admitted in 1874, was the first of the long line of Australians who have made their way to the College, providing it with some of its best oarsmen and at least two of its poets.

Research into graduation lists shows that, of the 1,290 men admitted, only 848 (or slightly less than two-thirds) took degrees. We must realize, however, that by no means all the others were idlers or failures. In those days it was quite common for a man to enter a university with no intention of staying long enough for a degree. This was particularly true of members of the landed classes and of men going into the army. A degree was of no particular value to them and the letters 'B.A.' after a man's name had not yet acquired the almost mystical significance that they now have in the eyes of the man in the street. Some of the most able and conscientious men of Corrie's time never took degrees.

Of the 848 who graduated, only 217—just about a quarter of the graduates, or 16 per cent. of the total number of men admitted —took honours degrees. Here again we must be careful before we draw parallels with the present day. We must remember that an honours degree was of commercial value to very few men other than schoolmasters, and not to all of them. Further, the only honours course open to undergraduates when Corrie became Master was in Mathematics. The Classical Tripos, previously confined to Bachelors, was opened to undergraduates in 1850. There was no other honours course until the Law Tripos was established in 1858. Natural Sciences and Moral Sciences were opened to undergraduates in 1861, Theology and History not until 1874 and 1875. There were no other Triposes in Corrie's time, except Semitic Languages and Indian Languages, founded in 1878–9 and later fused into the Oriental Languages Tripos.

Of the 217 men who took honours, Mathematics had a long lead with 118 men. Classics came a poor second with 36, Law and Theology accounted for 18 each, Natural Sciences for 12, History 10, and Moral Sciences 5.

Of the honours men, 24 became Fellows of the College. Two-thirds of these, either through marriage or for other reasons, did not stay in residence long, but took up careers as barristers, schoolmasters, inspectors of schools, or parish priests. Those whose lives were bound up with the College for long periods of time included Arthur Gray, J. H. H. Goodwin, for many years Bursar, E. H. Morgan, outstanding in the life of the College for nearly forty years, Alexander Nairne, subsequently Dean and Regius Professor of Divinity, H. Shield, Bursar of the College and Liberal Member of Parliament for the Borough of Cambridge, and William Welsh, Senior Wrangler and Smith's Prizeman.

The subsequent careers of about half of Dr Corrie's men are known. No fewer than 448 of them—slightly more than a third of the whole—took holy Orders. Five of these became bishops, a number became cathedral dignitaries, and one abandoned the cloth for gold-mining in South Africa, but the great majority were parish priests, or schoolmasters, or a combination of the two.

A number of laymen also became schoolmasters, but the big majority of those who entered the teaching profession were in Orders. About 90 became barristers, seven of them rising to be judges, and 49 became solicitors. Over 100 were landed proprietors, farmers, graziers, or planters, a number of the landowners being also probably in industry. No fewer than 52 became army officers. The Home, Colonial, and Indian Civil Services absorbed 33. The remainder can be classified as follows: medical 30; academical 20; journalists, authors, and publishers 10; engineers 6; stockbrokers 6; architects 4; artists 3; naval officers 3; musicians 2. Very few of these figures can be regarded as complete, with the exception of the clerics and probably the lawyers, doctors, military officers, and civil servants.

The five men who became bishops were scattered to the four corners of the earth. Only one (E. Hoskyns, of Southwell) was appointed to an English see. T. E. Wilkinson, whose portrait hangs in the College Hall, was the first Bishop of Zululand. C. P. Scott, famous as a cricketer in early life, was Bishop of North China for a third of a century. Cecil Wilson, also a celebrated cricketer, who played eight years for Kent, was a bishop in the southern hemisphere for forty-four years, the first seventeen of them in Melanesia. His account of his voyages among the numerous islands of that diocese, where many of the inhabitants were cannibals, makes interesting reading and is sometimes also entertaining. H. W. Williams, a New Zealander by birth, returned to his native country after ordination and became Bishop of Waiapu and a leading authority on the Maori language.

Of the inferior clergy, the most remarkable was Cecil Tyndale-Biscoe, who was indeed one of the most remarkable men in the whole history of the University. Something of his great achievements as an educational pioneer and social reformer in Kashmir can be gathered from his autobiography and from his son's book, *Fifty Years Against the Stream*. When he first went to Kashmir as a missionary the pupils at his school—many of them married men with families—would not play ball-games, because Brahmins were forbidden to touch leather; neither would they swim, row, or help to put out a fire, for fear of losing caste by performing what was considered coolies' work; and as a result the lives of many Kashmiris were thrown away when accidents took place on land or water. Tyndale-Biscoe succeeded in changing all that, by sheer moral courage, by disregarding public opinion, by his obvious love for the people, and by his keen sense of humour. He even succeeded in breaking down the deplorable taboo on the remarriage of child-widows by offering dowries to men who would marry them. His school developed in time into a group of schools with 1,800 pupils of both sexes, and in them were trained many who were ready to be leaders of Kashmir when India became independent.

Tyndale-Biscoe would have escaped William Everett's strictures on the Jesuan Puseyites; not so H. B. Bromby, twenty years Vicar of the celebrated Anglo-Catholic church of All Saints', Clifton; J. N. Burrows, for thirty years at St Augustine's, Haggerston, an Anglo-Catholic stronghold in East London; Lambert Woodard, of great influence as Vicar of St Paul's, Bedford, for thirty years; and Orby Shipley, sometime Vicar of St Alban's, Holborn, a voluminous writer and a translator from Latin, French, Spanish and Italian. Another prolific writer was H. M. Luckock, for some years a Fellow and twice Vicar of All Saints', Cambridge—the first time of the old church opposite St John's College, the second time of the new church opposite Jesus. He was largely responsible for the building of the latter in 1863 and is said to have fixed the weather-cock at the top of the high steeple with his own hands. Afterwards the virtual founder and first Principal of Ely Theological College, he became finally Dean of Lichfield, where he inaugurated the movement which gradually led to the triumph of Puseyite principles in all English cathedrals. Two other theologians, A. C. Jennings and A. L. Williams, were as remarkable for the number of University distinctions which they gained during residence as for the extent of their writings when they had gone down.

Among the schoolmasters, clerical or lay, must be mentioned Richard Lee, Headmaster of Christ's Hospital for twenty-six years, L. H. Lindon, Headmaster in turn of Geelong G. S. and Christ's College, Tasmania, for a total of over thirty years,

A. L. Francis, Headmaster of Blundell's for no less than forty-
three years, and James Robertson, who went from an assistant-
mastership at Harrow to the headship of Haileybury. He and
Francis were both Fellows of the College for a time, as was also
R. C. Seaton, who became an assistant at Harrow and wrote a
defence of Sir Hudson Lowe, Napoleon's gaoler at St Helena.

Bernard Pitts was the most distinguished of those who took to
a medical career. As an undergraduate he was a versatile man: he
rowed, boxed, played football, tennis, and cricket, and 'was one
of the few who have hit sixes from Jesus Close over the trees on
to Midsummer Common'. During the Balkan War of 1876 his
medical skill was placed at the disposal of both Turks and Christians; but his greatest work was at St Thomas's Hospital, where
he was a pioneer in more than one branch of surgery.

J. D. Bourchier, who migrated from Jesus to King's, was connected with the Balkans for a much longer time than Pitts, but in
a different capacity. He was chief correspondent of *The Times*
there for nearly thirty years and claimed to have been the origin-
ator of the Balkan League which resulted in the almost complete
expulsion of the Turks from Europe in 1912–13.

C. M. Brochner (afterwards St Amory), the only Jesuan of the
time who is known to have made the stage his career, was both
an actor and a composer of light operas, including *The Swineherd
and The Princess*.

E. A. Bowles, who began residence during Dr Corrie's last
days, became one of the foremost horticulturists in the country.
His garden at Myddelton House, near Enfield, was famous for
its beauty. He was the author of a number of charming books on
horticultural subjects.

Among the few who are known to have become architects is
George Gilbert Scott junior, the son of the better-known Sir
George Gilbert Scott and the father of the contemporary architect, Sir Giles Gilbert Scott. He came up in 1863 at the age of
twenty-four after studying architecture under his father, won an
oar in the Lent Races, was top of the Moral Sciences list, and was
elected to a Fellowship, subsequently vacating it through marriage. Essentially a scholarly architect, he has never had proper

recognition and is not in the *Dictionary of National Biography*, for instance. His *Essay on the History of English Architecture* covers a much wider field than its title suggests. It contains, for example, valuable chapters on the orientation of early churches and on the aesthetic and artistic element in primitive Christianity, giving information difficult to find elsewhere. Burne-Jones obtained one of his first commissions for ecclesiastical work through the good offices of Gilbert Scott. It may have been he who introduced Burne-Jones and William Morris to the College, where they did so much work.

Another architect, W. M. Fawcett, admitted in 1868, is little remembered today but he changed the face of Cambridge, for good or ill, not a little. His buildings include, for instance, the old Cavendish Laboratory, the 1875 range at Queens', Chetwynd Court at King's, the Master's Lodge at St Catharine's, the Syndicate Building at the Pitt Press, the Local Examinations building in Mill Lane, the Hostel at Emmanuel, King's College Choir School, the Perse School, many pavilions for college and university clubs, many boat-houses (including the old Jesus boat-house destroyed by fire in 1932), and Hughes Hall, unkindly described by Professor Pevsner as 'in the Neo-Dutch Norman Shaw London School Board style, with later additions'.

Of the literary men of Dr Corrie's time, Harold Cox, admitted in 1878, had a varied career—as a Socialist President of the Union in his undergraduate days, a University Extension Lecturer, a Lecturer in Mathematics in India, a Parliamentary journalist, a Member of Parliament, the author of several works on economics, and editor of the *Edinburgh Review*.

Charles Whibley, his junior in the College by a year, entered on a literary career as soon as he went down. His first published work was an admirable anthology, *In Cap and Gown, Three Centuries of Cambridge Wit*, in the introduction to which he makes the very true remark that 'the same stories against the dons which amused our great-grandfathers in their first term are told to the freshmen of today as entirely modern'. He soon began to assist W. E. Henley in editing *The National Observer*, a weekly paper distinguished for its die-hard Toryism. Later he joined the staff of *Blackwood's Magazine*, to which he contributed ultra-Tory 'Musings without Method' practically every month for over a quarter of a century. Henley's biographer, John Connell, describes them as being written 'with almost equal savagery and brilliance'. Like Harold Cox, he was elected an Honorary Fellow of the College in later years. He lived in College during term and would occasionally entertain visitors with an impassioned tirade against 'the foul principle of democracy' or would urge a return to the Golden Age that preceded the Reform Bill of 1832. The College portrait of him by Sir Gerald Kelly was presented by the artist.

Frederick John Jackson, admitted in the same year as Whibley, did not stay at Cambridge long enough to get a degree. After some years of roving in Kashmir and East Africa he entered the service of the newly incorporated British East Africa Company in 1888 and had an adventurous career in Uganda, of which he ultimately became Governor. His hobby was the study of the mammals, butterflies, and birds of East Africa. He became a recognized authority on the last of these in particular and at his death left a practically complete history of the birds of Kenya and Uganda. He was the original of the character called 'Good' in *King Solomon's Mines*, written by his intimate friend, Rider Haggard.

Steve Fairbairn, Jackson's junior in the College by a couple of years, might well have had a similar career of adventure and administration, but returned after graduation to his native Australia where, like four of his brothers who were at the College with him or before him, he became a grazier. Other Jesus men may have been even greater oarsmen than Steve, but he remains unsurpassed as a teacher of rowing. He was to return from Australia after some twenty years to coach the boats of his old College and send them on to victory after victory.

Charles Hose, admitted in 1882, was one of the most remarkable members of the College—remarkable both in achievement and in size; he must have weighed twenty-five stone in middle life. Going down without a degree (merely through not residing long enough to get one), he was given the honorary degree of

THOMAS CRANMER
artist unknown

LAURENCE STERNE
by Allan Ramsay

Plate IX

S. T. COLERIDGE
by James Northcote (1804)

STEVE FAIRBAIRN
by James Quinn (1926)

Plate X

Above: CEILING OF THE ANTE-CHAPEL, DESIGNED BY WILLIAM MORRIS

Below: left—CHIMNEYPIECE IN THE CONFERENCE ROOM
        right—A WINDOW IN THE OLD LIBRARY

Doctor of Science by the University years later. This was in recognition of his important ethnographical research in Borneo, where he spent most of his active life, and of his discovery of the cause of the dreaded disease, beriberi, from which he had himself suffered. He was also a great administrator. 'By his tact, fairness, and sympathetic understanding of their customs', says the *Dictionary of National Biography*, 'he succeeded in establishing friendly relations with the natives . . . and many of the more turbulent chiefs became his loyal friends. Head-hunting was gradually suppressed and a state of peace was inaugurated.' What the *D.N.B.* does not mention is that Hose, as befitted a Jesus man, succeeded in getting the Borneans to substitute boat-racing for warfare as a means of settling tribal disputes. The story has often been told of how he stopped one threatened war by merely sending a messenger to the opposing forces, to exhibit a pair of his enormous trousers and warn them that the man who wore them was on his way there. When Hose arrived, says the legend, the tribes had decamped in fear.

The undergraduate career of George Townsend Warner, admitted in 1884, overlaps into the next Mastership. Well known subsequently as the author of *Landmarks in English Industrial History* (published in 1899 and many times reprinted) and to schoolboys as one of the collaborators in 'Warner and Martin', he was very prominent in the life of the College while he was up, and was devoted to it. He was one of the founders of the Jesus magazine, *Chanticlere*, which started in the first term after Dr Corrie's death. In 1890 he was elected to a Fellowship and it is clear that he hoped to stay at the College for life; but, for some unknown reason, when his Fellowship ran out a few years later he was not re-elected. This was a great blow to him, and before he left Cambridge he expressed his feelings in a pseudonymous article which he contributed to *Chanticlere*. Many a Jesus man, many members of all colleges, must, during their last term at Cambridge, have felt as he felt, but no one else has succeeded in putting the 'going down' feeling so poignantly into words. He evidently felt the parting so keenly that he could not bring himself to write the words 'going down', but substituted for them the milder 'going away'. The more euphonious and fateful phrase is used here. It keeps breaking into the narrative like the tolling of a bell:

I may as well come to the truth at once. The fact is I am going down. I have banished the thought, and lost it in my work, and forgotten it in the company of friends—for a time. And in vain: for now and again It comes to me and whispers, 'You are going down'; and latterly It has been most faithful to me, walking at my right hand and insisting on being listened to. It writes itself large on my books, and stares at me. At night as I sit alone in my rooms It draws up my other arm-chair to the fire and sits down opposite me and says, 'Don't forget Me: You are going down'; and if in company some-one uses the words 'next year', It jogs my elbow and says, 'Do you hear? He talks of next year. There is no next year for you; this is your last year, for you are going down'. It is sad, and the saddest part is that no one will notice it. . . . Next October everything will go on the same, except that I shall not be here. . . .

People say to me, 'I suppose you are very sorry to be leaving Cambridge', but in so saying they do not understand the matter. It is not Cambridge nor the University that I regret. It is the College. . . . I am merely a passer by, nay, have already passed, with nothing more to do than to keep the place green in memory. I may fancy myself walking back across the new chapel court on a moonlit night, looking at the chapel with its sharp roof, long lancet windows, and sturdy tower, each angle touched with the moonlight, and perhaps the snow lying on it, seeming to throw into deeper darkness the shadows at the foot; and the long line of buildings stretching north-wards, with here and there a lighted window, and among them my own; and behind it all the spire of All Saints', piercing upwards into the clear frosty sky. Or again let me go in fancy through the front court just after sunset and look to the west where, in the distance, the tower of John's Chapel stands out black against the red evening glow, and the irregular line of chimneys and house-roofs gains a beauty from the hour, as the light fades, and the smoke from the town lies over them. I shall see it all again some day, but it will never be the same; for then it will only be a familiar view and a reminiscence. And now it is part of my daily life.

CHAPTER XIII

LATE VICTORIAN AND
EDWARDIAN TIMES

IN the Michaelmas Term of 1885 the Fellows of Jesus met for the first time in the history of the College to elect a Master. Their choice fell on Henry Arthur Morgan, nicknamed 'Black Morgan' from the colour of his hair before it turned grey. The nickname served to distinguish him from the Dean, Edmund Henry Morgan, the original colour of whose hair caused him to be nicknamed 'Red Morgan'. Black Morgan had entered the College as an undergraduate in 1849, a few weeks before Dr Corrie entered it as Master. In 1860 he was elected to a Fellowship and three years later was appointed Tutor. The rise of Jesus to the position of third largest College in the University during the late seventies had been largely due to his labours, and his success as a College officer and his attractive personality made his election to the headship a foregone conclusion. Although he was the thirty-first Master of Jesus, it is noteworthy that, so far as is known, only two of his predecessors had been undergraduates at the College. These were John Duport, Master from 1590 to 1617, and Lynford Caryl, Master from 1758 to 1781.

Dr Morgan's Mastership of twenty-seven years was, compared with Dr Corrie's, an uneventful period in the history of the College, the University, and the country. There was no fresh building at Jesus, no change of importance in the statutes of the College or the University, no war except the South African campaign of 1899–1902. The College, like the greater part of the nation, supported that little war with enthusiasm. One or two of the undergraduates and a number of old members fought in it—one of them, a South African, on the Boer side—and seven of them lost their lives.

Some interesting changes in the College buildings were made during Dr Morgan's Mastership. The first was that in 1886 the modern lath-and-plaster ceiling was removed from the Old Hall of the Master's Lodge (now called the Prioress's Room). This change greatly improved the appearance of the room, as it revealed the late-medieval joists, on which the sacred monogram had been painted in white at regular intervals, probably in Alcock's time. Bay windows were added to the dining room and the sash windows, introduced in 1718–20, were replaced by Tudor-style casements. In 1887 a second organ was introduced into the chapel. It was much bigger than the organ in the choir and stood in a loft at the west end of the nave, blocking two of the new Burne-Jones windows from view and spoiling the appearance of the chapel; but it stayed there for thirty-five years. In 1893 the entrance to the nunnery chapter-house, which had been walled up at the suppression in 1496, was rediscovered in the east walk of the Cloister. The walling was removed, leaving the beautiful Early English arches exposed to view.

The irony of an eleven years' Headship of the River occurring during the mastership of a severe critic of rowing and rowing men was repeated in reverse under Black Morgan, a keen and experienced oarsman. The Headship was lost in the very first summer after his election and was not regained until a few years before his death. In the Michaelmas Term following the loss of the Headship there were no fewer than seventy-one freshmen— the largest number in the history of the College until then. A critic of rowing men, writing in the College magazine, attributed this big entry to the collapse of the boat club, but he spoke too soon. The seventy-one freshmen were only a flash in the pan, for as the boat continued to fall year by year on the river, so the number of admissions fell with it. The boat, in fact, began to climb again before the number of admissions. It reached its lowest point—the eleventh place on the river—in 1897, after which it rose gradually. The number of admissions, on the other hand, did not reach its lowest point until 1901, in which year there were only twenty-two freshmen. By 1909 the boat was once more Head of the River. It kept the Headship in 1910, lost it in 1911, but regained it in 1912, a few weeks before Black Morgan died. The number of admissions reached its summit in 1910, with eighty freshmen.

Throughout the period of the decline E. H. Morgan continued to hold the office of Dean which he had held in Dr Corrie's time, and from the time of H. A. Morgan's accession to the Mastership he was Senior Tutor also. The two men, though possessing the same surname, were unrelated. Red Morgan was the more masterful character of the two and indeed the most masterful person in the College. One of the Fellows, Alexander Nairne, used to say in later years, 'We were all afraid of Red Morgan—all of us, including the Master'. F. J. Foakes Jackson, a Trinity man who was imported from a country curacy in 1882 to be Chaplain of the College, summed up the situation in a hitherto unpublished fragment of a play which he improvised one day when out walking with a colleague:

Red Morgan. I am the tutor, bursar, butler, dean:
I rule the College with imperial sway.
The very Master owneth me supreme,
The Fellows tremble and my rule obey.
Chorus. The Czar of Russia and our gracious Queen
Are not so potent as our noble Dean.

Red Morgan died in 1895, before the College or its boat had begun to rise again. The silver cross on the chapel altar was given in the following year in memory of him. Foakes Jackson, who was already a legendary figure among undergraduates, succeeded him as Dean and held the office for over twenty years. With his propensity for reciting the morning collect at Evensong and the evening collect at Mattins and other peculiarities, he corresponded to some extent—no one could do so entirely—to the popular idea of the eccentric and absent-minded don. Unlike Red Morgan, he was not both Dean and Senior Tutor. The latter office fell to Arthur Gray, who had been Junior Tutor under Red Morgan and had found life difficult.

The period during which the Jesus boat lay in the doldrums was a golden age for other sports in the College, particularly cricket and football, in both of which it produced a remarkable number of Blues and Internationals. At one time, there were as many as eighteen Blues in the College. W. N. Cobbold, an Association football Blue for four years running, played for England while a freshman and was captain of England while still an undergraduate. The Cambridge Rugby football and cricket teams which met Oxford during Black Morgan's Mastership frequently included four Jesus men, and the Rugby team in 1889 included no fewer than six of them. Several Jesus cricket Blues were afterwards captains of first-class county cricket teams. Among them were A. O. Jones, A. J. L. Hill, and the two greatest Jesus cricketers of all time—S. M. J. Woods and G. MacGregor. These last two were Internationals in both cricket and Rugby football, and can only be called geniuses at both games.

It would be a mistake nevertheless to imagine that Black Morgan's men did little or nothing but play games. Of the 1,348 men admitted during his Mastership, 134 took first classes in one or both parts of one or more Triposes, to which Medieval and Modern Languages, Mechanical Sciences, and Economics were added during this period. Mathematics headed the Jesus list with 46 men getting firsts. Next came Classics with 38, Natural Sciences with 24, and Theology with 19. The other Triposes were poorly represented among the first classes.

The number of men reading for honours in Theology was swollen from 1890 by the holders of Lady Kay Scholarships, founded in that year for ordinands in their third or fourth years and open to the whole University. Among those who came from other colleges to be Lady Kay Scholars was Edward Wynn of Trinity Hall, who became Chaplain of Jesus and ultimately, after his enthronement as Bishop of Ely in 1941, its much-loved Visitor.

The high table, too, was strengthened now and then, as in former times, by the election of members of other colleges to Fellowships. Foakes Jackson, J. C. ('Tommy') Watt, and Edwin Abbott—three very popular dons—all entered the College in this way in late Victorian times. The Edwardian introductions included W. R. Inge, who came to the College as a Professorial Fellow in 1907 but left four years later to become a famous

Dean of St Paul's. Before he left, S. C. Cockerell, Director of the Fitzwilliam Museum, had been elected to a Professorial Fellowship. His surname provided an obvious target for the undergraduate magazine of John Alcock's foundation, which acknowledged his arrival in these appropriate verses:

> Thrice welcome, brother, to our run!
>   The Fates to thee be gracious!
> For never have we hailed a one
>   So truly gallinaceous.
>
> Thy fellow roosters may'st thou see
>   To be of goodly breeding
> And thy election never be
>   Adjudged a foul proceeding!

The author of those lines may or may not have been a member of the Jesus club called the Roosters, founded in 1907, with the cockerel as the centre of its curious ritual and vocabulary of later years.

One of the last acts of Dr Morgan's Mastership was the replacement of gas lighting by electricity in 1912 throughout the College. Another was the foundation in the same year of a special library for undergraduates, to supplement the somewhat inaccessible and antiquated Old Library. Called the Shield Library after the Fellow who had provided part of the money needed to inaugurate it, it was housed at first in S. T. Coleridge's old rooms on the ground floor of 'D' staircase. Growing too big for its quarters, it was moved to North House in 1939 and from there to the top floor of 'A' and 'B' staircases in 1952.

Henry Arthur Morgan died at the Lodge in September 1912, at the age of eighty-two, having been a member of the College for sixty-three years. As his successor put it, few Jesus men had known the College so long, and none had been identified for so many years with every phase of its activities. He was not a great scholar but, as Charles Whibley wrote, he was 'a loyal champion of the honour and privileges of his college', and 'he tempered his patriotism with a profound knowledge of the larger world. If he succumbed willingly to the genius of the place, if he could not have lived happily beyond its precincts, he enormously increased its worth and dignity by the constant exercise of a wise devotion.'

Information about the after-careers of Black Morgan's 1,348 men is more plentiful for those admitted during the earlier part of his Mastership than for those admitted in the later years. No reliable conclusions can be drawn for the period 1901–12, but the subsequent occupations of over 70 per cent. of the 746 men admitted during the years 1885–1900 are known. As in Dr Corrie's time, those who took holy Orders head the list with 142, though their proportion to the total number of admissions has fallen from 34 per cent. to a little under 20 per cent. On the other hand, the percentage of lay schoolmasters has risen considerably. The legal profession still stands high, with 46 barristers and 31 solicitors. Business of all kinds, from brewing to stock-broking, accounts for over 50, agriculture and medicine for about 40 each, the Civil Service (Home, Indian, and Colonial) for 37, the Army 33, academical work 23, engineering and mining 19. Journalism and authorship account for 6. Three are known to have become chartered accountants, two actors. Architecture, painting, music, archaeology, and exploring are not known to account for more than one or two each. One man gave his occupation as 'horse-racing handicapper'. Another, reduced from wealth to poverty, was at one time a professional rag-picker living in a Salvation Army shelter.

Of those who took up academical careers, W. L. H. Duckworth and E. M. W. Tillyard became in turn Masters of the College; H. G. Wood became the first Professor of Theology at Birmingham, and his younger brother, Sir Robert Wood, became the first Vice-Chancellor of the University of Southampton. W. H. Mills, H. Spencer-Jones and W. B. R. King became Fellows of the Royal Society and E. M. W. Tillyard a Fellow of the British Academy.

J. M. Edmonds, a Fellow of the College and Lecturer in Classics, was the author of a number of striking war epitaphs published in 1917. One of them achieved world-wide fame and came into prominence again during the War of 1939–45, being quoted or misquoted in many books and reproduced (generally incorrectly) on numerous war-memorials throughout the world. The correct version runs:

> When you go home, tell them of us and say,
> 'For your tomorrows these gave their today'.

Among those who became eminent as theologians may be mentioned W. K. Lowther Clarke (sometime Fellow of the College), W. O. E. Oesterley (Professor of Hebrew at King's College, London), and E. C. Hoskyns (Fellow and Dean of Corpus Christi College, Cambridge). P. Gardner-Smith, Dean of the College during practically the whole of the next three Masterships, was celebrated throughout the University and beyond it as a teacher of theology, a witty and stimulating lecturer, and a preacher of the first order.

Among the mathematicians of Black Morgan's time Sir Harold Spencer-Jones, Astronomer Royal from 1933 to 1955, stands pre-eminent. He and G. H. Livens (afterwards Professor of Mathematics at Cardiff) were Smith's Prizemen. A third mathematician, A. W. Siddons, was the author of a number of text-books on geometry and algebra which enjoyed a very wide circulation for many years.

Several of Black Morgan's men entered Parliament, on both sides of the House. Among the Liberals was P. H. Illingworth, who attained Cabinet rank as Postmaster-General. Sir Mark Sykes, at one time a Conservative Member of Parliament, spent much of his life as a diplomat and explorer in the Near East. Another diplomat, Abdul Aziz Izzet, was for some time Egyptian Foreign Minister.

Of the writers, Arthur Lambton, who translated Maupassant into English and Sheridan into Italian, devoted a considerable part of his life to securing the passing of the Legitimacy Act by Parliament in 1926. Douglas Dewar, an Indian Civil Servant, produced thirty or more books, most of them dealing with Indian life and particularly with Indian birds, on which he was an authority. Joseph Hone, an Irishman, wrote on such Irish

authors as Bishop Berkeley, Dean Swift, George Moore, and
W. B. Yeats. Conrad Skinner was a successful novelist who wrote
on original lines under the pseudonym, "Michael Morris".

Among the journalists, B. F. Robinson was editor of *Vanity
Fair*, a celebrated weekly founded in 1868. A. H. Billing migrated to New York, where he edited *The World*. Another who
described himself as a journalist was no more than a racing tipster
writing for a popular Sunday newspaper under the pseudonym
of 'Larry Lynx'.

William Briggs, who came up at the age of twenty-eight—he
was a non-collegian for his first two years—read Mathematics
and Law for his degree, but was undistinguished in either Tripos.
This was probably because his energies were concentrated elsewhere—on the organization which he had already founded for
coaching for examinations by post. It proved highly successful,
ultimately drawing pupils from all over the world. Its founder
was a generous benefactor to the College.

A. F. C. C. Luxmoore read Law for his degree, was twice a
Rugby football Blue and, after he left Cambridge, a Rugby
International. One of his undergraduate pranks was to climb to
the roof of the College one quiet Sunday afternoon with his
friend E. S. Grogan in order to pour a bucket of water down another man's chimney and put his fire out. Unfortunately for
them, they poured it down one of their own chimneys by mistake. In view of this and other escapades and his athletic activities,
it is not surprising that Luxmoore took only a pass degree. He
nevertheless soon made his mark as a barrister and ended by becoming a Lord Justice of Appeal. E. S. Grogan distinguished
himself soon after he left Cambridge—he was not there long
enough to get a degree—by crossing the African continent from
south to north on foot in 1898, most of the way unaccompanied.
His exciting experiences among savage tribes, many of them
cannibals, who had never seen a white man before, are recorded
in his book, *From the Cape to Cairo*.

A number of the men who read Law for their degrees became,
like Luxmoore, distinguished members of the judiciary. Sir
Ernest Wild, Recorder of London from 1922 to his death in 1934,

was a man of great humanity but could be very severe at times. ('When Wild's wild he's —— wild' was found scratched on the wall of a released prisoner's cell.) William Watson, who came out near the bottom of the Law Tripos list in 1894, nevertheless rose to the top of his profession and became a Lord of Appeal in Ordinary, sitting in the House of Lords as Baron Thankerton. His recreations included knitting, at which he was an expert. J. S. C. Reid (Lord Reid) who belonged to Dr Morgan's later years, was unlike Lord Thankerton in that he took a first class in Law but resembled him in passing through the House of Commons on his way to the Upper House as a Lord of Appeal in Ordinary. Sir Godfrey Russell Vick, Q.C., whose undergraduate career extended into the next Mastership, became a Recorder of three cities in turn, President of the Bar Council, and a County Court Judge.

Other Jesus men of the first decade of the twentieth century include James Wood, the artist, to whom the College owes a portrait of one of its Masters; Sir Lawrence Pattinson, one of the first members of the Royal Air Force, and later an Air Marshal; John Boot (Lord Trent), who was not merely the head of a great trading company, with branches in almost every town in the kingdom, but also the chief founder (with his father) of the University of Nottingham and its first Chancellor; Sir Harold Scott, at one time Chairman of the Prison Commission and Commissioner of the Metropolitan Police, who also made his mark as a criminologist; and Sir Wilfrid Eady, another very distinguished Civil Servant, who was Chairman of the Board of Customs and Joint Second Secretary at the Treasury. He devoted his spare time for years to the Working Men's College, of which he later became Principal. His contemporary at Jesus, M. L. W. Laistner, for many years a Professor in the United States, became distinguished as a writer on classical and post-classical literature and history.

CHAPTER XIV

THE MASTERSHIP OF
ARTHUR GRAY (1912-40)

ARTHUR GRAY, who was elected Master of the College a few
weeks after Black Morgan's death in 1912, was the first layman
to hold the office. Born in 1852, he entered the College in 1870,
became a Fellow in 1875, a tutor in 1885, and Senior Tutor on
the death of Red Morgan in 1895. He had seen the undergraduate
population of the College double during his first ten years,
shrink to its former size of about a hundred during the next
twenty years, and reach two hundred again by the time he
became Master. He was the last Master of the College to hold
office for life. A revision of the statutes in 1926—the first since
1882, except for a few minor alterations—introduced age limits
for all office-holders, but they were not made retrospective. Two
other important provisions of the new statutes, it may be noted
here, were the institution of Research Fellowships and the abolition of the limitation on the number of Fellows, which had been
fixed at sixteen ever since 1559. The College could in future
have as many Fellows as it could afford, and within thirty years
they had doubled in number.

Within two years of Arthur Gray's election the number of
undergraduates shrank to a mere handful, owing to the outbreak of the War of 1914-18. The few who remained in residence shared the College with cadets in training for army commissions. The College is known to have contributed over 700 of
its members and past members to the armed forces during the
war, and nearly 150 of them fell. Most of these were inevitably
Black Morgan's men, including Bernard William Vann, awarded
the Victoria Cross for conspicuous gallantry in France.

A few undergraduates who had been in residence before the war came back when it was over to complete their degrees. Among them was W. N. Hoyte, who had been awarded the Military Cross and Bar during the war. His subsequent academical career gives the lie to the frequent charge that an undergraduate cannot both row and work properly; for during the May Term of 1921, on the days when he was actually sitting for the Natural Sciences Tripos, he rowed in the College first boat every evening, and he not only took first-class honours but also finished head of the river, as he had done in the previous year.

The College filled again rapidly as soon as the war ended, and for some time men who had been in the forces, holding every rank up to lieutenant-colonel, were in a majority. A number of them—it must have been the first time in history that such a thing happened—were recipients of government grants, without which a university education would have been impossible for them. No less than two-thirds of the undergraduates, however, had formerly been at one or other of the big public schools. The average number of matriculations at the College in the three years immediately before the war had been sixty-four a year. The average for each of the years 1918–39 was ninety-four, so that the population of the College between the two wars was more than 46 per cent greater than before 1914.

Edwin Abbott was Senior Tutor after the war, as he had been ever since Arthur Gray's elevation to the Mastership. A shy, sensitive man, he nevertheless commanded the affection of undergraduates of all ages and continued to do so until he retired from office in 1933. Foakes Jackson, who had gone to the United States during the war to take a Professorship, was succeeded in the office of Dean by Alexander Nairne, an ascetic, a Platonist, and a High Churchman. He allowed the pre-war rule requiring undergraduates to attend chapel a certain number of times in each week to fall into desuetude, and it was never afterwards enforced by him or by the Rev. P. Gardner-Smith, who succeeded to the office of Dean in 1922, when Nairne vacated it on becoming Regius Professor of Divinity. Chapel attendance thus became voluntary but continued to thrive. The Master, a staunch Anglican, set the example of attending chapel twice every weekday and three times on Sundays, taking the Sacrament every week. Compulsory chapel was abandoned at most other Cambridge colleges about the same time as at Jesus, but not at all of them.

One of the outstanding characters in the life of the College during the whole of Arthur Gray's Mastership was Sir Arthur Quiller-Couch, commonly called 'Q' from the pseudonym that he had long used in his numerous writings.

Originally an Oxford man, he had been appointed by the Crown to the King Edward VII Professorship of English Literature at Cambridge in 1912 and elected to a Fellowship at Jesus a few days after Arthur Gray's installation as Master. As striking in features as he was in dress, and distinguished also by a most sympathetic nature, a courtly manner, and a keen sense of humour, he soon became one of the best-known and most popular men in the University. His lectures, prepared and delivered with the care which he devoted to all his undertakings, were models of English prose, attracting large audiences of undergraduates, dons, and even non-members of the University to the lecture-theatre at the Arts School in Benet Street.

'Q' resembled Steve Fairbairn in one respect, if in no other. One of Steve's favourite slogans was, 'Enjoy your rowing, win or lose', and 'Q' similarly taught his pupils to enjoy their reading, just as he enjoyed his own.

Another Oxford graduate who was elected to a Professorial Fellowship at the College during the latter part of Arthur Gray's Mastership was Charles Harold Dodd. Renowned internationally as a New Testament scholar and as a broadcaster on religious subjects, he received honorary doctorates in theology from more than a dozen universities, British and foreign. His appointment as general director of a new translation of the Bible, undertaken by a joint committee representing many Christian denominations, reminds one that two Masters of the College—John Duport and Roger Andrewes—had been members of the committee of divines which produced the Authorized Version of 1611.

The great increase in the number of undergraduates after the war made Arthur Gray's Mastership, like Dr Corrie's, a time of much building, all of which was carried out from the designs of P. Morley Horder. Operations began in 1922, when the 1870 conveniences in Second Court were replaced by a staircase (four sets of rooms) and a block of bathrooms. These were the first to be erected during the eight centuries of the history and pre-history of the College. Until then, the only baths had been big circular tin saucers, about five feet in diameter, kept in bedrooms and trundled out into the keeping-room when required for use, if the bedroom was too small for the purpose.

The arch under the new staircase ('L') was adorned on the Chapel Court side with the former arms of the College (the Five Wounds of Christ) and on the other side with the modern (A. D. 1575) arms of the College impaled with those of the Master (a field of six pieces engrailed, with an eight-pointed cross between two roses on a bend). In the same year the second chapel organ which had blocked the west end of the nave since 1887 was removed. The loft on which it had stood was adapted by Morley Horder to make a gallery for the chapel of West-cott House. The organ was sold to the City Temple, where it was destroyed by enemy action during the War of 1939-45.[1]

A lull in building followed for a few years, except that in 1924 a cricket pavilion—there had been only a tent before—was built on the Close. In the same year the Ghost Room at the top of Cow Lane (officially marked 'G' Staircase) ceased to be used as a lumber-room and was restored to human occupation. Arthur Gray had made the room the scene of his best ghost-story, 'The Everlasting Club', included in his *Tedious Brief Tales of Granta and Gramarye*, which he had published in 1919 under the pseudonym of 'Ingulphus'.

Building was resumed on a large scale a few years later and in 1930 a new block of forty-five sets of rooms was opened in Chapel Court. It abutted on the Carpenter Building of 1885, turned through two right-angles, and ended a short distance from the chapel. Its eight staircases were numbered from 7 to 14, continuing the numbers of the six staircases of the Carpenter

[1] It was replaced in 1971 when Noel Mander built a new one in the adjoining chancel arch to that containing the Sutton organ. Peter Hurford, a former Organ Scholar with a worldwide reputation, gave the opening recital.

Building. These, however, had to be reversed to make the two sets of numbers run consecutively. The new range was decorated with Eric Gill's carving of the arms of Leonard White-Thompson, Visitor of the College at the time, impaled with those of his see of Ely. The angelic supporters of the shield soon caused the gateway below them to be called the Angel Gate. The appearance of the Carpenter Building was greatly improved about the same time by removing the iron gates from its tower and replacing them by high wooden linen-fold panelled doors copied from those at the old entrance to the College, which probably date from Alcock's time.

The alterations of 1930 were completed by an enlargement of the Close. This was brought about by incorporating in it a triangular piece of land, bounded by Victoria Avenue and Jesus Lane, which had been used in past centuries by the townsmen for archery practice and was hence called Butt Green. In exchange for this the College gave to the town some land adjoining Midsummer Common lower down the river and surrendered its ancient rights over New Square. A new approach was then made from Victoria Avenue to the Carpenter Tower. It was entered through wrought-iron gates given in memory of Dr Morgan by his widow and four daughters, who also planted the new road with chestnut trees. These maintained the tradition of 'the flowering chestnuts of Jesus' mentioned by Edward Fitzgerald in his *Euphranor* as the home of nightingales.[1]

In 1932 the greater part of the College boat-house, built by Fawcett in Swiss-chalet style in 1883, was destroyed by fire. Morley Horder's new boat-house on the same site incorporated the clock-turret and two of the walls of its predecessor. He provided more accommodation for boats and oarsmen, which was badly needed, and shower-baths where there had been none before. His last architectural work for the College was carried out in 1934, when he provided the Fellows with a private entrance to the Combination Room. Until then, they could get to

[1] The Morgan gates fell into disuse for all but pedestrians when the tremendous growth of traffic along Victoria Avenue made the exit there so difficult that a new one had to be established in Jesus Lane.

it only by going through the Hall—a way which had always been inconvenient and had been more so than ever since the institution of a daily lunch in Hall in 1929. Horder cut a doorway through the east wall of the Cloister, between Cow Lane and the Chapter House arches, and ran a staircase from there to the Combination Room. The new entrance was fitted with doors carved with linen-fold panelling copied from Alcock's door at the north-west entrance to the Chapel. Architectural taste changes rapidly; but Morley Horder's reputation, so far at least as his work at Jesus College is concerned, has stood the test of nearly fifty years of criticism.

The revival of Jesus rowing which had marked Dr Morgan's last years went from strength to strength throughout the Mastership of his successor, chiefly because of the brilliant coaching of Steve Fairbairn, who spent most of his time in England after his return from Australia in 1905. There were very few years between that date and his death in 1938 when he did not coach the College boats for at least part of the year, and often the whole of it. As he grew older his enthusiasm for rowing became, if possible, greater than ever, so that the sport seemed to be his religion. He had the satisfaction of seeing the College finish Head of the River fourteen times out of a possible twenty-three during Arthur Gray's Mastership and Head of the Lents thirteen times out of a possible twenty-two. What is perhaps even more remarkable is that from 1905, when he took over the College coaching, until his death a third of a century later, the Jesus May boat was never lower than fourth on the river and the Lent boat never lower than third. Of the numerous Blues whom he produced, H. B. Playford was distinguished by rowing in three successful races against Oxford and rowing Head of the River for the College in the same three years. One of Steve's later pupils, P. N. Carpmael, distinguished himself by winning the Wingfield Sculls in 1948 and again in 1949, when he was forty years old. He was still winning victories in first-class rowing during his fiftieth year.

When Steve Fairbairn died in 1938 Arthur Gray was over eighty-five but had not had a day's illness in his life and was full of vigour. He had outlived many of his junior colleagues, including Welsh, Watt, and Nairne. At the last graduation lunch that he ever attended he described himself as 'a great traditionalist and a great radical'. There was much truth in this self-description, but he was an iconoclast rather than a radical, and his iconoclasm grew with the years. In 1935, for instance, it induced him, in his *Earliest Statutes of Jesus College*, to essay the impossible task of proving that John Alcock had not founded the College. He went even further, suggesting that it had been founded by someone else, whose name had never before been mentioned in connection with the history of the College, even by Arthur Gray himself in his published history.

He celebrated his eighty-seventh birthday a few weeks after the outbreak of war in 1939. Although he did not live much longer he was active to the end, presiding over the meetings of the College Council and sometimes acting and speaking as though it were legally a despotism instead of a democracy. He seemed impervious to the climate, and continued to walk slowly through the College courts and the town streets without an overcoat in what was one of the bitterest winters ever known, even during snowstorms. He continued to smoke cigarettes all day long and to amuse the Combination Room with his admirable stories of Cambridge characters of the past seventy years and with his denunciations of Red Morgan, who had been dead for forty-five years. In March 1940 he made one of the best bump-supper speeches that he had ever made, weaving into it the pathetic story of the aged Barzillai the Gileadite and holding his undergraduate audience to the end with his oratory, his humour, and his obvious devotion to the College. He died in his sleep on 12 April, having worked even on the day of his death. In keeping with the custom of the College at the burial of a Master, his coffin was wheeled through each of the College courts in turn, with his family and the Fellows walking behind. He had been a member of the College for seventy years, all but a few months, and no one in all its long history had ever loved it more.

The total number of men admitted during Arthur Gray's Mastership was 2,350. Information about the subsequent careers of the great majority of them is not available, but it is safe to say that their occupations were far more varied than those of the men admitted during any previous Mastership. The percentages of clerics and of officers in the regular army were certainly much smaller. The percentage of lawyers and doctors probably remained about the same as before. The percentage of lay schoolmasters on the other hand, increased greatly; and many new openings were found in local administration, business, industry, engineering, journalism, publishing, and the new career of broadcasting.

The mid-Victorian accusation that the College excelled in nothing but rowing had been amply disproved in Dr Morgan's time, and was even more strongly disproved by the achievements of Arthur Gray's men. It is noteworthy, for instance, that no fewer than four of them—L. A. Pars and three of his pupils (A. E. Green, I. J. Good, and D. R. Taunt) won the Smith's Prize—probably the highest award that the University can confer on any of its junior members. One man (M. P. Charlesworth) won the Chancellor's Classical Medal and in later years was elected a Fellow of the British Academy. A considerable number of Arthur Gray's men were appointed to Professorships at Cambridge and other universities, both at home and abroad, in scientific subjects and also in the humanities. E. S. Abbott became Warden of Keble College, Oxford. W. T. Astbury, T. M. Sugden and W. H. Thorpe were elected Fellows of the Royal Society.

Among scholars and men of letters produced by the College B. L. Manning made a mark as an ecclesiastical historian and as a doughty and witty Christian apologist, M. P. Charlesworth as a writer on ancient history, C. H. Wilson as an economic historian, and A. H. Armstrong (Professor of Greek at Liverpool) as a writer on ancient philosophy. Gerald Bullett was a versatile writer, with a reputation as a novelist of English social life, as poet, critic and anthologist. B. D. G. Little succeeded in packing a great deal of information into his numerous works on English topography without becoming dull. J. M. Reeves made a special niche for himself with his delicate studies of English literature, his anthologies, and his stories for children.

V. C. Clinton-Baddeley, one of the first to become prominent in English broadcasting, became known also as a writer of plays and the author of books on music and drama. Alistair Cooke, who in his undergraduate days founded the Mummers (the first University dramatic club at Cambridge open to both sexes), became one of the best-known of all broadcasters, being particularly successful in presenting the American scene to British people. J. Bronowski, who came into prominence as Director of the Central Research Establishment of the National Coal Board and as a broadcaster on a variety of topics, achieved a high reputation also as a literary critic, a writer of radio plays, and of the television series *The Ascent of Man*. Another prominent broadcaster, Sir Jack Longland, who abandoned an academical career for educational administration, became well known through his membership of the Mount Everest Expedition of 1933.

A number of Arthur Gray's undergraduates, as befitted the Mastership of so keen a churchman, rose to ecclesiastical distinction as prebendaries, canons, archdeacons, deans, principals of theological colleges, and bishops. N. B. Nash became Bishop of Massachusetts, S. F. Allison Bishop of Chelmsford and then of Winchester. Three others became suffragan bishops—G. E. Ingle (Fulham, and later Willesden), S. W. Betts (Maidstone), and J. A. T. Robinson (Woolwich); and E. S. Abbott became Dean of Westminster.

In the armed forces one must single out two who became Air Marshals—Sir Philip Livingston and Sir Victor Goddard, the former being head of the Air Force medical services.

In civil affairs, Sir Paul Sinker was First Civil Service Commissioner and afterwards Director of the British Council. Of the diplomats, Sir Saville, later Lord Garner, became Permanent Under-Secretary of State at the Commonwealth Office and Head of the Diplomatic Service, Sir Humphrey, later Lord Trevelyan, British Ambassador to Egypt, Iraq and Russia, and Don Carlos Sardi Ambassador of the Republic of Colombia to Great Britain. Sir Chintaman Deshmukh, after many years in the Indian Civil Service, rose to the high position of Minister of Finance in the Government of India after his country attained independence. Among British politicians, the most eminent Jesuan of his time was Gwilym Lloyd-George (Viscount Tenby), who was successively Minister of Fuel and Power, Minister of Food, and Home Secretary.

Brian O'Rorke, who was in residence at the College immediately after the War of 1914–18, rose to eminence as an architect and was elected a Royal Academician in 1956.

CHAPTER XV

THE WAR OF 1939-45 AND AFTER

In May 1940 the Fellows met in the blacked-out Chapel to elect a successor to Arthur Gray. Their choice fell on W. L. H. Duckworth, who was already seventy years old and could not have been elected but for emergency statutes covering the war period. He had been born on St Boniface's Day and was therefore christened Wynfrid—the saint's original name—but his relations always called him by his second name Laurence. Everybody liked him. Tall, spare, and very abstemious, he was a mirror of old-fashioned courtesy, with a gentle humour of an unusual kind. He had a great knowledge of the College and its traditions, having been a member of it since 1889 and possessing a remarkable memory, and was unlike all previous Masters in being a Doctor of Medicine and also being a Doctor of Science. For many years Lecturer and Reader in Anatomy, he had a great reputation as a teacher of the subject. Practically all medical men in the University for more than forty years had been taught by him, and had a great devotion to him. He was an enthusiastic anthropologist and a pioneer in some branches of the science. During the early 'nineties he had made unaccompanied skull-measuring expeditions into remote parts of Crete and Montenegro, where unprotected travelling was difficult and even dangerous.

A great deal of the precise language which the new Master had long used in his scientific lectures had become absorbed into his daily speech and writing. This mode of expression perhaps began as a jest. However it began, it had long since become second nature, with the result that he never seemed to say anything in one word if he could say it in six, or to use a short word if a long word would do. 'You will remember' was consequently transformed into 'It will be within the recollection of the members of the Council, will it not?' and boys' camps became 'camps for juvenile individuals'. Another striking characteristic was the extent of his knowledge on every kind of subject, which never failed to startle visitors. They were invariably impressed, too, by his kindness, to which there appeared to be no limits.

Just before the outbreak of war in 1939 the number of junior members in residence at the College was slightly less than 300. By the end of the war it had fallen to a bare hundred. Most of the war-time undergraduates were cadets sent to Cambridge for a six-months' university course as part of their training before being commissioned. Unlike the resident cadets of 1914–18 they matriculated as members of the University. The remaining undergraduates—the only men in residence for any length of time—were mostly working for degrees in Medicine, Natural Sciences or Engineering under government instructions before being drafted into national service, military or civil. Conspicuous among the latter was D. H. Wilkinson, who came up in 1940, became a Fellow in 1944, was elected a Fellow of the Royal Society at the early age of 34 and Professor of Nuclear Physics at Oxford a year later. He was knighted in 1974 and became Vice-Chancellor of the University of Sussex in 1976.

All who were in residence, both dons and undergraduates, did their utmost to keep the College life and traditions going throughout the war. Most of the academical, social and athletic clubs continued to function and Chanticlere continued to appear every term—perhaps the only College magazine at Cambridge of which that could be said. Unfortunately it did not survive the peace, the last issue appearing in 1960 after nearly three-quarters of a century of publication. The short-course men took part in all these activities with the greatest zest and absorbed the spirit of the College rapidly. Many of them returned after the war to complete the University's requirements for a degree.

Although the number of war-time undergraduates, even including the short-course men, was small after the first twelve months, the College was nevertheless full to the brim. This was because the rest of the buildings were occupied, almost until the end of the war by members of the Air Force—at first by a training

wing, later by a maintenance unit, including members of the
Women's Auxiliary Air Force. On one or two evenings during
the early part of the war an airman on guard with fixed bayonet
outside the Porter's Lodge happened to be a Fellow of the College,
who was passed unrecognized by his colleagues on their way in or
out during the blackout.

Early in the war the medieval glass in the Old Library and the
Burne-Jones windows in the chapel were sent away into the
country and the majority of the College portraits and medieval
manuscripts were dispersed to married Fellows' houses and elsewhere, so that they might not all be destroyed by bombs if things
came to the worst. There were 242 air raid alerts at Cambridge
during the war, in the course of which the enemy dropped 118
high-explosive bombs and about a thousand incendiaries, and
29 people were killed. The Round Church, the Union Society,
Whewell's Court at Trinity, and houses in Jesus Lane were hit,
but the College buildings came through the war unscathed.

Foakes-Jackson, who was still in America, died in December
1941 and Bernard Manning a week later. B. L. Manning had
held office for over twenty years, first as Bursar and afterwards as
Senior Tutor, and his death when he was still under fifty years of
age was a great blow to the College. 'Q', who entered the College
as a don in the same term (Michaelmas, 1912) that Manning had
entered it as an undergraduate, kept his eightieth birthday in the
autumn of 1943 and died in the following spring. He had resided
in College until the previous term.

In the spring of 1945 the members of the Air Force and their
auxiliaries marched out of the College. Despite the oft-repeated
stories of vandalism by troops billeted in beautiful old buildings—
of ancient panelling ripped from walls to be burnt, and of
ancestral portraits used as dart-boards—there was not a scratch on
the panelling or a cut in the venerable oak tables in Hall when
the airmen moved out of the College, although they had used the
Hall during part of every day for five-and-a-half years.

The war ended a couple of months later. The lives of 124
members of the College had been sacrificed in it, all but fourteen
of them being Arthur Gray's men. One of the bravest of them

was John David Graves, a lieutenant in the Royal Welch Fusiliers, who was killed in action in Burma in 1943. He and two of his men had attacked and captured a strong Japanese position, but his companions were wounded and unable to go farther. He thereupon attacked a second position single-handed and carried it, killing all its defenders, but was himself killed while attacking a third position on the same day. Another outstanding man was Lambert Charles Shepherd, who went down with H.M.S. *Hood*. He had already accomplished a remarkable feat in 1940, when he was still a civilian, by twice rowing a small boat alone across the Straits of Dover, bringing back each time several soldiers during the evacuation of the hard-pressed British forces from the Dunkirk beaches.

To commemorate the fallen, their names were cut into the south wall of the Cloister, close to those of the men who had fallen in the War of 1914–18. A further memorial followed a few years later. *Lux perpetua luceat eis.*

Dr Duckworth's period of office expired about the end of the war; and in June 1945, for the second time in five years, the Fellows met to elect—and for the first time to pre-elect—a new Master. They elected Dr E. M. W. Tillyard. He had entered the College as a Classical Scholar in 1908 and had been elected a Fellow in 1913, after carrying out research in classical archaeology at Athens. During the War of 1914–18 he served with distinction in the army in France and Greece. On his return he changed to English Literature and a few years later was appointed to one of the new University Lectureships in English—a subject which was developing rapidly in the University at the time. During the greater part of the War of 1939–45 he was Senior Tutor of the College. A Doctor of Letters and a specialist in Shakespeare, Milton, and the epic, he enjoyed an international reputation for scholarship.

As after the Napoleonic Wars and the War of 1914–18, so after the War of 1939–45 the resident membership of the University grew considerably. The increase was greatest during the first first few years, owing to the presence of a large number of men whose academic careers had been interrupted or delayed by war service. The annual number of matriculations at Jesus during the first twelve years after the war varied from 127 to 76, the average being 108. It was noticeable how well the undergraduates, of very different ages, social backgrounds, and experiences settled down together. Men who had held commissions for several years and fought on more than one front, objectors to military service, men who had begun residence before the war, married men with families, boys straight from school, men from the big public schools and from the municipal secondary schools, rich men and poor men—all these lived together in amity.

Even when the men of the post-war 'bulge' had gone down the University continued to be considerably larger than it had ever been before. This was mainly because of the great increase in the amount of financial help given by national and local government authorities to the cause of higher education. State scholarships had been given before the war, but there were far more of them now; and if a College Entrance Scholarship was inadequate for maintenance the State was prepared to make good the deficiency. The composition of the University consequently became much more representative than it had ever been. Working class boys were now able to enter it in considerable numbers for the first time. The competition for places became in consequence very keen, and the former stream of wealthy or middle-class men who had entered the University with no intention of working for anything more than a pass degree was now suppressed in favour of men reading for honours, regardless of social class. The University, anticipating this state of affairs, had already (during the war) ruled that all undergraduates, except a small minority falling into special categories, should in future read for honours.

Those who confidently asserted that the virtual elimination of the pass degree man would ruin College rowing at Cambridge would find it difficult to explain away the record of the Jesus Boat Club during the years 1946-72. During this period the College was Head of the Lents thirteen years out of twenty-seven, and Head of the River seven years out of twenty-seven. It won the Coxswainless Fours five times, the Fairbairn Cup seventeen times, and Ladies Plate three times. All these, it may with justice be said, were victories over other college crews; but the same cannot be maintained about the Club's three victories in the Putney Head of the River Race, in which as many as 275 eights from all over the British Isles, including such great clubs as London and Thames, have taken part in one year; nor, above all, can it be maintained about the Jesus victory in the Grand Challenge Cup at Henley in 1947. The College had many times before come within a few feet of winning this, the most coveted of all rowing trophies; but the odds against any college crew ever winning it are so great that Jesus, though a leading rowing college, had done so only twice before—in 1879, and again in 1885, when the captain of the Club was Steve Fairbairn, with C. E. Tyndale-Biscoe coxing. The victorious 1947 crew were D. C. Bray (*bow*), G. S. S. Ludford, D. V. L. Odhams, F. L. Whalley (*capt.*), G. C. Thomas, J. P. Whalley, N. S. Rogers, C. B. R. Barton (*stroke*), and D. S. M. Harriss (*cox*).

In other sports a record was established in 1965 when the College appeared in the four finals of both Rugby and Association Football, hockey and athletics, winning the cup for the last two.

To those who knew the College both before and after the war the most striking change in the daily life of the undergraduates was in the provision of their meals. Before the war, they were required to dine in Hall at least five times a week. Apart from that restriction, they could have breakfast, lunch, tea, or dinner sent to their rooms from the kitchen as often as they liked, or they could get their own meals. They had the alternative of lunching in Hall if they wished, but breakfast was not provided there except for crews or teams in training, and tea was never provided there. After the war breakfast was served in Hall and undergraduates with rooms in College were for a time charged for it whether they went to it or not—and in consequence they generally went. They could either lunch in Hall or get their own meal. No meals at all were sent to their rooms. One consequently no longer witnessed the familiar pre-war sight of kitchen porters carrying meals to undergraduates' rooms on their heads in trays covered with green baize, or of boys carrying tea, coffee, or groceries from the buttery.

The shortage of labour in colleges which accounted for this change accounted also for another—the disappearance of the bedmaker's 'help' from the scene. Before the war, each staircase had been normally worked by two women— a bedmaker and a help. Both arrived at an early hour and stayed until about eleven o'clock. The help came alone in the early afternoon to clear away lunch, make up the fire, set the tea, and do whatever else was necessary. The bedmaker came alone in the evening, to clear away tea, attend to the fire, and turn down the bed-clothes. After the war the bedmaker had no help and came only in the morning. She was compensated for the loss of her former assistant by the introduction of such labour-saving machinery as vacuum cleaners, instead of the old dustpan and brush, and by the replacement of coal fires by gas fires throughout the College in 1951 and the years immediately after. These were in turn super-seded by central heating and by 1975 only a few of the older buildings lacked this amenity.

In 1959 Dr Tillyard retired and was succeeded by Professor D. L. Page, a Doctor of Letters, Fellow of Trinity, and Regius Professor of Greek in the University. The first Master since Dr Corrie to come from outside the College, he had been a Scholar and then a Student of Christ Church. During the Second War he was on Special Foreign Office Service, part of the time as Head of a Command Unit of the Supreme Allied Command in South East Asia. From the first he threw himself into the life of the College and both he and his wife entertained on a lavish scale at the Lodge, which had been modernized and altered to accom-modate them and their four schoolgirl daughters.

Modernization of the College kitchens and the buttery also took place when Small Hall (built in 1875) and the kitchen annexe under it were demolished. To compensate for the loss of dining space, the two sets of Fellows' rooms adjoining the Old Library were reconverted into one big room (Upper Hall) which seated 56. The lath and plaster ceilings were removed, revealing the fine oak roof with carved early sixteenth-century bosses, and some new carvings were added showing the date 1962 and the letters D. L. P.—the Master's initials— and his arms as Regius Professor of Greek. A gallery at the west end of Hall provided a link between the two halls and extra seating space.

Various improvements in the undergraduates' lot was brought about during both Dr Tillyard's and Professor Page's masterships. In 1946, for instance, a College nurse and surgery were introduced and both undergraduates and dons soon began to wonder how they had managed without them before. A second Common Room ('the Junior Parlour') was provided in East House in 1949 and was moved to Pump Court with the addition of a Music Room in 1965. Another Common Room incorporating a bar and television room was opened at the same time on the site of the old Buttery Shop. One very great improvement was the transference of the undergraduates' library from its cramped makeshift quarters on 'Q' Staircase to the top floor of 'A' and 'B' Staircases in 1952. This was the indirect result of a fire which broke out there early in 1950. The top floor dated from 1718–20, when it was added to the founder's former Grammar School for the choristers, which was originally the nuns' almonry. After the fire it ceased to be used as sets of rooms and was transformed into a beautiful and commodious War Memorial Library, designed by Marshall Sisson on the same lines as the Old Library. The floor below the new library was at the same time converted into single-room sets (connected by a corridor) for Fellows normally living out of College. One of the two sets on the ground floor of 'A' became a post room, the other an office for the Head Porter. The two sets on the ground floor of 'B' remained in undergraduate occupation. The whole building was provided with central heating and the disused chimney stacks were removed, their disappearance being apparently unnoticed by most visitors.

A few more undergraduate sets of rooms were now available on 'Q' Staircase as a result of the removal of the library to 'A' and 'B'. A much larger increase in the number of sets was brought about in 1950-53 by an internal reconstruction of the Carpenter Building in Chapel Court, where there had always been a great deal of waste space. The partitions between the rooms there were rearranged in such a way that twenty-seven additional sets were contrived, the new sets being aptly described as 'something half-way between a normal set and a bed-sitting room'. The new rooms had what the old ones had never had—hot and cold water laid on and wash-basins.

The greatest increase in accommodation came, however, in 1963 with David Wyn Roberts's design for a three-storey, three-sided court with the open side facing south towards Jesus Lane and sited so as to leave Pump Court open to the west. It was named North Court and contained six staircases which housed 73 undergraduates and incorporated the sick bay and surgery, bathrooms, changing rooms, and two sets of Fellows' rooms. This great undertaking ensured that, for the first time since the war, every man could have at least two years in College.

The lot of the Fellows was also improved after the war—in 1946 the Old Hall of the Master's Lodge was transferred to the jurisdiction of the College Council and thus became available to all members of the Society. The master retained his private entry to the room (renamed the Prioress's Room), and any member of the Society could now reserve it for a lecture, a meeting, or a lunch or dinner party whenever he wished. An annexe with a fine timber ceiling and fitted with a serving bench was added in 1969. The room was also available for those attending the conferences which became an important source of revenue during vacations.

In 1949 the one small set of rooms on the first floor of Cow Lane, previously occupied by an undergraduate, was re-orientated on the Fellows' private staircase and converted into a second Combination Room. In view of the great increase in the number of Fellows, such a room was badly needed. It was also very useful for meetings of committees of the College Council.

The Fellows had not merely increased in number since the war but also showed much greater variety of subject and of academical origin than before. Of the thirty-two members of the Society at the end of Dr Tillyard's mastership, fourteen had been undergraduates at Jesus, nine at other Cambridge colleges, seven at other British universities, one in Australia, and one in the United States. The complement of Fellows had risen to over fifty in 1976 when it included the Professors of Modern History, International Law, English Law, French, Drama, and Morbid Anatomy; Readers in Engineering, Iranian Studies, and Pharmacology, as well as twenty-four University Lecturers. Among the last was Lisa Jardine, the first woman Fellow of the College, who was elected in 1976.

The College courts were made more attractive than ever in 1951, when the numerous coats of arms carved on the walls during the course of centuries were painted in their heraldic colours—most of them for the first time. The same year saw the beginning of the practice of hanging baskets of flowering plants from each of the Cloister arches throughout the summer. They made a delightful addition to the Cloister, which without them had been rather gloomy. It had already become the setting for a series of plays produced in it every May Week from 1948 onwards, the first performance being a production of Milton's *Comus* and Purcell's opera *Dido and Aeneas*. The following December saw the first modern performance of medieval nativity plays in chapel. These were equally successful and became an annual event in the life of the College until musical concerts took their place.

The chapel provided a wonderful setting for these performances. The combined ravages of time, damp, and the accumulated candle-soot of a hundred years had tarnished the decorative work of Pugin and Morris, but the interior of the building shone again in all its beauty when a four-year process of cleaning and repairing was completed in 1957. Professor B. W. Downs says in his *Cambridge Past and Present*, 'From 1845 until the present day, restoration and beautification of the building have been in perpetual process, undertaken with piety, skill, and taste, for which there must be few parallels in this or any other country.' The Rev. B. D. Till, who had succeeded the Rev. P. Gardner-Smith as Dean, was followed by the Rev. P. R. Baelz (afterwards Professor of Moral and Pastoral Theology at Oxford), in whose time ripples of reform began to appear in chapel. The holy table was moved away from the east wall and the priest celebrated the liturgy facing the congregation. On Ascension Day 1965 there was an evening Celebration as well as one in the morning—probably for the first time in the history of the chapel. The basis of the religious establishment was widened and permission was given for services other than those of the Church of England to be held.

In 1978 the Master and Fellows gave a dinner in honour of Mr Gardner-Smith's ninetieth birthday. He spoke with the special brand of humour for which he was famous and included reminiscences and personalities of the six masterships during which he had served the College.

Dr L. A. Pars, who celebrated his eightieth birthday in 1976, continued to take an active part in the life of the College where his warm welcome and lavish hospitality continued to be enjoyed by old and present members alike.

In 1969 Dr Frederick Brittain, one of its most devoted and well-loved members, died in College. Known to all as Freddy, he had been up for half a century (as a Fellow for 32 years of the time) and was at various times Steward, Librarian, Praelector, and Keeper of the Records. Hundreds of Jesus men subscribed to present him with his portrait by William Narraway and later to provide the beautifully carved oak doors at the bottom of Hall stairs as a memorial to him. He was a prolific author, and his own memoirs *It's a Don's Life*, give a vivid picture of life at the College during the half century of his residence there.

The Master, who had been knighted in 1971, retired two years later. He was succeeded by Sir Alan Cottrell, Chief Scientific Adviser to the Government, and destined to become the first Jesus Vice-Chancellor of the University for more than 100 years. Early in his mastership the statutes were revised to include undergraduates on the College Council and to abolish the ban on women becoming members of the College. Thus the wheel came full circle and by the end of the decade women were again in residence at St Radegund's.

The 800 years between the foundation of the Priory and the mid-twentieth century were bridged in 1947, when the wisdom of the nuns in building where they did was given ocular proof. That winter was the most severe in living memory in England, its chief feature being heavy and frequent snowfalls and continuous frost. For practically the whole of the Lent Term snow and ice covered every blade of grass on the Close and in the College courts, where it would have been possible to skate. Towards the end of the term a thaw set in, accompanied by very heavy and continuous rain. As a result, Cambridgeshire suffered severely—the Fens disastrously—from a double flood of melted snow and rain-water. Queens' and other colleges along the Backs were flooded out and their inhabitants had to go about in boats but Jesus was more fortunate. The Cam, it is true, expanded into a broad lake, which covered the whole of Jesus Green and Midsummer Common up to the very boundary of the College Close; but owing to the foresight of the founders of the nunnery in building on slightly higher and firmer ground, the College itself escaped flooding, as it had evidently done throughout the centuries.

PROSPERUM ITER FECIT FACIAT

Index

Coleridge, S. T. 111, 120–1, 124, 130–
139, 141, 148–9
his rooms 134, 189
play by 136
poems by 133
Combination Room 93, 102, 143,
145, 150
new entrance 198
second 212
Commissioners
Edward VI's 46
Elizabeth's 41–2, 54
Queen Mary's 44
Victorian 164–5, 168–9
Common Rooms, undergraduates'
209
Communion, Holy 53, 156
Conclusion Book 115
Conference Room 18
Constance, Countess 6
Cooke, Alistair 202
Corbels, Hall 27
Corrie, G. E. 108n., 161–84
on rowing 172
on Royal Commissions 164, 168
on Sunday trains 165
Cottrell, Sir Alan, 214
Coursing 108
Cow Lane 102, 197–8, 212
Cox, Harold 181–2
Cranmer Society 173
Cranmer, Thomas 30, 35, 37–41
Cricket 108n., 167, 172, 178, 180,
187–8
pavilion 197
Cripps, J. M. 139, 141–2
Cycling 172

Daily services 92, 156
Dark Entry 19
Dean 49, 64, 156, 168, 212
Degrees taken 103–4, 114–15, 152,
176
Deshmukh, Sir Chintaman 202
Dewar, Douglas 191
Dinner hour 128, 150, 173
Discipline 151–2, 171
Dissenters—see Nonconformists

Dividend, Fellows' 47, 62–3, 73–5,
155
Dod, John 59, 71
Dodd, C. H. 196
Dogs 173
Dolphin Inn 38
Doncaster School 175
Dormitory nunnery 19, 20
Downs, B. W., quoted 167, 212
Downs, Geoffrey 40
Dowsing, William 80, 118
Dress 36, 98
Drinks 36, 69, 91–3
Duckworth, W. L. H. 190, 203–7
Duport, John 57–8, 60–1, 92, 112, 196

Eady, Sir Wilfrid 193
East House 169, 211
Eccleston, John 39
Edmonds, J. M. 190–1
Edmunds, John 40
Education Act of 1902 175
Edwards, Thomas 122, 124, 132
Edyll, Dr 51n.
'Eight hours' work' 166
Electric lighting 189
Eliot, John 66, 71, 164
Ely, Bishops of, their rights in Col-
lege 32, 48–9, 162, 168–9
Ely Fellow 49, 162
Erasmus 38–9, 137
Essex, James 145
Evangelicals 113, 158, 179
Everett, William (quoted) 163–4, 179
Exceedings 29, 91
Expenses 35, 90–2, 109, 175

Fairbairn, Steve 182, 196, 199, 209
Fair Close 11, 17
Fanshawe, Sir Richard 82
Fasts 73, 91
Fawcett, W. M. 181, 198
Fawkes, Francis 112
Feasts 69, 150
Fellow-Commoners 35, 49, 50, 64, 81,
93, 104–5, 108, 151–2, 158, 174–5
Fellows
counties of 49, 154–5

Fellows—*contd.*
  ejected 80, 81, 84, 100
  election of 48, 86, 162, 168
  first woman, 213
  number of 23–4, 31–5, 43, 47, 81,
    86, 154, 194, 212
  reinstated 86
  research 194
  residence 38, 74, 148
  stipends of 31–2, 34, 47, 62–3, 73–4
Fen Ditton 87, 89
Fire-places 67
Fisher, Osmond 158–60
Fishing 4, 108n.
Five Wounds 28, 197
Flamsteed, John 95
Floods 4, 214
Foakes Jackson, F. J. 187–8, 195,
  206
Foley, T. P. 119n.
Fontibus, John de 8
Food 69, 91–2, 208
  complaints about 174
Football 70, 94, 108, 172, 187–8, 192,
  209
Forms for seats 102, 168
Francis. A. L. 173, 180
French, William 151–2, 156–8, 163–4
Frend, William 111, 120–32, 138
Fulborne, Joan 15–16
Fuller, John 44, 47

Garden, Fellows' 93, 142
Gardner-Smith, P. 191, 195, 213, 214
Garlick Fair 11
  Lane 11
Garner, Sir Saville (Lord Garner,) 202
Gas Fires 209–10
Gas light 149, 189
Gascoyn, Edward 52
Gate Tower 28, 30, 117
  crosses on 44
Ghost Room 197
Gibson, Charles 102
Gibson, John 158–60
Gidding, Little 87
Gill, Eric 198
Glass—*see* Windows

Goddard, Sir Victor 202
Golf 172
Good, I. J. 201
Goodrich, Thomas 40
Goodwin, J. H. H. 177
Goring, Lord Charles 81
Gower, Humphrey 99, 106
Gown, Rustat 98
Grammar school 17, 25, 30–1, 49,
  57–8, 75, 117, 209
Grammar, teaching of 31
Graveley 43
Graves, J. D. 207
Gray, Arthur 173–7, 187, 194–203
Greek 39
Green, A. E. 201
Green, Charles 157
Green Croft 3, 4, 6, 7, 11, 212
Greville, Fulke 56
Greyne, Thomas 29
Grigg, William 105, 107–9
Griggson, Edward 29
Grimbaldston, W. 99
Grogan, E. S. 192
Grove, Jesus 79, 133
Guest rooms 28
Gunning, Henry (quoted) 124, 130–1,
  141, 148–9
Gyp rooms 67, 167

Hall, the 19
  floor 117, 174
  life in 67–8
  new entrance 168
  oriel 27, 168
  roof 27
  screen 68
  seating 68
  tables 143, 205
  windows lengthened 146
Hall, Stephen 80, 86, 89
Hallifax, Samuel 114
Halliwell-Phillipps, J. O. 84, 154
Hall-Stevenson, J. 112
Harman, Richard 40
Harriss, D. S. M. 209
Hartley, David 103, 110–11, 133
Hastings Fellowship 32